Job Search
The Total System

KENNETH M. DAWSON
SHERYL N. DAWSON

John Wiley & Sons
New York • Chichester • Brisbane • Toronto • Singapore

Published by John Wiley & Sons, Inc.

Library of Congress Cataloging-in-Publication Data:

Dawson, Kenneth M.
  Job search: The total system

  1. Job hunting. I. Dawson, Sheryl N. II. Title.
HF5382.7.D38 1988   650.1′4   88–42
ISBN 0-471-60078-4
ISBN 0-471-60079-2 (pbk.)

Printed in the United States of America

10 9 8 7 6 5 4 3 2

This book is dedicated to:

*Our sponsoring companies who have
entrusted their employees to us;*

*Our individual clients who have proven
that our system works;*

*Our staff who serve as a model of the
qualities and techniques that create success;*

*Our parents who taught us to excel
and encouraged us to achieve;*

*Ourselves for believing in each other
and making our dreams reality.*

Foreword

Donald C. Vaughn

President and Chief Executive Officer,
The M.W. Kellogg Company, Houston, Texas

Success in today's intensely competitive business world, more than ever before, depends on careful preparation and effective presentation. The M. W. Kellogg Company is well known as a progressive engineering and construction firm, an international leader in its field. Yet we don't take our reputation for granted. Each prospective new project calls for extensive information gathering, careful attention to detail, and our very best sales effort.

The same rules must apply to those seeking successful job placement and subsequent advancement. Certainly, applicants cannot depend on simply presenting a résumé of past activities and waiting for someone else to do something about it.

Job Search: The Total System is written expressly for those seeking positions in today's highly competitive job market. It is designed to prepare an individual to be a winner in that environment. The formula is based on the professional knowledge and proven experience of Ken and Sheryl Dawson. As management consultants, they have worked with major corporations in the outplacement field and in developing corporate and executive excellence programs. I know first hand of their expertise through their association with the M. W. Kellogg Company as consultants.

The major skills addressed in this book are important not only in finding new employment but also in achieving career advancement. Professional commitment, interpersonal skills, and expertise in negotiation are qualities that any business prizes in its employees.

Job Search: The Total System is an especially valuable resource because job seekers must prepare so diligently for their task. Mergers, acquisitions, and cost cutting have eliminated many jobs and made many professional positions even more demanding. Business has become leaner and more streamlined. The job candidate must take the same approach. Technical competence, education, experience, and individual accomplishment are of great importance. But they are not necessarily enough to land a sought-after position. Before knocking on the door, you must learn a great deal about the firm you seek to join. Who are the clients? What are the company's needs and opportunities? Where could you fit into the organization? Employers are looking for a high level of commitment and interest. They want prospective employees to be knowledgeable about the firm's business objectives and standards. These factors are as important as the degree of technical competence.

Because business has become increasingly competitive, companies must do their homework as never before in looking for prospective employees. Every single job applicant must be evaluated not only in terms of technical knowhow but also in terms of how he or she will fit into the culture of the organization.

Recognizing that the employment process is a two-way street, progressive companies require prepared job seekers. Thus, our firm welcomes pertinent questions from the job candidate and makes every effort to respond as fully as possible. Remember, too, that input from the job seeker can be of great value to a company in assuring that the right person is placed in the right job.

The M. W. Kellogg Company makes every effort to prepare individuals for advancement and success. At the same time, we greatly value individual initiative and a strong sense of accountability in our employees. In the final analysis, it is your own responsibility to take control of your career. This is true regardless of whether you are currently an employee of a firm or are looking for a position in a new company. *Job Search: The Total System* can be a great ally as you take control of your career. I wish you every success as you explore its contents and put its valuable lessons to work.

Preface

Job Search: The Total System is your guidebook to your next profitable, successful, and rewarding position. If you are unemployed or are dissatisfied with your present position, or if you are merely thinking about making a job change, this book will prepare you to achieve your ultimate career goal.

We are the Dawsons. As outplacement specialists, we have assisted individuals at all organizational levels, in a wide spectrum of functional areas, and across many industries with excellent results; our clients' average time-to-placement is 3.2 months, almost half the industry average of six months. The advice and techniques we recommend to our clients to achieve *a better job, in a better company, for better pay* are contained in this book. We are not a search firm and we do not find jobs for our clients, but their successes have proved that the assistance we provide is far more valuable. Every job search technique that we teach relates to the concept of *psychological leverage*. At each step in your job search, you must be mentally a step ahead. Psychological leverage enables you to be proactive, better prepared, more aware, always anticipating your next action. Begin now to build psychological leverage by making up your mind to take control of your job search. When you realize that placement is up to *you*, the job hunter, this book will become an indispensable guide. *Job Search: The Total System* provides the tools for your successful job search.

With companies restructuring because of acquisitions, mergers, divestitures, and other organizational changes, it's a fact of life that job security has gone the way of the dodo bird. The phenomenon of the dual-career couple also has made it increasingly difficult for individuals to plan their careers in only one organization, which may frequently demand relocation for promotion. Rapid technology advancements and the wholesale shift in employment opportunities from agricultural and manufacturing to service-oriented jobs has made job and career change a way of life for virtually every employee. A generation ago, an individual may have looked for a job only once in a career; now, however, job and even career changes may occur several times throughout one's working life.

Although they are especially geared to the executive, manager, and professional, the techniques and skills presented in this book apply to any job seeker, whether a new graduate or an ambitious employee seeking that first supervisory opportunity. The earlier in your career that you develop effective job search skills, the more quickly your career will advance. For the senior executive who thinks that his or her needs are unique, consider the fact that whereas once only 40 percent of executives responded to search firm inquiries, now only 10 percent dare ignore such calls. This book will enlighten you to the fallacy of relying strictly on executive search firms and will provide a dynamic system for you to take control of your next job search.

As professional career counselors and management consultants, we have helped thousands of employees to develop their careers within organizations and to find new jobs and career opportunities when their current employers presented them with pink slips. In case such services are new to you, the latter is called *outplacement.* Although getting a pink slip used to be a notice of incompetence, and being jobless was the same as wearing a badge of dishonor, today unemployment is an accepted reality of a constantly changing work force. Corporate conscience has motivated many organizations to recognize that it is their responsibility to hand out more than just pink slips. As part of their severance packages, terminated employees are provided professional assistance to find new employment in another company, a consulting opportunity, or their own business. Key phases of outplacement include career assessment and counseling, professional resume preparation, job search organization, networking and interviewing skill development, as well as spouse and financial counseling. In addition, a comprehensive range of support and administrative services for executives is provided in a positive and professional environment. The objective of outplacement is to assist the displaced employee in finding *the right position within a short period of time and with a minimum of trauma.*

Because our services are offered only through corporate sponsorship, we have felt at a loss to help individuals who are not sponsored by corporations in their job searches. These individuals are at a disadvantage in the job marketplace because they lack the proper skills and knowledge to conduct a job search effectively. *Job Search: The Total System* solves that deficiency and provides a means for us to help, cost-effectively, the vast majority of job seekers who lack company sponsorship in outplacement programs.

In case you are contemplating a passive approach to your job search, bear this statistic in mind: Only 10 to 20 percent of jobs are secured through classified ads or placement agencies. Unless your propensity for risk is to accept ten-to-one odds against you, this book is for you. On these pages we will challenge you, stretch you, force you into an eyeball-to-eyeball confrontation with yourself. To that end, we are unyielding, unrelenting, and dogmatic in our approach to teaching job search techniques. There is good reason for such a demanding regimen—today's job market is a Darwinian environment. In our Houston outplacement facility, we've created a system that gives our clients an advantage in the *survival-of-the-fittest* challenge. It works so well for us and our clients that we'll attempt to win your allegiance by setting it out in this book. Only the committed will make the cut.

Believe this, and you've taken a giant step toward survival in job search: Short cuts, gimmicks, and dramatic innovations simply do not exist. No doubt, you'll find charlatans peddling a variety of search techniques with the promise that they will simplify and expedite your job campaign. We stand on our previous statement. Information is out there in abundance, but much of it is misinformation. In terms of helping your search for a new position, much of it is pure tripe.

Make no mistake about this—you'll not find any "warm fuzzies" or meaningless "feel-goods" on these pages. Do you remember this country's guiding philosophy of the 1960s?—"If it feels good, do it." Alarmingly, although our society has grown through that phase, job search still seems mired in the concept. For example, suggestions such as "Take a couple of weeks off to rest and let your psyche heal" or "Go to the beach, sit on a pier, and watch the tides; contemplate where you want to go next" are common-place in the job search world.

That kind of theoretical nonsense might sell a few books for its authors, but it won't do much else. And it most assuredly won't help your search. We won't challenge the idea that you need time for reflection and assessment; you have an important decision in your immediate future. Our point is, however, that you don't arrive at realistic solutions by sitting at the end of a pier, awaiting a message in a bottle to wash in with the tide. You prepare for important decisions by researching, planning, analyzing, networking, and undergoing a professionally administered battery of assessments.

In any high-stress or difficult situation, we all must rely on our sub-conscious minds for guidance and direction. But understand this: You get out only what you put in. Unless you spend time putting valid information in, you won't get any substantive conclusions in return. The most valid information about job search is traditional, time-tested. The tactics that work best today are those that have worked for fifty years and will continue to work best for fifty years into the future. *Dedication, discipline, courage, preparation, self-confidence, consistency, and professionalism* stand as the drive wheels for success in any phase of career or life. But their importance expands geometrically during job search, when emotions are taut, time is pressing, and second chances are few. As a result, we seek—*demand*—an intensive short-range time and energy commitment from you, coupled with a pledge to plan and use your time efficiently.

And we guarantee that those who won't buy into our principles, who can't make a commitment without reservations, will simply be screened out by natural selection. That's the toughest news: We can help only the strong, or those who would be strong. But the good news is that survival in the world of job search—unlike in nature—isn't based on intrinsic qualities or good fortune. Everything you need to know to be fit for survival is learnable. And we are the teachers. As the student, all you need to do is continue reading and follow our guidelines to job search success.

Note: Throughout *Job Search: The Total System,* we provide examples to illustrate specific techniques. All names used in our examples have been changed to respect the confidentiality of our clients.

KENNETH M. DAWSON
SHERYL N. DAWSON

Contents

CHAPTER ONE

Setting the Stage: Where You've Been, Where You Are, Where You're Going

In the pages of this book, you'll learn more about the nuances of job search and your career than you ever thought existed. To categorize the information, we can say that all we know, all we teach, fits under the umbrella of our two great commandments of job search. If you have a stone tablet handy, carve these down: *linkage* and *positive thinking*.

THE FIRST COMMANDMENT: LINKAGE

Typically, job search is approached as a series of freestanding, unrelated events. Resume writing, networking, interviewing, and negotiating are generally written about or taught as a series of independent occurrences. This is not so. By adapting our principle of linkage and putting it into action, you'll begin to see job search as a series of interlocking steps, each inexorably linked to the previous event and the subsequent one.

Linkage means that you approach your job search with a specific game plan. A series of unrelated plays, no matter how great, is not likely to result in a win. Linkage requires that each step in your job search be thought through and carefully planned, for itself and in relation to the other steps, just as athletes look at each play as part of an overall strategy to win the game. A great resume may get you an interview, but if you are unprepared to back up your accomplishments with solid evidence during that interview, you've failed to use linkage. Or if you've obtained a reference letter from a former employer but didn't prepare him for a reference check by a potential employer, you've failed to use linkage. In effect, linkage in job search is a tightly structured plan of action to achieve a specific career objective or objectives. Nothing is left to chance as you take control of your job search game plan.

For example, although you want to impress a potential employer during the interview that your skills and strengths are limitless, your answers to interview questions don't come from a box of Wheaties—they come from your resume. Likewise, when you wonder what one of your references might say about you, stop wondering and use linkage to take control: Prepare a draft of a reference letter and submit it to your former employer for the appropriate signatures.

When you're negotiating compensation, you don't throw a number on the table and expect the employer to go after it like a famished German shepherd. Your *research* should have already firmly established your negotiating position as fair, reasonable, and consistent with industry and company norms. Moreover, your interviewing *performance* will have so impressed the hiring authority that you are being aggressively pursued as a valuable member of the team. Consequently, you will have psychological leverage to negotiate a mutually satisfactory compensation package.

THE SECOND COMMANDMENT: POSITIVE THINKING

If you do not think positively, you will not succeed at job search. We exercise autocratic authority in this regard at our outplacement facilities. If you can't maintain an upbeat, positive attitude, you're just not welcome there. Those who want to bathe in negativity must do so at home, where they can screw up only their own job search, no one else's.

We recognize that losing a job can be a tough blow psychologically. Typically, a termination will drag you through a five-step process:

1. *Denial*—This can't be happening to me.
2. *Anger*—How can they do this to me when old Mr. Slowpace does only half the work I do?
3. *Bargaining*—Can I take another job at lower pay?
4. *Depression*—No one's hiring; there's no use trying.
5. *Acceptance*—OK, they cut me loose. Where do I go from here?

For a few people—generally those with serious disorders predating their career disruption—that process is a steep slide downhill. They never rise to step 5. For those cases, we recommend a therapist or a psychologist to help sort out the problems. But for the rest of us—the vast majority of people—we can reach the point of "Let's get moving." This is a problem of *attitude*, and it's controllable. We believe your attitude can be controlled as surely as your behavior can be controlled. We stress to clients that there are three time periods to life: the past, the present, and the future. Two of those you can control, but the past is history. So why get depressed and confused for weeks following termination? Certainly, you can work through the five-step process, but we believe that's a task measurable in hours or perhaps days, not weeks or months. Go beyond the past—deal with the present and your future.

Don't lay more psychological weight on this event than it need carry. Have you ever experienced the death of a child, a spouse, a best friend, or a parent? Those are truly devastating psychological traumas; each could be a life-shattering event. Moreover, they are irreversible. Not so your job loss—that is a salvageable situation. Remember, you've lost your job, not your talent or your career. How many other cities can you target your skills toward? How many other industries might use your talent and background in an area you haven't yet investigated? Don't get depressed, get busy. That's the best cure for any attitude problem. Don't allow yourself to wallow in self-pity. Don't get angry, get assertive. When you do, you begin to build momentum, which begets positive thinking, which begets hard work and effort, which begets success.

We watch that scenario unfold every day in our facility. In fact, we see it happen so often that we like to suggest to just-terminated clients: *Rather than the worst thing, this could be the best thing that's ever happened to you.*

We base that belief on the notion that termination is seldom a surprise. If indeed you're shocked by it, it's probably an indication you just haven't been aware of what's happening around you. More important, however, we have the evidence; we see a consistent pattern of placement that verifies our proposition. Our clients who utilize these principles of job search do land better jobs, in better companies—for more money. And keep in mind that many of our clients come out of the "oil patch," where conditions in Texas and the Southwest for the past few years have been virtually postnuclear. Yet the application of our principles of positive thinking and hard work boosts these displaced workers to their next career step—frequently without a hitch. Often that next step is another (frequently better) job. Occasionally, a person who is released from a position will decide to become an independent business owner or a consultant.

Witness the experiences of two recent clients in our facility, both engineers from the oil field supply industry. They entered our program weighted down with fear and uncertainty about their future.

Joe Williams, in his early 40s, was so paralyzed over the prospect of making cold calls to seek out job opportunities that he had trouble picking up a phone, let alone talking into it. Initially, Joe came to us to ask if we'd be willing to place that first, tough telephone call to break the ice for him.

The other client, Hank Turner, who was past 60, was conditioned to believe that he'd have to slide into retirement after his termination because no one, anywhere, was being hired in the oil industry—and especially not people over 60. The market was too overpopulated with young hotshots for that to happen.

Rather than succumbing to the deceptive warnings of many so-called experts who say that it will take one month of searching for every $10,000 you earn, let's look at the facts instead.

The younger engineer, Joe, applied himself fully to our program, bought into our concepts, bonded with our staff, and within two months was working the phones as though he'd done it all his life. More important, within another month he'd generated three fine job offers. Incredibly, Joe orchestrated the pace and timing of those offers so that all three were on the table on a Friday afternoon—every *t* crossed and every *i* dotted, ready for his evaluation and final answer. He took the weekend to discuss the offers with his family, came back on Monday and said yes to the company he thought offered the best opportunity.

This was a textbook case—in three months, he'd progressed from ground zero to the top one percent of all job hunters. And he relished the entire process. Joe transformed the worst event of his life into a turning point in his life—for the better. Now he's living in a community of about 20,000 people—just what he and his family had wanted. He's working for a small engineering company, which he preferred over a multinational corporate giant. And he's working in municipal construction, where business and the new company is booming—away from the strangling atmosphere of an industry in trouble.

Hank, the engineer past 60, took his search in another direction but nonetheless generated similar positive results. Cut loose from his firm, Hank spent the first forty-five days networking, reestablishing contact with people all over the world. Ultimately, of course, he didn't have to accept early retirement. Instead, he was placed in a senior engineering consulting role with a foreign steel manufacturer.

The startling part of this story is that his new employer had an absolute, international hiring freeze in force. Yet Hank networked his way into the firm, pushed his contact—in this case, the chairman of the board—to the limit, and got the offer. So not only did he get another job, but it was a better job, with more responsibility and more money and with a better company. Even the term *better job* doesn't touch upon the magnitude of his accomplishment, however. What Hank created was his *ideal job*. He analyzed what the steel company needed in order to get where it had to go. Then he built a scenario detailing how his skills could help it get there. And he sold the idea. He created his own new job, structuring for himself a position of duties that included those he had always enjoyed performing while eliminating those he didn't enjoy. What might have been the end of his career, in fact, had been transformed into an opportunity to make the last five years of his career the best five years of his career.

One aside: During his job search, Hank kept hearing one objection repeatedly: "You're too experienced." Of course, that's a polite and legal way of telling an applicant "You're too old." So Hank conceived the best answer we've ever encountered to the underlying objection. When he sensed that the interviewer was building toward the stock objection, he would preempt it by saying, "Well, I have thirty-five years of engineering experience and that's what you need. The fact is, if you want someone with thirty-five years' work experience, you're going to have to hire an older man." Not only was his response clever, it met the test of any selling statement. Rather than trying to shield or minimize a negative perception, Hank faced the potential objection head-on and diffused it by transforming it into a positive with a bit of humor.

IT'S UP TO YOU

Both of these engineers met our test of what makes people succeed in job search. They, along with hundreds of other clients we've helped this year, organized and implemented a personal assault on the job market. We take considerable pride in contributing to that success—our time-to-placement and our placement rate are the best in our industry. Both of these clients were placed within a three-month period—our average is 3.2 months. That dispels the one month-per-$10,000 myth. But we don't presume to take all the credit, because we don't conduct their job searches for them. We push, pull, lead, and counsel—whatever is most needed. The individual does the work, investigates the company, conducts a needs analysis, then devises a sales presentation designed to convince the company that he or she can solve their problems.

Just as the engineers did it, you should do it. We can't tell you the precise words to say, because it's *your* background you're selling. We can't tell you which companies are hiring or which to use as networking contacts—that's your job. If you do it well, you'll have access to those jobs a step ahead of the rest of the job search world. You'll catch those jobs before they "go public" with listings in state employment services, search firms, and newspaper ads.

You will have identified the company's needs, you will have orchestrated a scenario establishing that your skills and background can benefit the company in an area of need, and you will communicate those facts in your networking, cold-calling, and interviewing opportunities. This is how you find jobs. In subsequent chapters, we'll discuss extensively how each element works. But prepare yourself to accept the fact that *you* must do the work. We'll put up some signposts, guardrails, and speed limits to help you through the tough parts and keep you on course.

It's central to our philosophy of job search that you take on this responsibility for your own campaign. Remember, *you will find a job*. Anyone can do that—almost everyone does eventually. That's not an issue in your search. *What* job you find is an issue. Now we're getting into variables. What job you get and how long your search takes are controlled primarily by you, not by market conditions. It doesn't take a mathematical genius to figure out that if you work five hours a day and find your new position in six months, you might find that same position in three months if you work ten hours a day. What you do with those hours is as important as the basic decision to use them for work. For example, during prime business hours, you work the telephone, networking and cold-calling. In the evenings and on weekends, you read, research, answer newspaper ads, and otherwise use the time when you won't be able to reach most people by phone. That's how you build a winning job search formula. And that's how you achieve placement in record time.

THERE'S NO MAGIC FORMULA

We know our principles work. They work so well, in part, because they're so old. Like bad cars, bad ideas never have a chance to get old. Don't assume that you must "reinvent the wheel" to find a job. People search endlessly for the final solution—some hi-tech innovation that will beat the traditional methods of job search. The fallacy of this approach, however, is that there's nothing wrong with the traditional steps. People fail with them not because of the methods but because of the implementation. In other words, they don't find new positions because they don't work hard and long enough and because their ability to communicate their skills and attitude aren't yet ready for a nose-to-nose and toes-to-toes session with an employer.

In contrast, you can build your own cycle of success. If you work hard, you'll take pride in what you're doing. When you're proud, you're confident. And when you're confident, you become more proficient at job search and more attractive to employers. That's *linkage* in action. You eliminate negative attitudes because you're busy locating job openings or networking into new companies. If you follow our advice to the letter, you'll start your search a step ahead of about 99 percent of all job hunters.

Let's look briefly at some concerns with which job hunters must deal.

Severance Benefits

You negotiate going into a job, so don't think it out of place to negotiate when you go out. You should initiate discussions with your immediate superior and provide a list of what you need to make the transition to your next position easier. At the top of most lists would be salary continuation and health insurance coverage. Often, the use of company office space and administrative support is suggested as part of the package, but we don't recommend that. If you're history at that company, don't hang around. You're striving for psychological leverage in your job search, and using the office of a former employer is not conducive to that attitude. Instead, you can get those benefits much more effectively, along with other essential services, from a quality outplacement service. Outplacement is one of the most valuable negotiable severance benefits—ask for it. Other negotiable items might include mortgage assistance, flexibility in the company's pension policies, or continued use of a company car. In essence, there are no rules here. If you think a severance benefit would be helpful in your search, go for it. After all, at this point, what more have you got to lose?

Budget

You probably already have a workable budget for your household. If you don't, institute one immediately. You'll need it now, more than ever, during your job search. For your current purposes, however, you don't use a budget simply to monitor income and outgo. During job search, your budget becomes a key player in the goals and time periods you establish for each step in your campaign. For example, if your budget calculations indicate that your household can continue operating for six months on reduced income, you can plan on establishing a six-month job search campaign. Like every other phase of our instructions, your budget links with the time frame you've set to regulate your entire job search calendar.

Goal-Setting

We're assuming that you've utilized goal-setting as an important component of your professional success to this point. Don't abandon it now. Like all goals, your job search goals should be realistic, specific, timed, and measurable. (To assist you in goal-setting from the beginning of your job campaign, Exhibit 1.1 provides a form for getting started. As you read the chapters that explain the tasks outlined on the form, set your goals for completion and monitor your own progress.)

Changing Careers

Career change is certainly a viable option for someone coming out of a moribund industry. But be sure that you comprehend the parameters. If you have grown tired of petroleum engineering because there has been little engineering and too much petroleum, and you are thinking of electronics or computers, think again. That's not a profitable, wise career change. Jump from a slow industry if that's best for you, but be certain that you pick a landing spot that can utilize your skills. Otherwise, you'll walk into a lineup with the rest of the rookies. Build on what you've done, what you can bring to the table. Don't chuck it all just because of a transitory economic slowdown. To assist you in evaluating the possibility of changing careers, answer these questions:

- What specific careers hold the most appeal for me?
- What are current market conditions in those careers?
- Are there related occupations I need to learn about?
- Whom do I know in this field? Whom do they know?
- What about other options—independent business, entrepreneurial organization, consulting?

Assessing Strengths and Weaknesses

Ideally, career assessment should be done professionally. Frequently, universities and colleges have assessment centers where you can complete a professional career assessment very cost-effectively. If you must do it yourself, first make a list of your likes and dislikes. When you've identified a

EXHIBIT 1.1
Personal Marketing Plan: Getting Started

TASKS TO COMPLETE	GOAL	DATE COMPLETED

(1) ASSESSMENT
  (A) Evaluate career goals
  (B) Explore independent business options
	(A) _____
	(B) _____
		(A) _____
		(B) _____

(2) RESUME
  (A) First draft
  (B) Second draft
  (C) Final draft
	(A) _____
	(B) _____
	(C) _____
		(A) _____
		(B) _____
		(C) _____

(3) GENERIC LETTERS
  (A) Cover
  (B) Search Firm
  (C) Ad response
	(A) _____
	(B) _____
	(C) _____
		(A) _____
		(B) _____
		(C) _____

(4) REFERENCE LETTERS
  (A) Boss
  (B) Boss's boss
  (C) Peer and others
	(A) _____
	(B) _____
	(C) _____
		(A) _____
		(B) _____
		(C) _____

(5) NETWORKING
  (A) Personal/professional contact list
  (B) Target companies (initial list)
    (i) A priority (high)
    (ii) B priority (medium)
    (iii) C priority (low)
	(A) _____
	
	(B) _____
	
	(i) _____
	(ii) _____
	(iii) _____
		(A) _____
		
		(B) _____
		
		(i) _____
		(ii) _____
		(iii) _____

(6) SEARCH FIRM LIST		
(7) IDENTIFY AD RESPONSE SOURCES		
(8) PRACTICE INTERVIEWING		
(9) IMPLEMENT PERSONAL MARKETING PLAN		
(10) PLACEMENT (NEW POSITION)		

potential direction, then the work really starts. Do your research and networking to discover the career possibilities in the chosen area.

SELF-ASSESSMENT

To evaluate *where you've been, where you are, and where you're going,* complete the following self-assessment questionnaires. They are designed to help you focus on the factors that are important in targeting your job search.

Personal Assessment

1. How do you feel about your current situation?

2. How does your family (spouse, children, parents) feel about your current situation?

3. What people or groups do you feel will be most supportive to you at this time?

4. How would you describe your energy level at this time? (Consider physical and psychological factors.)

5. What three personal qualities do you consider to be your greatest strengths?

    a.

    b.

    c.

6. What three personal qualities would you most like to change about yourself?

    a.

    b.

    c.

7. Have you begun to make these changes? (If not, why not?)

8. How do you use your personal time?

9. What topics do you enjoy reading and talking about?

10. What must you achieve during your lifetime in order to consider yourself a success?

Past Career Assessment

Also critical to this process is a self-analysis of what you've done in the past. This is a good time to separate personalities from actual occupational problems. For ten years, you might have thought you were out of place as a computer programmer. Now, in retrospect, you might discover that programming is fine—it's the ingrate you worked for all those years that made your life miserable. Part of our conviction that job search is a positive experience is rooted in the idea that this is the perfect time to sort out all these emotions. Evaluate all the data, then set a new course.

1. Why did you select the career opportunities or jobs you have held in the past?

2. Have you been doing what you felt you *wanted* to do or what you *had* to do?

3. List the titles of the jobs you have held throughout your career, in order, from your first job to your most recent.

4. Do you feel you were well suited to your most recent position? (Why or why not?)

5. What did you like about your most recent position?

6. What did you dislike about your most recent position?

7. What skills or personal qualities have you been complimented on by previous employers?

8. What, to your knowledge, have employers, co-workers, and/or subordinates found fault with? Did more than one person have the same complaint?

9. Have you held a position in the past that you would describe as your ideal job? (If so, what was this position and what characteristics of this job made it ideal for you?)

Future Career Assessment

1. Which of the following occupations are of special interest to you? (Circle your choices.)

Accounting	Building construction and maintenance
Acting	
Agriculture	Business administration
Architecture	Clerical
Art	Communication
Banking	
Biological sciences	

Dairying

Dancing

Decorating

Dentistry

Domestic and personal services

Education

Engineering

Finance

Fine manual work

Forestry

Government and public service

Graphic arts

Health services

Home economics

Insurance

Landscaping

Languages

Law

Law enforcement

Library

Machine operation and repair

Manufacturing and industry

Mathematics

Mechanical design and construction

Medicine

Ministry

Music

Office administration

Personnel

Physical sciences

Production

Publishing and printing

Selling

Social sciences

Social work

Systems and procedures

Transportation

Writing

Other:

_____

_____

_____

2. How do you rank the following in terms of importance to you? (Rank the most important as 1 and the least important as 12.)

_____ Earnings

_____ Working conditions

_____ Tasks of the job

_____ Status of the job

_____ People I'd work with

_____ Chance to do important work

_____ Supervisor I'd report to

_____ Job security

_____ Opportunity for advancement

_____ Benefit program

_____ Opportunity to use abilities and interests

_____ Opportunity to learn

3. How would you describe your ideal job today?

4. Which of the following *skills and abilities* do you have that would make this an ideal job for you? (Circle your choices.)

Analyzing/synthesizing

Artistic/design

Communications/verbal (speeches, presentations, teaching, languages, etc.)

Conceptual

Controlling

Coordinating

Data/details (figures, records, systems, controls, research)

Directing

Idea generation (creative, original)

Interpersonal (people sensitivity)

Intuitive

Judgmental

Leadership (directing, supervising, motivating)

Listening

Making money

Mechanical/manual

Memory

Negotiating

Observant

Organizing

Planning   _____

Problem identification/solving   _____

Others: _____

5. What special *knowledge and experience* do you have that would make this an ideal job for you? (Circle your choices.)

Accounting

Acquisition

Administration

Advertising

Business development

Customer relations

Customer service

Data processing

Distribution

Economic analysis

Engineering, technical specialties, industrial applications, etc.

Financial planning

Government contracts/relations

Law

Maintenance

Management information services

Marketing/sales

Merchandising

Organization planning

Packaging

Personnel administration (recruiting, training, compensation and benefits, employee relations, staffing, manpower development, union/labor relations, etc.)

Policy development

Product/process design, development

Production (planning, scheduling controls)

Project management

Promotion

Public relations

Purchasing

Quality control/assurance

Research/investigation

Safety/housekeeping

Strategic planning

Systems analysis (methods, procedures, controls)

Taxes

Teaching

Technical services

Visual/graphic arts   _____

Warehousing   _____

Others: _____

6. Which of the following *personal qualities* do you have that would make this an ideal job for you? (Circle your choices.)

I am:	Fair
Accurate	Flexible/adaptable
Alert	Gregarious
Authoritative	"Hard-nosed"
Calm	Independent
Cautious	Individualistic
Conceptual	Innovative
Consistent	Intelligent
Cooperative	Loyal
Courageous	Lucky
Creative	Methodical
Decisive	Organized
Discreet/tactful/diplomatic	Participative
Diligent	Patient
Deliberate	Perceptive
Dedicated	Practical/realistic
Dependable/reliable	Professional
Direct	Punctual
Economical	Quality-conscious
Empathetic	Receptive
Enterprising	Resourceful
Enthusiastic	Thorough

Versatile

Other:

_____

_____

_____

I can:

Anticipate problems

Delegate well

Follow through

Get things done

Get to the core of problems

Keep current (knowledgeable)

Keep others informed

Meet deadlines

Resolve conflicts

See the "big picture"

Take and give orders

Take calculated risks

Think quickly

Use time effectively

Work well under stress

Work with minimal supervision

Other:

_____

_____

_____

I have:

Energy/drive

Initiative

Sense of timing/priorities

Other:

_____

_____

_____

7. What additional capabilities, experience, or educational qualifications would you need to acquire in order to be well prepared for your ideal job?

8. What are your greatest strengths on the job?

9. How can these strengths benefit an employer?

10. What are your potential weaknesses on the job?

11. How can you eliminate these potential weaknesses or turn them into a benefit for an employer?

12. What is your long-term career goal (for the next ten or twenty years)?

13. What is your short-term career goal (for the next one to five years)?

14. How do your career goals relate to the career and life goals of your family members?

15. Do you believe that your ideal job is attainable today? (If so, please explain.)

16. If not, what major obstacles stand in the way?

17. Can you overcome these obstacles to achieve your career goals? (If not, please explain.)

18. Would you relocate for the right career opportunity? (If so, where are you prepared to relocate?)

19.   What specific jobs have you targeted for your employment search?

20.   Are the jobs you have targeted realistic career goals, given the nature of the current marketplace?

21.   Do you prefer a small, medium, or large firm?

22.   Do you want to work in a highly charged environment or a more evenly paced one?

23.   What leadership style is compatible with yours?

24.   Are you willing and able to risk joining a relatively new company?

25.   Have you targeted specific companies you would like to join? (If so, list these companies and state the factors that attracted you to them.)

26.   How hard would you be willing to work to join one of these companies?

27.   Do you want to explore consulting, independent business, or other opportunities? (If so, why?)

28.   Have you set a personal goal regarding when you expect to be employed or earning income from consulting or a business venture? (If so, what is the date? If you have not set a date, please explain.)

29. How many hours per week do you plan to work to achieve this goal?

CAUTIONS

Lists of do's and don'ts are ubiquitous in job search advice. Although we set world records for emphasis on positive thinking, a few *don'ts* can help eliminate grief and streamline your search.

• *Don't take time off.* You don't deserve a reward until you're placed in a new position.

• *Don't assume that your closest networking contacts know all there is to know about you.* Even your best friend may have misconceptions about what you can do and where you've done it. You must tell them explicitly what you're aiming toward and what you want them to do for you.

• *Don't take rejection personally.* It's a normal by-product of job search. Learn to transform an initial *no* answer into a positive conclusion for you. Obviously, the majority of the contacts you make will not have an opening, and if you stop there you will be wallowing in negative feedback. We insist that your contact shouldn't stop with a no. Push the phone call forward. If you can't get a job offer or a lead, get additional names you can contact. In that way, almost every call becomes positive. One of the job search theories we dislike most is the Mickey Mouse exercise called "the rule of no's." The idea is to write the word *no* on a piece of paper several hundred times, then write *yes* at the bottom, and paste the paper on your wall. Then, each time someone tells you no, rejoice and cross one *no* off, because you're even closer to your *yes*. We dislike that because it's a juvenile escape. If your phone calls are all ending in no's, the problem is you. Learn to cold-call (Chapter 7), improve your technique, and meet your goals. If you won't be satisfied with a no, we guarantee you won't hear it as often in your job search.

• *Don't count on one hot lead working out.* The most encouraging network contacts—the hottest leads—turn up stone cold more often than not. Never sit by the phone waiting for one contact to bear fruit. Keep pushing and keep making your contacts. Remember, you don't have a job, and your search isn't completed until you have an offer, have accepted it, and have started working in your new position.

• *Don't expect search firms and classified advertisements to do all your work.* Combined, these two sources account for at most 10 to 20 percent of jobs. Yet most people spend 100 percent of their time working these sources. When you read about rejection, depression, and endless searches for new jobs, the victimized people are almost without exception the people who rely on search firms and ads. That is the easy way, the lazy way. But it doesn't work, because you're competing with the whole world. Also, be aware that when you use a search firm, although you're dealing with someone who professes to be able to assist you, in reality he's an agent of the employer and is looking out, first, for the interests of the company. The people who network and cold-call are the people who get the best jobs first.

• *Don't keep the bad news to yourself.* If you've been terminated, don't be embarrassed about telling close friends and family members. They can help in two ways. During the initial period, when you're dealing with your emotions, they are your best support system. Then they become the first names on your networking lists.

• *Don't call a lawyer.* We teach job search as a win-win proposition. Filing suit against your former employer violates every rule of positive thinking and smart planning that we teach. By engaging in a lawsuit, you're focusing on the past. Remember, that's beyond control. Even if you win a lawsuit—and ten years from now get back pay, reinstatement, or a settlement—so what? You've wallowed in bitterness and anger for all those years, and that's not any way to live and work. Termination isn't a disaster; it's an opportunity. Get on with your future. Let your former employer be a jerk or a violator of the law, but don't let him have an impact on your life from this day forward.

Now for the last caution before you begin structuring your job search:

• *Don't fall prey to the snake oil artists.* Be careful! Don't touch the ink on this page. If our passion about these guys has been transmitted through the printing process, it may be poisonous—dangerous to your health. Even if the ink is toxic, however, it's not nearly as hazardous as the charlatans who are waiting out there to rip you off. Anyone who wants your money up front for job placement or counseling services is suspect in our view. Regrettably, many of these firms attempt to do what we do. Frequently, they are called management consulting, outplacement, or executive consulting services, but whatever their title, they share a common bond. If they want your money first, stay away from them like the plague—because that's just what they are.

Everyone has to make a living. Our firm is funded by the sponsoring corporations of the individual clients. A legitimate employment agency or reputable search firm is paid by the company listing a job. In some cases, the individual job hunter pays the freight—but only after services have been rendered and you have a job. There are other ways to spend money—needlessly, we think—on resume preparation, for example. Resume services will likely not give you a professional resume, but we won't suggest that they're crooks. Beware, however, of any others who want to take your money up front for job search advice or services; they *are* crooks. Don't get hooked up with some charlatan who'll give you a resume and a computer printout, plus a stack of pamphlets with acronyms for titles. Typically, you'll take a hit of between $2,000 to $10,000 for these "services." They'll get rich. You'll get nothing.

We can't mention anyone by name, unfortunately, because, like most crooks, they're rich; and these guys have a lot of legal horsepower. One of them, in fact, is suing the state of Texas over attempts to regulate and curtail the abuse job hunters are suffering. For now, until these people are finally nailed to the ground for good, your only protection is to keep your money in your pocket. If you're tempted by a sales pitch, first contact your local Better Business Bureau, your state attorney general's office, or any other consumer protection agency in your area.

Now that your income has stopped, you need to monitor your cash flow more than ever. It would be tragic to blow it on some thief who will not help your job search. We recall one client whose experience sums it up best:

After completing our outplacement seminar as a corporate-sponsored client, Bill Brown commented that several years before, he'd fallen prey to one such job search consulting service. The experience cost him nearly $6,000. Bill told us, "You people do what they promised they would do. I spent all that money and got nothing but a half-baked resume in return. I'm really ashamed to admit I did that. I'm a lawyer. I'm supposed to know better than that."

Now, with the main issues and cautions on the table, let's move on (with wallets untouched by the pickpockets) to the first actual step of job search—deciding if *a job* is really what you want!

CHAPTER TWO

Before You Search: Explore Independent Business Options

It's only Chapter 2, and already we're telling you not to look for a job—at least not yet. (We promised this wouldn't be run-of-mill career advice.) The fact is that we want every true professional who's looking for a new position to consider consulting or entrepreneurial ventures first, before plugging back into the corporate environment. We don't want to push anyone into a field for which he's not suited, but it's imperative that you look at entrepreneurship now, seriously, if you've ever had an interest in it. After you're placed in a new position, you'll only be second-guessing whether you might have succeeded independently. So stop now and analyze whether or not your skills and personality might drive a small business or consulting operation.

We won't attempt here to outline and clarify all the legal, financial, and technical elements of creating your own business. Rather, we will share our ideas on the personality and motivational aspects of life as a free agent. Our hope is to give you a better understanding of what you're looking at—why some people succeed and others fail—when you consider independent business options.

Before all else, however, you'd best discover if you have the personality suited to an independent business career. That's what we'll attempt to help you sort out in these pages. Do you know how to tell the difference between a consultant and an employee? A staff engineer following design specs gets $200 today to put the swizzlecam on top. A consulting engineer gets $1,000 a day to come in tomorrow and say, "The swizzlecam doesn't go on top. Take it off and put it on the bottom."

Besides the ability to analyze placement of the swizzlecam, consider the following traits you'll need as a consultant or entrepreneur:

- *Enthusiasm and energy level:* Success as a consultant may require that you have the stamina to work long hours for sustained periods.
- *Self-reliance:* You need self-confidence, a belief in your ability to achieve goals, and a sense that events in your life are determined primarily by you.
- *Calculated risk-taking:* Entrepreneurship is generally equated with risk-taking, and properly so. You don't have to act like a riverboat gambler, but much of the dependability regarding income and benefits will be eliminated from your professional life, at least for the short term.
- *Aiming for high goals:* You need the ability to set and reach goals and objectives that other people might consider too challenging.
- *Enjoyment of problem solving:* You must have an intense and consistent desire to drive toward completion of a task or solution of a problem.
- *Long-range commitment:* You must be able to commit yourself to completing projects that will require two to five years of intermittent work.
- *Ability to set the tempo and take charge:* You need the desire to seek and assume initiative and to put yourself in the middle of situations in which you are personally responsible for the success or failure of the project.
- *Growing from setbacks:* You must be able to use failures as learning experiences. Setbacks must not discourage or frustrate you.
- *Maximum utilization of talent:* You must be able to effectively identify and nurture the expertise of others. You can not be so intent on meeting your goals and independent accomplishments that you fail to delegate responsibility.
- *Optimism:* If you can't be totally positive about yourself, your skills, and your business idea every day, why in the world would you want to be an entrepreneur? Starting and running a new business successfully is one of the most difficult propositions you'll ever face in your professional life. You must believe in yourself without equivocation before you start and every day you operate your business.
- *Sales skills:* You must either have sales skills or learn them if you expect to succeed in any venture. Businesses don't survive unless someone is selling the products or services. And make no mistake—when you're independent, that someone is you.

Those are only a sampling of what's required to operate a business. We suggest that you approach any assessment of your personality more thoroughly than any book can profile you. For example, part of the outplacement counseling process in our Houston facility is a battery of assessments. Our senior clients receive a professional, accurate, introspective look at how they work at work. With this comprehensive assessment, they can go forth confident that they've picked the best of the three options available—another company, independent business, or consulting.

But you're making a fatal error if you assume that only your personal characteristics, attitudes, and aptitudes dictate success as an independent business operator. You must also look at the marketplace potential before you jump. For example, our favorite illustration of a marketing disaster in the flesh is the story of a petroleum engineer who opened a bait camp because he liked to fish. And then there was the systems analyst who bought into a hot dog restaurant franchise because he always loved to eat hot dogs. That is not proper targeting in the marketplace, let alone market research. Use all your networking contacts (Chapter 5) and your cold-calling skills (Chapter 7) to learn how your ability and background will sell in the marketplace before you venture out.

As for the specific building blocks of a small business, you can find volumes of information in the library—enough books and government pamphlets to fill a warehouse—all to guide you through the creation and operation of a business. That's why we've elected not to compete with those books.

FINDING HELP

For guidance in the mechanics of going into business for yourself, we highly recommend that you consult an attorney, an accountant, and other professionals concerning legalities, accounting, financing, taxes, patents, contracts, copyrights, and the like. Do not rely on books as your sole source of information. That would be like performing a triple coronary bypass with a scalpel in one hand and a medical text in the other. If you expect to succeed in your new business, get a legal eagle to advise you as well as a number cruncher who can make the dollar signs sprout on trees.

Then utilize all the educational materials. This is when the books can help, as a supplemental source of information. Remember, also, that most chambers of commerce have small business or entrepreneurial committees that sponsor workshops and business lead sessions. Moreover, the Small Business Administration (or what's left of it) conducts frequent seminars for independent business owners. For perhaps the first time, you will have ultimate responsibility for finance and accounting, marketing, sales, production, managing growth, personnel administration—in short, every event that comes up in small business (and then you come to the second hour of the day). Given the fact that four out of five new enterprises go out of business in the first year because of mismanagement or undercapitalization, commit yourself, first, to doing the necessary research to get your embryonic business off the ground and running in the proper direction.

If you feel that you fit the mold thus far, perhaps you're ready to consider some of the positives and negatives of consulting or entrepreneurship.

SOME POSITIVES

- It is a chance to be truly your own boss, with minimum involvement in organizational politics and red tape.
- It can allow you to control your time—the number of hours you work and the time of day or night you work.
- It presents the opportunity for varied work settings and travel.
- Consulting can require minimal capital investment.
- It does not have a mandatory or traditional retirement age.
- It has great potential to be financially very lucrative.

SOME NEGATIVES

- Because it is so attractive, the competition is intense.
- Because you are on your own, you do not have the support system of an organization.
- Because you are outside the power structure of an organization, you lack the authority to impose solutions on others.
- Because you can control your time, you do not have the aid of a regimen or schedule with which you must conform.
- Because your time is your own, you may find that the distinction between working time and leisure time is lost; your time may actually become your client's time.
- Because financial resources are frequently difficult to obtain, cash flow can be a serious problem in a small business.
- Because of the risks, job security is very low and the potential for failure is high.

BASIC SKILLS

In addition to weighing the pluses and minuses of consulting or entrepreneurship and considering whether your personality traits match those of successful independent businesspeople, you must bring to the table a basic set of skills before you bet your career on independence. We like to consolidate them into the following four categories.

Interpersonal Skills

You must be able to relate well to the client or customer and to his or her staff. Your communications skills must be sufficient to persuade the client that your analysis, problem identification, and proposed solution are valid and worth acting on. You must assume responsibility for reducing any friction in the client's office or plant that results from your presence, positioning yourself as a problem-solver who will benefit the company and its employees. Finally, you must communicate effectively in the jargon of the industry and the company, and you must be prepared to do this at all levels of the organization.

Marketing Skills

You must have confidence in yourself and in what you're doing. And it's imperative that you communicate that confidence always, everywhere. As an independent consultant or entrepreneur, you not only maintain a formal marketing program for your company and utilize sales skills to generate new business, but you also become a spokesman for your business in every phase of your life. Whenever and wherever you meet people—at parties, conventions, or professional meetings, or across a backyard fence—they become potential clients or leads to potential clients.

Technical Skills

Your skills in a professional discipline are, of course, the basis for your confidence and marketability. Quite naturally, these skills should be a given for anyone opting for independence. But be aware that if your corporate background portrays you as a *generalist*—the type of person whose versatility and flexibility are invaluable to organizational efficiency—perhaps corporate life is just where you belong. Your potential client most likely doesn't need a generalist. Someone like that is probably already on staff. You must have specific technical skills—preferably on the cutting edge of technology—to be able to attack the client's problems successfully.

Consulting Skills

At first glance, a requirement for consulting skills may seem a redundancy. Actually, however, consulting skills and technical skills differ dramatically.

For example, simply because you're the finest reservoir engineer in the world doesn't mean that you're worth a three-legged alley cat as a consultant. The difference lies in the consultant's communications skills, leadership, problem-solving ability, and personal motivation. A consulting engineer's area of concern is not just the reservoir—how much is there and how to get it out—but in focusing his expertise on how that information relates to the client's company and staff.

MAKING YOUR DECISION

We've given you a great deal to evaluate before you leap to independence. Although much of the information we've provided may seem like pitfalls, we don't mean to discourage you from considering the entrepreneurial/consulting option. Much of the advice you'll encounter from consultants and networkers will be negative, but you should consider the source carefully. In some cases, successful consultants may be reluctant to provide you with a favorable picture of their operation—for obvious competitive reasons. So don't be scared off, but do evaluate fully what you're walking into before you take the first step. And remember that the correct answers for your life and career aren't in this book or any other book. Nor are they found in what the members of your network advise. Until you've been through a professional assessment of your attitudes and aptitudes, you're not ready to hang out your shingle. And until you've worked in conjunction with a lawyer and an accountant or financial analyst, you're not ready to unlock the door under that shingle.

If all signals are go, however, we'd like to share with you—as a potential cornerstone of your fledgling business—our custom-designed consulting proposal. Quite naturally, we like it because we created it, but also because it's simple.

The necessary elements of a consulting proposal include:

- A brief heading used as a title
- A synopsis of the client's problem, supported by a brief analysis of your documentation
- A brief outline of your proposed solution
- A statement of the benefits the client will realize as a result of following the course of action you recommend
- An outline of the first step of the solution, which should be simple and should involve you personally
- An estimate of the time to completion for the first stage of the project

- A full description of your ongoing role—gathering further information, overseeing the first stage of the solution, diagnosing other manifestations of the problem, analyzing results following completion of your suggestions, and so on
- A statement of your fees

Whether your answer is yes, no, or maybe to the consulting or independent business option, don't stop reading. Whether you're a consultant, a small business owner, or a corporate employee, you'll need a resume. Turn one more page, and you'll discover a new world of resumes—*the resume*, to be precise. We are confident that ours is the finest resume in the American job market.

Likewise, whoever you are, wherever you go, you'll need our networking, cold-calling, interviewing, and negotiating skills. Although you may already be a world-class consultant or a proven, fast-tracking corporate employee, over the next eight chapters you will become a world-class job campaigner.

CHAPTER THREE

Beyond Resume Platitudes: The Foundation for Goal Setting

Before you even think about writing a resume, do yourself a favor. Purge from your mind any advice you've ever heard or read about the subject— how to write a resume, how to avoid writing one, how to get a better job without one. When you put pencil on paper to create a resume, make sure your brain is free of clutter.

It's a sad fact, but a fact nonetheless, that almost every piece of advice you've ever received about resumes is useless. When you go looking for any kind of information in books, you're going to find some good, some not so good, and a small percentage downright bankrupt. With resumes, the bankrupt advice dominates the field. As the reader, your greatest responsibility is to discern quality advice from the garbage being peddled by unemployed hucksters. If you've learned a bunch of "trendy" junk from such pseudo-career counselors, exorcise it from your brain and your library.

If you've done any serious research on conducting a job campaign, you're familiar with the verbal effluent with which many "authors" or "consultants" flood the job marketplace. The theories parallel this line of thought: Resumes don't work. . . . Corporations get hundreds, or thousands, every week. . . . Yours won't be read, . . . so don't use one. The rationale continues that a "savvy" job hunter makes direct contact with the hiring authority, uses an alternative marketing letter to generate interviews, and never sends a resume to the company.

There's a grain of truth in that scenario: It acknowledges the value of networking. But networking doesn't replace your resume; they are two tools that complement one another. So if you swallow that trendy line and follow it, you're not as savvy as you think. You're listening to people who don't understand resumes, who probably have never written or read a truly good resume, and who can't even conceive of the multiple benefits an effective resume can produce for your job campaign. In short, our conviction is that *your resume drives your entire job search*. Certainly, it will if you'll agree to do it our way. Any other suggestion will not provide legitimate guidance for your campaign. In fact, it's not really job search advice at all. Most likely, it's intended to generate book sales, lecture tours, and television talk show appearances for the purveyors.

HOW THE RESUME WORKS FOR YOU

Honor your resume; understand that it summarizes your work life and charts your future. A resume is not just a calling card. That's one of its important functions, but many people limit it to that. Nor does the resume simply attract the employer's attention and allow you access to the hiring authority, although that is one of its primary jobs.

More important, however, the procedure you use for creating an effective resume reinforces the process of self-evaluation and goal setting. Your resume sets the tone and direction for all that you do in your job search. When you complete the preparations for creating a resume, you will have on paper how your skills and experience can benefit both you and your next employer.

Properly prepared, the resume will introduce you and sell your skills. Moreover, it will be an ally that will never fail you in any facet of the job campaign. In particular, the resume will assist during interviews, provided that you write it correctly and learn how to use it.

WHY MOST RESUMES ARE OVERLOOKED

Admittedly, the platitudes many of the snake oil artists peddle are based on a truth—corporations *are* inundated with resumes. It's therefore logical to assume that when you submit a resume you're playing a numbers game, with the odds stacked against the job hunter. In fact, only four or five out of every hundred resumes survive the corporate cut. The problem, though, isn't with the concept. It's not the pieces of paper that render a resume ineffective. Nor is it the competition from hundreds of other resumes on the same desk that makes yours get lost in the shuffle.

What renders resumes useless is what's in them. The world of job hunting may be smothering in a choking cloud of resumes, but it's a cloud of bad resumes. In general, they are as poorly written and ill-conceived as the "expert" advice that tells job hunters to eschew them. The one overriding reason that 95 out of 100 resumes don't work is that 95 out of 100 aren't worth reading.

Can you buy into our theory? Can you commit the next two or three days of your life to writing the best resume you've ever seen? That's just what you'll get from this chapter. But if you can't follow our advice by burying all the disinformation about resumes you've heard previously, our relationship, writer to reader, is in deep trouble for the rest of this book. Without an effective resume, built according to the formula provided on the following pages, nothing works. Our approach to job search is driven by our approach to resume writing.

THE GOSPEL OF RESUMES ACCORDING TO DAWSON & DAWSON: THERE IS ONE WAY, ONE TRUTH, ONE RESUME

- *The format is chronological order* (most recent experience first).
- *The resume is two pages long.* (On occasion, administrative support people, or workers in a trade, can fit their professional lives into a one-page resume.)

End of resume alternatives.

Beyond that single exception, never deviate from the formula. You could probably list many different resume formats—most people say five or six. Some "resume services" offer a menu with choices of ten or twelve different styles. Please, don't fall into the trap of selecting your resume from a list of alternatives. If you write any other resume format—functional, hybrid, targeted, or our favorite aberration, the "alternative marketing letter"—you're not acting in your best interest.

Beware: All variations in format are designed to accomplish one goal— to smokescreen weaknesses in your background. A termination? A new job at a reduced salary? A cut in responsibility? Job hopping? A gap between jobs? A functional resume, for example, can effectively create the illusion that you had management experience with IBM, when in fact it was as a board member of a PTA school group. On the surface, that's great. But guess what? The person who reads resumes at a major corporation isn't an idiot. Her first thought upon picking up a functional or targeted or hybrid resume is, "Let's see what we're hiding here."

Aside from resumes with different formats, there are the gimmick resumes. You know the scenario. A candidate wants her resume to stand out from the others and wants to catch the employer's eye, so she sends it inside a tiny coffin, with the note, "I'm dying to get this job." Or a guy sends a resume rolled up inside a shoe, with a note on the sole, "I'd walk miles to get this job." Don't waste your time. Those are gadgets. They have no place in a professional job search. More ominously, they suggest to the employer instantly that you are a promoter who needs to embellish the facts on your resume to compete with other, more qualified, candidates. A resume introduces and sells you to the employer, so a gimmick won't work—unless you're applying for a job as a ringmaster with Barnum & Bailey or a bouncer in a Tijuana strip joint.

Remember, your resume gets only about fifteen or twenty seconds of reading time. You get one chance to make a good first impression. And you do that best with a resume illustrating your experience, knowledge, professionalism, and maturity. When you think about sending a resume to an employer, keep one thought uppermost in mind. It's as though the company is asking, "What can you do for us?" You can't be there to answer the question, so your resume must speak for you. To that end, a two-page, chronological format serves you best.

We won't ask you to invest time in picking a resume format. Instead, the Appendix to this book presents samples of thirty different resumes. This is not a contradiction. They're all in the same format—chronological. But each represents a different function, industry, or level in the workplace. Moreover, we are confident that they are the best examples of resumes you've ever seen.

If you're an engineer, look at the sample engineering resume. A manufacturing manager can follow one example, a computer programmer another, a corporate planner another. The point is, that's the only choice you need make. Pick the function that fits your career, shoehorn your professional information into the format, and be confident that you have a real heavy-hitter on your side in your job search. Your resume will serve as the basis for your entire campaign.

If you haven't yet referred to the sample resumes in the Appendix, do so now. Concentrate on the occupational function that fits you, but also check the other resumes. You'll probably be able to borrow phrases and ideas from some or all of them. Plan to spend a couple of dozen hours preparing your resume. But please, don't try to write it yet. There's more to learn. If you don't also understand how to utilize the resume in your job search, you might as well send the employer that old shoe or that miniature coffin.

Recall our *First Commandment of Job Search: Linkage*. Restated, it means that every step you take in job search ties in with the previous step you took and the next one you plan. Each phone call, each networking contact, each letter of reference, each resume you send, each interview— they are all linked. And *your resume is the key link* in this process.

FORGING THE FIRST LINK

If you think ahead to the interview as you write your resume, you will see that what you put in the resume, and how you structure it, determines how you will answer the most important questions put to you when you're sitting across the desk from the hiring authority.

Don't fail to grasp this concept. In most job searches, the job hunters prepare their resumes independently of the other job search activities. Consequently they send a resume, follow up with a phone call, get an interview appointment, go to the interview and talk for an hour, and go home without an offer. That's how job search works when you don't understand linkage.

In Chapter 8, we'll discuss in detail all the facets of interviewing for a job—including, of course, the tough questions. But consider for a moment the traditional opening question in a job interview—and for many candidates the toughest—"Tell us about yourself." That's a signal for most people to launch into a rambling, disjointed biographical statement. More often than not, this response is a self-incriminating litany of every reason why no one, anywhere, would ever want to hire this person. But you can be different. When you complete your resume a couple of days from now, you'll be able to answer that opening question with a response that gets you off and winging with confidence on your interview. It's really not difficult when you link your resume to the interview.

Your answer should consist of four parts, and you should talk roughly two to three minutes. All you really have to do is state what's in your resume, starting from the bottom of page two and moving to the top of page one.

- Start with your early history—where you were born, where you grew up, how long you've lived at your current place of residence. If you served in the armed forces, include that here.

- Part two is your education. Tell where you went to school and what degree you received. (If you don't have a degree and work in a profession that normally demands one, you should be attending school and working toward a degree. State that in your answer.)

- Part three consists of a brief description of your early jobs out of school, explaining the transitions between jobs. Then get to your most recent (or current) position, explaining how your skills and experience relate to this opening.

- Finally, part four is a brief explanation of why you and this company would be a good match, reflecting facts you learned in your advance research on the firm. In closing, mention what a first-rate company this is and that you are pleased to be interviewed for a position in the firm.

Voila! Your answer is complete. You not only got through—in all likelihood, you knocked them out of their chairs. Confidence boosted, you're ready for the subsequent interview questions. It's so simple, it mystifies us why more people don't do it.

The resume will serve you equally well all through the interview. Any time you get into trouble (you will—we all do, sooner or later), count on the resume to rescue the interview, as surely as a lighthouse guides a foundering vessel to port. That's linkage in action. That's how a powerful resume sets the stage for a winning interview. But enough about interviewing—you have a resume to write.

IT'S TIME TO START WRITING

To answer the tough questions so adroitly, you must know your resume and what's in it—forward, backward, upside down, inside out. Of course, you're dead if you try to read from it during the interview, so you must know every word that's in it by heart. Obviously, it follows that you must write it yourself. Paying some laid-off secretary or unemployed personnel clerk—or, worse yet, some resume service—to write your resume short-circuits the process and guarantees a bad start for your job campaign. It's your life, your career. And it must be your resume if you're to utilize it to full advantage.

Write it. Rewrite it. Cut it down and rewrite it again. Polish it. It's probably still five pages long, so let it cool off overnight, then cut it down and rewrite it again. If it remains more than two pages long, rest assured that it's full of information no one will read, so cut it again. Follow the models and principles set out for you in this chapter. Take the resume to a friend or colleague who's good with the language and get an evaluation, but again, steer clear of the charlatans in this consulting business who prey on job hunters. Most important, don't set sail on your job search with a bad resume or a resume written by someone else.

Thus far, this has been a chapter full of theory. But one of our bedrock beliefs about job search is that people shouldn't be overdosed on theory. Hands-on, real-world training works best. So let's get to that. Here's how to build the two-page, chronological resume that will get your job search moving in high gear.

Start at the top of page one by centering your name, mailing address, and phone numbers, with area codes. Your home number is a must; include a business number if possible.

YOUR PHONE *MUST* BE ANSWERED

Be certain that your phone will be answered during business hours. If your only contact is a home phone, and no one will be available to answer during the workday, your job search is already in trouble.

Let's assume that a company has selected your resume as one of five out of 350 to follow up on for interviews. How many times do you think they will call back if there is no answer? Your best bet is to answer the first call. When you're out interviewing or doing library research, don't allow even one caller to miss you. To that end, use an answering service, get a message recorder, or arrange with your spouse or a friend to cover the phone while you're gone. One excellent method is to use an executive office arrangement as your job search headquarters. Our Houston facility has individual offices for executive clients as part of our corporate outplacement service. Clients get full administrative support, with a complete library, as well as individual counseling. If you can arrange outplacement support like this through your former employer, so much the better. But whatever your circumstance, make the logistics work to your advantage.

A SAMPLE RESUME

Look at Exhibit 3.1, Sample Resume A (Paul Lee). Lee's resume identifies the applicant, tells where the company can reach him by mail or phone, then moves immediately into professional qualifications. *Never* include your height, weight, marital status, or any other personal information in a resume. Remarkably, some people walk around carrying an occupational death wish—*Height: 4' 10"; Weight: 210; Marital Status: Divorced mother of eight children*. Incredible, but it happens every day. You might just as well walk into an interview with a scarlet letter on your chest. The point is that none of that information has any bearing whatsoever on your ability to do a job. If

EXHIBIT 3.1
Sample Resume A

PAUL LEE
Address
Home #
Business #

OBJECTIVE

Director of Marketing

SUMMARY

Over twenty years experience in planning, developing and implementing sales of various steel mill products.

PROFESSIONAL EXPERIENCE

MOC INC.   1968-Present

Manager, Houston District Tubular Products - Houston, Texas - (1985-Present)

• Managed salesmen and developed short and long range sales objectives for total yearly sales of $60-$70 million.

• Increased market share of apparent domestic supply by 2%, or $1.5 million.

• Developed three new accounts, which resulted in sales of $5 million.

• Reduced selling and administrative costs within responsible territory by 3% for a $10,000 net reduction.

• Developed marketing information on competitive situations and market trends by territory which increased effective sales planning.

Resident Manager - Oklahoma City, Oklahoma - (1979-1985)

• Managed sales office with a staff of four and yearly sales of $60 million.

• Increased total yearly sales by 14% or $5 million for the district.

• Increased market share on all products by 4% or $2 million within sales territory.

• Negotiated quarterly contracts for two major accounts amounting to new business of $7 million.

• Coordinated marketing, credit, technical services and mill operations for the selling team within the district.

<u>Senior Product Specialist</u> - Kansas City, Missouri - (1977-1979)

- Developed and formulated commercial policy for the sale of hot rolled bars, structural and semi-finished products.

- Broadened the product line to include the production and sale of alloy bars and semi-finished alloy bars.

- Developed claims handling procedure for entire Kansas City works.

<u>District Sales Representative</u> - Wichita, Kansas - (1969-1977)

- Increased sales of territory by 10% to $12 million.

- Developed a distributor network for the sale of wire products and tubing products which increased market share by 8% for sales of $1 million.

- Developed and implemented a sales training program for the inside staff which resulted in a 5% increase in sales in the amount of $1.1 million.

<u>Sales Correspondent</u> - Dallas, Texas - (1969)

- Managed inside sales for all steel mill products.

- Handled pricing, order entry, expediting orders, claims and written quotations.

- Assisted outside sales in implementing sales plans and meeting sales forecast and objectives.

<u>Sales Trainee</u> - Middletown, Ohio - (1968)

MILITARY

U.S. Army, Lieutenant Colonel,
Company Commander 4th Armored Division - 1965 - 1967
Deputy Chief Personnel and Administration,
75th U.S. Maneuver Area Command - 1985 - Present

EDUCATION

B.B.A., Texas A & M University, College Station, Texas - 1965
Graduate Command & General Staff College, Fort Leavenworth, Kansas - 1977

information isn't job-related, it doesn't belong in your resume. Another favorite trivial redundancy is the phrase at the top of many resumes: "Resume of Qualifications." Now *that's* a revelation! You can be certain that an employer isn't going to mistake a resume for your last will and testament, so it's not necessary to label it. Your cover letter will introduce the resume anyway.

Moving along to the meat of the resume, the *Objective* tells what job Paul Lee wants to get. Period. Don't include a lot of extraneous nonsense about a "challenging career position with a dynamic, growth-oriented company." Similarly, the *Summary* is direct and to-the-point. It doesn't drag the reader through every detail of Lee's life; it simply states what he's done to qualify for the job objective stated above. It's brief, well-organized, and complete. Again, there are no extraneous words cluttering up the page and stealing time from the fifteen to twenty seconds Lee has in which to grab the reader's interest.

ANALYZING THE SAMPLE

In the Lee sample resume, within five to seven seconds the employer could learn the applicant's name, that he wants a job as a Director of Marketing, and that he has twenty years' experience in marketing steel products. Always remember that the people who read resumes are busy and that yours is competing with hundreds of others for their attention. Almost every other resume either will be abysmally unprofessional or will consume all fifteen to twenty seconds of reading time just to discover who the applicant is. Instantaneously, you've achieved a competitive advantage.

That advantage isn't confined to just reading time required, however. Don't you agree that the sample resume is a high-impact, professional piece of work? We're not claiming originality. Our resume format is nothing but a compendium of effective features we've encountered throughout many years of human resources counseling. Still, one of the hardest lessons to get across to applicants is that no one but their mothers enjoys reading their resumes.

In this sample, the professional data is excellent. Equally important are the ample white space, brief statements, plus right and left margin justification. You get this tailored look on a word processor and *only* a word processor. If you don't have access to one, go to the expense of hiring an operator on an hourly contract basis to prepare your resume. That's the only way to get a tight, professional, organized appearance.

In addition, a word processor gives the flexibility you must have at the top of a resume. As you turn the page you will notice some italicized type ahead. Yes, that means that Dawson & Dawson are getting ready to blow another resume platitude out of the water: *Another Dawson & Dawson Commandment: Don't Waste Time on a Completed Resume.*

Although a resume should be custom-designed for each job opening, redesigning your entire resume for every job lead is an absolutely stupid waste of time. Time is the ultimate, finite resource for us all. Don't rewrite a resume after you have arrived at the final, polished draft. Many so-called consultants feed that kind of garbage to job hunters, telling them to tailor their resume to each job opportunity. You're supposed to be busy researching, networking, getting job leads. Wasting time on a completed resume won't accomplish anything but delay in your job search.

To custom-design a resume, all you need to do is change the objective and possibly rephrase the summary. This is where the flexibility of a word processor is essential in producing your resume. Having produced hundreds of resumes for our clients, we guarantee that the word processor will streamline your job search. Your basic resume remains intact. The operator can quickly punch in the new information to lead off the resume, and instantly you have a custom-tailored document ready to help you get that interview.

A good human resources executive can tell all she needs to know about you from your resume. That's why our firm stresses the importance of the complete package, custom-designed. Beyond your professional qualifications, the employer can tell how well you'll fit the corporate culture just from the appearance of the resume. A real pro can gauge your professionalism, your maturity, how much effort you put into preparing the resume, and a myriad of other impressions that virtually jump off the page for a trained interviewer.

Most of all, the interviewer is looking for excuses to stop reading. That's why it's so important to ensure that your resume presents you as a solid professional. *That's* what complements your technical skills and experience—not some gimmick or eye-catching departure from format. For example, on the Lee resume sample, the interviewer can quickly tell that Paul Lee is a pro, just from the overall impact. Then the reader learns immediately his *Objective*—Director of Marketing. If that objective doesn't fit the company's needs, the resume is culled. (See, now, the paramount importance of custom-designing the top of your resume?) If the objective fits, the reader moves along to the *Summary.*

The Summary must justify Lee's desire to fill his job objective. If it does that, the reader continues. If not—if the summary of experience isn't heavy enough to qualify for the position targeted—the resume is tossed aside. The summary pushes the reader along to *Professional Experience.* Quickly and cleanly, Lee tells where he worked, when, and what he did. But here's the critical part of the resume—the selling statements for Lee's skills. *It's not what he did in terms of duties, but what he did to help MOC INC. make more money!* Read that again, underline it, commit it to memory. That's the part of your resume that catches the employer's attention. It's what causes her to put your resume on the "good" stack rather than the "bad" one.

ANOTHER SAMPLE: SIMILARITIES AND A DIFFERENCE

Now look at Exhibit 3.2, Sample Resume B (Joseph Jenkins). Jenkins's objective and summary are presented similarly to Paul Lee's. Below that, however, the two samples differ slightly. This style variance is the only discretionary element for clients in our offices. Both resumes list the company and length of service, then break out jobs within the organization as transfers and promotions occur. (*Note:* Both resumes use years only, not months. Never use months on your resume. That causes the reader to focus on short-term details rather than long-range accomplishments in your career.) Here is the writer's discretion: Lee gets right into his accomplishments and incorporates his job duties into those statements. In contrast, Jenkins briefly summarizes his responsibilities before listing accomplishments: "Project Manager/Brazil—Directed staff of 40 professionals," and so forth. Either format is acceptable. Both work. Just be certain that you don't clutter up the accomplishment statements with a list of duties.

Note that both resume samples address *problems* faced in their jobs, what *actions* they took to solve the problems, and what *resulted* from their efforts. Refer back to Lee's resume: "Increased market share . . . $1.5 million," "Reduced selling and administrative costs . . . by . . . $10,000," "Developed three new accounts, which resulted in sales of $5 million." Similarly, Jenkins's resume informs the company that he helped his previous employer by reducing penalty charges by 35 percent, reducing operating downtime 50 percent, and developing a service group that reduced expatriate costs by $300,000.

Two points in common are evident in the two resumes, and you should adapt the same idea for yours. Both Jenkins and Lee express their job performance or results in terms of numbers—either percentages or dollars. Those are *quantitative* accomplishment statements. If your resume doesn't have that type of forcefulness, it's not yet ready for the employer to read. There are exceptions, however. Some professions just don't lend themselves to the use of flat quantitative accomplishment statements. In such cases, use *qualitative* accomplishment statements that indicate results, such as "substantial reductions," "significant increases," "improved results," and so forth. In short, the reader should infer from your accomplishment statements that you are a walking, talking, breathing bundle of management and/or technical skills. That's what your accomplishments implicitly communicate.

WHAT'S IN IT FOR THE COMPANY?

Many people can't shake loose from the concept of what they did on the job—their duties or responsibilities. But to write solid accomplishment statements, you must think in terms of *values* to the employer. The following accomplishment statements include some of the values that will push the hot button of any company:

- Contributed to profit increase, cost reduction, increased sales or market share
- Increased productivity and quality; improved product or service
- Improved relations with customers, consumer groups, governments
- Improved employer/employee relations
- Improved teamwork and resolved conflict
- Improved communications and information flow
- Reduced operating downtime, streamlined operations
- Developed new technology or administrative procedures
- Anticipated a need or problem and initiated effective remedial action
- Planned or directed in an innovative manner
- Implemented an important program or acted with significant benefits
- Increased return on investment

The common denominator isn't difficult to determine in that list of accomplishments. It is, of course, the corporate bottom line. The only reason a company wants to hire you is to solve its problems and enhance its profitability. The foregoing accomplishments illustrate that you know how to do both. Generally, a true accomplishment must meet one of the following tests to aid the company:

- Achieved more without utilizing increased resources
- Achieved the same but reduced resource utilization
- Achieved improved operations or relations
- Achieved a goal for the first time under existing conditions
- Achieved resolution of problems or conflicts with little or no negative effect

EXHIBIT 3.2
Sample Resume B

JOSEPH JENKINS
Address
Home #
Business #

OBJECTIVE

Sales Manager

SUMMARY

Over fifteen years experience including eight years in planning, developing and implementing sales/marketing plans internationally and domestically. Extensive involvement in joint ventures, licensee agreements and agent contracts. Broad field experience in drilling and production, onshore/offshore.

PROFESSIONAL EXPERIENCE

SURPLUS COMPANY - Houston, Texas   1982-Present

Project Manager/Brazil - (1984-Present)

Directed staff of 40 professionals in the manufacture, assembly and installation of subsea production systems to Petro.

- Reduced penalty clause charges by 35% through timely delivery of units.

- Reduced operating downtime 50% and scrap rate 50%; improved efficiency of original design 35%; all resulting in streamlined operations.

- Developed Brazilian service group thereby reducing expatriate costs by $300,000; instituted wage/salary structure which reduced payroll by $50,000.

- Formulated and administered company policies and procedures that resulted in no absences and increased productivity by 50%.

Sales Engineer - International - (1982-1984)

Planned, developed, and implemented sales/marketing efforts in Canada, Latin America and Mexico.

- Increased market penetration 25% and reduced cost of sales by 35%.

- Conducted sales/marketing/engineering support to South East Asia and Europe/Africa offices, which improved customer relations.

- Trained customers through special presentations in subsea drilling and production and standard wellhead systems, which improved customer knowledge.

- Developed and maintained exclusive agent agreements in India, Latin America and South East Asia, which increased market penetration.

JOSEPH JENKINS

TOC OFFSHORE, INC. - Houston, Texas   1979-1982

Sales Engineer - Latin America

- Achieved a 50% increase of subsea market in Mexico and 35% in Argentina and Chile.

- Developed and evaluated licensee agreements and foreign investments in Argentina and Mexico, which increased profits.

- Coordinated with project engineering on special customer project, which improved customer relations and administrative procedures.

DAE PUMP - Bartlesville, Oklahoma   1976-1979

Application/Sales Engineer - London - (1977-1979)

- Increased sales in North Africa 30% and reduced cost of sales by 25%.

- Improved relations between customers, agents, and government offices in North Africa and Europe, which improved operations.

- Improved client relations by aiding in service work in the Sahara.

Application/Sales Engineer - Bartlesville, Oklahoma - (1976-1977)

- Coordinated the business plan and capital justification for a joint venture in Mexico and a licensee agreement in Argentina, which increased sales.

- Developed and implemented sales strategies in Latin America, which increased market share.

RING PETROLEUM CORPORATION - Houston, Texas   1973-1976

Field Engineer/Assistant to Manager of drilling department involved with all phases of drilling and production operations onshore and offshore.

EDUCATION

B.S., Mechanical Engineering, Texas A & M University - 1970
Chinese, Continuing Studies, Rice University - 1983

LANGUAGE

Spanish, Italian, French, Portuguese

PROFESSIONAL

American Petroleum Institute
American Institute of Mechanical Engineers

49

THE RIGHT WORD IN THE RIGHT PLACE

The importance of measurable results in your accomplishment statements has already been addressed. Think of the statements as flags waving at the top of a fortress. But you need a foundation for each statement—the word that starts each phrase. Without fail, that word must be a strong, active-voice verb. Look over the following lists of suggested verbs, and use them in your resume. Again, refer to the Lee and Jenkins sample resumes. The opening word of each accomplishment statement captures the reader's attention and encourages the eye to move along toward the critically important dollar or percentage figure that illustrates the job hunter's potential worth to the employer.

Action verbs that address your *planning* skills include:

Conceived	Formulated	Projected
Created	Initiated	Reorganized
Designed	Innovated	Revised
Developed	Instituted	Scheduled
Devised	Invented	Solved
Engineered	Justified	Systematized
Established	Laid out	Tailored
Estimated	Organized	Transformed
Experimented	Originated	
Formed	Planned	

Action verbs that address your skills in *directing* employees include:

Administered	Determined	Ordered
Approved	Directed	Prescribed
Authorized	Guided	Regulated
Conducted	Headed	Specified
Controlled	Instructed	
Decided	Led	Supervised
Delegated	Managed	Trained

Action verbs that suggest that you have skills in *assuming responsibility* include:

Accepted	Arranged	Attended
Achieved	Assembled	Audited
Adopted	Assumed	Built

Checked	Gathered	Overcame
Classified	Halted	Performed
Collected	Handled	Prepared
Compiled	Improved	Produced
		Received
Constructed	Implemented	Reduced
Described	Initiated	Reviewed
Developed	Installed	Sold
Doubled	Integrated	Simplified
Established	Maintained	Transacted
		Tripled
Evaluated	Made	Used
Experienced	Operated	Utilized

Action verbs that embody an ability to provide effective *service* include:

Carried out	Explained	Provided
Committed	Facilitated	Purchased
Delivered	Furnished	Rewrote
Demonstrated	Generated	Sent
Earned	Inspected	Serviced
Exchanged	Installed	Submitted
Expanded	Issued	Transmitted
Expedited	Procured	Wrote

Interactive skills with people are suggested by the use of these action verbs in your accomplishment statements:

Advised	Coordinated	Negotiated
Aided	Counseled	Participated
Apprised	Helped	Promoted
Clarified	Informed	Recommended
Conferred	Inspired	Represented
Consulted	Interpreted	Resolved
Contributed	Interviewed	Suggested
Cooperated	Mediated	Unified

Finally, your *investigative* skills emerge with the use of these action verbs:

Analyzed	Evaluated	Reviewed
Assessed	Familiarized	Searched
Calculated	Investigated	Studied
Computed	Observed	Verified
Correlated	Proved	
Discovered	Researched	

That's only a sampling of the types of words you must include in your resume. Use these lists or use other verbs to communicate your skills and how they generated accomplishments. Just be sure that you use a strong action verb to open every statement.

HITTING THE BULLSEYE

Note the ● symbols that precede the accomplishment statements in the following list as well as in all the sample resumes in the Appendix. They're called *bullets*, and your job is to see that each one of them hits the target. It will if it is followed by a winning accomplishment statement. The target is that small pile of resumes on the desk of the human resources staff person that are put aside to be followed up instead of discarded.

Your completed accomplishment statements should read like these:

- Achieved a 25% cost reduction by creating and installing a complete accounting system by department in a large agency.
- Created a profit and loss statement, by product, resulting in substantial increase of sales in the high-profit products.

(Do you recognize the categories of those first two? The first is *quantitative*; the second is *qualitative*. But they both work.)

- Managed a professional group in creating a sales organization after identifying a $300 million market.
- Conceived a new management information services procedure that made vital operations reports available to management the following day.
- Prevented a potentially volatile ethnic incident from erupting in a racially sensitive community.
- Developed a community acceptance campaign in San Francisco (a hostile market), resulting in the reduction of processing time by nearly 25%.

- Saved millions in possible damages, and prevented embarrassment by discovering potential bankruptcy of a supplier.
- Proved that a $2.2 million inventory shortage predated the acquisition of a division, resulting in corrective action.
- Formulated policies and procedures for the administration of zoning petitions, resulting in the reduction of processing time by nearly 25%.
- Created and administered more than a million lines of free newspaper and magazine publicity, helping to maintain top television ratings.
- Reduced rework by 20%, eliminated schedule delays, and doubled in-house manufacturing capability through reorganization and introduction of methods and systems.
- Designed supporting equipment and techniques for a new process that raised product market potential from $5 million to more than $20 million per year.
- Promoted a new concept in welding procedure that reduced labor costs by $100,000.
- Discovered $190,000 overstatement of a division's inventory, enabling corrective action by management.
- Reduced turnover of personnel from 17% to 9% per year.
- Installed a cost system for complex fabricating process, saving $75,000 per year.
- Revised shipping procedures and introduced improvements that substantially reduced cost and shipping time.
- Instituted a wage and salary program especially tailored to improve morale while eliminating waste, reducing payroll by $40,000.
- Developed and installed a unique laboratory organization that eliminated duplication, encouraged cooperation, and reduced costs by $50,000.
- Trained new employees in laboratory procedures and use of equipment, resulting in more effective and efficient job orientation.

This list is intended only to get you into the right frame of mind to state your accomplishments in terms of dollars and percentages. Review your career and pick out your accomplishment highlights. If you're telling yourself, "I didn't do anything like that," welcome to the crowd. That's the initial reaction of most people facing resume writing. Push beyond those initial doubts. Jot down notes and thoughts and phrases as they occur to you. This is a building process, and it takes time, reflection, and effort.

Remember, we require a couple of dozen hours of commitment as your investment in your resume for the benefit of your career. This is where you'll spend the bulk of that time. One good way to get off dead center is to go ahead and write down your duties. That's probably the only way to deal with them, because most people are so preoccupied with their responsibilities that they can't get beyond the tasks of their job to highlight their achievements.

When you have the duties down on paper, begin to think through them. Recall results and benefits to the company that your duties generated. That's what goes into your accomplishment statements. Do not attempt to translate each responsibility into an accomplishment, however. Some responsibilities may not generate any significant accomplishments, while others may produce two or three.

To help you move along with the process, divide a piece of paper into three columns. At the tops of the columns, write these headings: *Action Verb, Action Taken, Benefit to Company*. In the *Action Verb* column, write a verb that indicates your intensity of effort, demonstrates the power required to achieve the result, or illustrates your level of responsibility. Be certain that you use a variety of verbs. Refer to our lists for ideas. They include more than 150 verbs, and of course you're not limited to those alone. On the contrary, be as creative as possible. And be aware that even a strong action verb becomes diluted if it is repeated in your resume. In the second column, under *Action Taken*, write *what* you accomplished. This should be a short, concise statement about what you did. It should not be a description of *how* you did it. Finally, in the column under *Benefit to Company*, write the result or impact of your achievement on the company's business. This is the payoff. This is where you use dollars and percentages at every opportunity. This is what makes you valuable to a prospective employer.

Remember, throughout this process, that the reader will look at each entry in your resume in one of three ways: it improves your chance to get an interview; it detracts from your chance; or it's a push, a neutral. Your primary job as a resume writer is to pack as many positives into the document as your memory, imagination, and the truth will allow.

Finally.

THE TRUTH?

There's that word. In your resume, you must tell the T-R-U-T-H—as in "the truth, the whole truth, and nothing but the truth." We don't agree, however—at least not in the context of "the whole" and "nothing but." You don't write a resume with one hand on the Bible. So we present *Dawson & Dawson's Final Commandment of Resume Writing: They Don't Know What You Don't Tell Them.*

Do tell the truth as it relates to your ability to do the job. Certainly, we're not suggesting that you lie, cheat, or steal to get a job. Aside from the ethical and moral questions, you'll be saddled with work you're not qualified to perform if you falsify your background or experience.

We *are* telling you to get smart. Leaving some point out of your resume is not lying. We all make mistakes in our professional lives. We all have elements in our personal lives that we wouldn't run up and confess to a stranger. Nonetheless, people will confess to just about anything—up to and including the organizing of the Arab oil cartel—when they're looking for a job. You're not in a confessional and you're not defending your past errors of judgment. Tell the truth—fine. But don't look for a job the way a Kamikaze pilot flies an airplane. If the information will hurt you, leave it out of your resume. Period. That's not a lie.

We've already mentioned our philosophy of using years, never months, in presenting your career history. That's a good illustration. Suppose that you worked at Dry Hole Oil Exploration from November 1985 to January 1986. If you put those months in your resume, you've probably made yourself into instant history as an applicant. However, if you put that you worked at Dry Hole from 1985 to 1986, you're not placing yourself in dire jeopardy immediately. Make no mistake, you'll have to address your brief tenure at Dry Hole during the interview, but at least you haven't prematurely removed yourself from consideration with one careless entry on a resume. Did you lie? Of course you didn't. You simply told the truth in terms that make you most attractive to the employer. If your mother or your old scoutmaster doesn't like that approach, that's too bad. Do some good turns and make it up to them later. First get a job.

FIRST THINGS FIRST GETS YOU WHERE YOU SHOULD BE

Now that you understand the truth as it relates to getting a job, get back to your accomplishments. You should include four to six entries under your most recent job. Remember, don't try to include everything you've ever achieved in that job, just the highlights that make you a more attractive candidate. With proper margin alignment and white space between each element we've discussed thus far, you should be at the bottom of page one. And that's proper—that's the way we construct a resume. Your last position and your accomplishments in that job are most critical. Your other jobs will go on page two.

Jenkins's resume is the best example of this. He held two positions with the same company over the past four years, and it's all on page one.

On page two, Jenkins lists three previous positions. Continue the same philosophy with accomplishment statements, but don't go back more than about ten years chronologically or two-thirds of the second page graphically. If you're a trooper with thirty or thirty-five years' experience, just summarize in one brief statement all the work experience and your accomplishments prior to the last ten years. Refer to the engineering resume in the Appendix (number 17) for an example of this technique. This engineering manager took his accomplishment statements back to 1977, then summarized four job titles with one-line descriptions of his duties. Another acceptable presentation is to omit the job titles and dates and write one summary statement of duties in a short paragraph form. Following the last accomplishment statement, you could state: "During the period from 1960 to 1968, held progressively responsible positions within the organization following on-campus recruitment as entry-level management trainee." See the administrative assistant's resume in the Appendix (number 28) for an example of this style.

The point is that if the information is more than ten years old, no one really cares about it. Summarize information that is dated; otherwise, you'll be cluttering up your resume with entries that won't be read because they're obsolete and/or irrelevant. We recognize that you may earnestly feel that you want to include a critically important accomplishment from 1958, but believe us, it won't help. Summarize it, undated, and keep your resume to two pages.

"JUST THE FACTS, PLEASE"

Next, list your *Military* background, but only if you were an officer (this indicates leadership capabilities) or if you served in a career-related enlisted rate (this implies hands-on training and experience). For example, an MIS degree coupled with prebaccalaureate working experience on a military data processing system can enhance your attractiveness as a candidate. (Note in Exhibit 3.1 that Lee lists his military background as a commissioned officer.) These entries should be brief and concise.

Cover your *Education* similarly. If you have advanced degrees, list the highest degree attained first, then any undergraduate degrees. If you graduated with honors, include your grade point average; otherwise, leave it out. Do not list training courses or seminars under *Education*. As we mentioned earlier, if you're working in a field that requires a degree and you don't have one, put in your resume that you're working toward the required degree, and give the projected completion date of your studies. (Again, don't lie. If your profession requires a college degree and you haven't completed school yet, do something about that. You're on borrowed time—enroll. Get a degree plan in action so that your resume won't be lying.)

The next resume entry is *Professional Affiliations*. Include here any societies, institutes, or other *Professional Associations* to which you belong. This shows the employer what you are when you aren't working. It implies civic involvement. Also, any certifications you have achieved should be listed here.

Finally, wrap up your resume with any other important job-related data. Note in Exhibit 3.2 that Jenkins is fluent in four foreign languages. That's an excellent punctuation mark for his background—good solid stuff to conclude the resume. It's also permissible to include an entry on community involvement. But be certain that the information enhances your impact on the employer. Did you coach Little League baseball? That's great, but it doesn't belong in a resume. If you served on a mayor's committee to study the community benefits of youth sports programs, that should be included. Do you serve on the PTA board at your child's school? Leave it off. If you're an elected member of the community's school board, put that in under community involvement. Get the idea? The employer will buy into activities that either lend prestige to the firm or illustrate skills you can transfer to the workplace. The employer doesn't want to read entries in your resume that indicate priorities that will take time and energy away from your career. (Refer to sample resume 15 in the Appendix for the best example of the types of civic activities to include in your resume.)

Again, omit all personal information. Marital status? *No*. Number of children. *No*. Salary? *Never*—you'll cover that in the interview and in the cover letter if necessary. Reason for leaving a job? *No*. Hobbies? *No*. So you like hunting, boating, and camping—*who cares*? What does that have to do with your ability to do the job? Health? *No*. That one is a real joke. Have you ever seen a resume on which an applicant wrote "Health: Below Average" or "Health: Poor" or "Health: Terminally Ill"? No—everyone writes "Health: Excellent." Therefore, it means nothing. And it doesn't belong on your resume, so keep it off.

WHEN YOU COME TO THE END, STOP

Finally, we come to the traditional closing statement on 98 percent of all resumes: "References available upon request." Remember, we don't want your resume cluttered up with useless information, which is just what this is. It's implied—you don't write it in a resume. There might be one or two human resources managers in the world who don't understand that references are always available upon request. But cluttering up a resume on the remote possibility that some idiot might read it is not a smart approach. If the guy reviewing your resume is such a rook that he doesn't comprehend this, you probably don't want to work at that company anyway.

You are now at the end of two pages, which means that your resume is complete. "But," you say, "what about my publications and the training courses I've taken?" Don't panic! For those of you who have additional career information that you feel is relevant to your qualifications as a candidate for a position, place such data on a third page. However, as a supplemental page, it should not be sent out with the resume but should be presented at the interview. Your resume should remain two pages and only two pages. (Exhibit 3.3 is a sample supplemental information page showing the various categories that are pertinent to career advancement.)

THE PERSONAL TOUCH

Now your resume is complete, but your work has just begun. Stay with us while we construct a good cover letter to introduce your resume, or else all your work will have been in vain. As good as your two-page resume will be, by its nature it's impersonal. Your cover letter will solve that problem. With a cover letter, your resume is targeted to a specific individual in the company. Always find out the name of the hiring authority. If you're an engineer, address the letter to the engineering manager, by name. If you're in sales, send it to the sales and marketing manager, and so on. No cover letter should carry the salutation "To whom it may concern." It will concern no one if you don't personalize it. The surest way to get the information is to find the name in trade journals or in *The Standard & Poor's Register, The Dun & Bradstreet Directory*, or other directories. Failing all that, call the company and ask for the name of the appropriate person. If you're responding to a blind advertisement, open with "Dear Sir/Madam."

Think of your cover letter in four parts, and write a maximum of 200 words in three paragraphs. (Exhibits 3.4 through 3.8, at the end of this chapter, provide examples of cover letters.)

The first paragraph introduces you and gives your purpose for writing. Perhaps you got the company's name from a networking contact or from an ad, or maybe you read an article in a trade journal about the firm's plans for expansion or introduction of a new product. Whatever your reason for sending a resume, this is where you state it.

In the second paragraph, briefly summarize your experience as it

EXHIBIT 3.3
Sample of Supplemental Information

MILITARY

U. S. Army

OTHER PROFESSIONAL COURSES

Graduate level courses; University of Houston

Introduction to Petroleum Engineering

Reservoir Engineering

Experimental Stress Analysis

INDUSTRY SCHOOLS

Well Planning, Prentice & Records, Lafayette, LA
Well Completions and Workovers, Prentice & Records, Lafayette, LA
Well Control (MMS Certified), Prentice & Records, Lafayette, LA
Rig Crew Training School, IADC, Abilene, TX
Wellhead School, Gray Tool Company, Houston, TX
Applied Drilling Systems, Adams & Roundtree, Houston, TX
Well Quality & Inspections, ASM, Houston, TX
Metallurgy in Oil & Gas Industry, ASM, Houston, TX
Hughes Drilling Seminars, Hughes Tool, Houston, TX
Oil Well Cementing, SPE Short Course, Houston, TX

PUBLICATIONS

"HP 41 CV Simplifies API Leak Resistance Calculations". Published in June,
1984, issue of World Oil.

"Value Analysis in Well Planning; A Systems Approach to String Design".
Presented at SPE Computer Technology Symposium, Lubbock, TX

PROFESSIONAL AFFILIATIONS

Member, Society of Petroleum Engineers (SPE)
Member, American Society of Mechanical Engineers (ASME)

LANGUAGE FLUENCY

Fluent in French, working knowledge of Spanish.

CIVIC ASSOCIATIONS

Chamber of Commerce

relates to this company's needs. In this section, you're attempting to hook the company's interest by answering the question: "What can this person do for us?" Also in this paragraph (or in a short, separate paragraph), you address salary if you're answering an ad that demands salary history. You must not ignore such a request. That might disqualify you from consideration. But at the same time, don't be too specific. We suggest that you use a range as a framework for your salary requirements. Use a $5,000 range if you earn less than $40,000, a $10,000 range if your income is from the mid-$40,000's to the $90,000's, and a $20,000 to $40,000 range if you earn $100,000 and above. (See Exhibit 3.4.) You don't, of course, pick numbers out of the air. First, research the company and the industry, and learn approximately what the position will pay before you respond. We'll cover how you do that in Chapter 9.

In the final paragraph, close with a proactive statement. This means that you take the initiative for the next contact. Don't leave it to the company. For example, many cover letters close with the statement, "Please contact me if you think my skills would help," and so forth. No—that's the wrong approach. That's reactive. When you're proactive, you write, "I'll contact you the week of July 7 to arrange an interview," and so forth. Don't ever be passive when you write a cover letter. You'll sit on your hands and wait forever. Be assertive. Be professionally persistent. Go for it. (Two exceptions to this rule are cover letters to a search firm—Exhibit 3.8—and in response to an ad—Exhibit 3.4.)

The fourth section of the letter is our favorite innovation. Save your one grand slam accomplishment to mention in a P.S. Studies of business letters prove conclusively that the segment of a letter that is most often read and retained is the first sentence, and the second most read is a P.S. For example, if a company is establishing a new sales territory, and its needs mesh with your experience, you could write "P.S.: As Marketing Vice-President for Weaktread Tire Corp., I supervised product introduction to the western U.S. First year sales topped projections by 65%."

Spend a few extra bucks and have your cover letter, like your resume, prepared on a word processor. Much is made of the importance of first impressions in job search—all of it valid. Few people stop to realize, however, that the format and style, plus the opening few words of a cover letter, actually constitute the very first impression they'll make on the company.

Your cover letter should be a product of your resume and your networking efforts. We've discussed cover letters in about 300 words and we've included five samples at the end of this chapter, while you've read maybe twenty times that much about resume writing in this book. That's not to minimize the role of a cover letter—there's just not that much to say about it. However, the cover letter is of critical importance, and you should strive for excellence in creating it, just as you do with your resume.

ACCEPT THE CHALLENGE

Striving for excellence is an imperative for your entire job search (and your life, as well). Follow the standards of excellence that we've set out for you in resume preparation, and adhere to the same conceptual approach in every step of your job campaign, up to and including the acceptance of an offer. Don't be discouraged by the bombardment of negatives you'll be hit with in your search. Certainly, there are thousands of others looking for jobs. Of course the market is tough—maybe tougher than ever before. But don't hide from the competitive nature of job campaigning. Respond to it. Challenge the numbers. Most of all, have confidence—both in yourself and in our principles of searching for a new job. The fundamentals are the same as they were thirty years ago and as they will be thirty years into the future.

Having lived in Texas for many years now, we can safely adopt one of the building blocks of Texan philosophy: "If it ain't broke, don't fix it." So it is with resume preparation. Snake oil artists are loose on the streets trying to sell you other ideas. But the tried-and-true system works. The only problem is that most people don't use it correctly. Strive to do it right. Expect to win. If you can't go into a competitive endeavor (which job search certainly is) expecting to win, don't play. It's the positive expectation of success that fosters success. If you don't expect to get the job offer, that attitude will show in all that you do, including your resume—especially your resume. The principles of positive thinking work every day in our offices. They will work for you, as well. Expect to get a job—not just any job, but the right career position for you.

Stop now and absorb what we've covered. Refer to the sample resumes and cover letters. Take the next two or three days to create a winning resume. Then come back and we'll make that resume work as hard for you as you worked at writing it.

EXHIBIT 3.4
Sample Cover Letter: Response to Ad

PAUL LEE
8212 Sandpiper
Houston, Texas 77072
(713) 999-1212

DATE

Mr. Thomas B. Clements
Vice President, Marketing
Northwest Supply Company
P. O. Box 1379
Los Angeles, CA 90036

Dear Mr. Clements:

Your advertisement, a copy of which is enclosed, caught my attention and I am interested in learning more about the position.

As my resume indicates, I have built a strong record of significant achievement in progressively more responsible sales and management positions during a 17-year career. My background includes planning, developing, and implementing sales of tubular products for MOC, Inc. In addition, my management responsibilities involved supervision of a staff of 18 in a three-state district.

My compensation requirements for this position are in the range of $60,000 to $70,000. (Note: If the ad requests salary information or salary history, this is how you respond.)

Should you have any questions, you may reach me at the above address or phone number. I look forward to hearing from you to discuss your organization and how my experience can contribute to its success.

Yours truly,

Paul Lee

PL/pp
Enclosure

EXHIBIT 3.5
Sample Cover Letter: Network Referral

PAUL LEE
8212 Sandpiper
Houston, Texas 77072
(713) 999-1212

DATE

Mr. Thomas B. Clements
Vice President, Marketing
Northwest Supply Company
P. O. Box 1379
Los Angeles, CA 90036

Dear Mr. Clements:

Mr. Kevin O'Hagan of IMC Corp. suggested that I contact you concerning a potential opportunity in sales management with Northwest Supply.

As my resume indicates, I have built a strong record of achievements in progressively more responsible sales and management positions during a 17-year career. My background includes planning, developing, and implementing sales of tubular products for MOC, Inc. In addition, my management responsibilities involved supervision of a staff of 18 in a three-state district.

Should you have any questions, you may reach me at the above address or phone number. I will take the liberty of telephoning you early next week to find a mutually convenient time for a meeting, and I look forward to discussing your organization and how my experience can contribute to its success.

Yours truly,

Paul Lee

PL/PP
Enclosure

EXHIBIT 3.6
Sample Cover Letter: Telemarketing Follow-up

PAUL LEE
8212 Sandpiper
Houston, Texas 77072
(713) 999-1212

DATE

Mr. Thomas B. Clements
Vice President, Marketing
Northwest Supply Company
P. O. Box 1379
Los Angeles, CA 90036

Dear Mr. Clements:

Thank you very much for taking time from your schedule to speak with me today. As you suggested, I have enclosed a copy of my resume for your review.

As my resume indicates, I have built a strong record of significant achievement in progressively more responsible sales and management positions. My background includes planning, developing, and implementing sales of tubular products for MOC, Inc. In addition, my management responsibilities involved supervision of a staff of 18 in a three-state district. As district manager, I developed three new accounts resulting in sales of $5 million, while reducing selling and administrative costs by 3%.

Should you have any questions, you may reach me at the above address or phone number. I will call you early next week to set up a mutually convenient time for a meeting, and I look forward to discussing your organization and how my experience can contribute to its success.

Yours truly,

Paul Lee

PL/pp
Enclosure

EXHIBIT 3.7
Sample Cover Letter: Cold Contact

PAUL LEE
8212 Sandpiper
Houston, Texas 77072
(713) 999-1212

DATE

Mr. Thomas B. Clements
Vice President, Marketing
Northwest Supply Company
P. O. Box 1379
Los Angeles, CA 90036

Dear Mr. Clements:

My investigation indicates your company would provide an excellent opportunity to realize my career objectives.

I am interested in a position which offers substantial challenge and a high degree of involvement and which provides the opportunity to contribute to the accomplishment of key organizational objectives. I offer an extensive background in marketing and sales management of a diverse range of steel mill products.

Enclosed is my resume for your review. I will contact you early next week to discuss your organization and how my experience can contribute to its success.

Yours truly,

Paul Lee

PL/pp
Enclosure

EXHIBIT 3.8
Sample Cover Letter: Search Firm

PAUL LEE
8212 Sandpiper
Houston, Texas   77072
(713) 999-1212

DATE

Ms. Dianne McAlister
Search Consultant
Executive Search Company
P. O. Box 4545
Houston, TX   77210

Dear Ms. McAlister:

I am interested in reviewing employment opportunities in the Houston area. I have extensive experience in planning, developing, and implementing sales of a diverse range of steel mill products. For the past nine years I have managed MOC, Inc.'s sales in Oklahoma City and at the district office in Houston, with a consistent record of increasing sales volume and market share.

I am now seeking new and challenging responsibilities in order to continue this career path in an organization that will demand maximum use of my skills, abilities, and experience. My compensation requirements are in the range of $60,000 to $70,000, and I am open to relocation.

Enclosed is my confidential resume for your consideration. Should you have a client assignment matching my background or would like to set up a mutually convenient appointment, please contact me at the above address or phone number.

Yours truly,

Paul Lee

PL/pp
Enclosure

CHAPTER FOUR

The Art of Preparing References: It's Not Just a List of Names

With deference to American Express, we suggest that you adapt the famous credit card advertising slogan for your job search: *"References—Don't Leave Home Without Them."*

Not surprisingly, our view of gathering references links with every other facet of our job campaigning advice—that is, plan and prepare for each step of the process. Coach your references on what you'll be telling interviewers, and elicit their assistance in supporting those statements. Then carry your detailed preparation work a step further. The critical part in the entire reference-gathering process comes when you write the reference letter about your own professional background. Sounds strange, doesn't it? It's not at all strange, but it is a unique approach.

Most often references are barely mentioned in job search advice, except to verify that they are needed and to suggest that you write at the bottom of your resume: "References Available Upon Request." Having written your resume our way, you already know that statement is for use by amateurs only. In contrast, we rate the gathering of references as an imperative in successful job campaigning. Make no mistake about it, if an employer does nothing else in the way of a background check, he will verify your education and check your references. One recent survey indicated that a company's average total cost-per-hire is more than $7,500 for each new salaried employee and can exceed $45,000 at the executive level. The company must get the right person at the right time for that kind of money. Therefore, you must effectively manage the flow of information from your references to potential employers. That's how you make references work for you rather than for the employer.

Obviously, this step is tough, complex, and subtle. If your relationship with a former boss ranged somewhere between quiet resentment and open hostility, the process becomes even more difficult. But make it happen—there is no alternative. Even if the resume you've just created jumps off the desk into the employer's hands, and even if the interviewing techniques you'll learn in Chapter 8 convince the company that you're their last hope, the job offer you were riding high on could crash and burn if your former boss indicates that your personal interactive skills more closely resemble Moammar Khadafy's than Mother Theresa's.

That's why we consider references an art, not just a list of names. Since for most job hunters our reference process is an untapped resource, successfully managing the complete scenario can position you for a huge advantage over the competition in the job market. For example, studies indicate that when job hunters endure a long, unproductive search, poor references are the root of the problem in about 40 percent of the cases.

Knowing that, why leave such a critical step to chance? Commit the extra effort and time to ensure that you get a reference letter, along with oral confirmation of the information, that will serve as a powerful complement to your winning resume and interview responses.

The only foolproof way to accomplish that is to write the reference letter yourself. The sequence is as follows:

- Prepare a draft.
- Send it to your former associate with a cover letter inviting him or her to review and edit the draft and asking that the final draft be returned on company letterhead.
- Put the resulting document in your job hunting tool kit, and you're beginning to stack some odds in your favor.

If you have any remaining doubts about the validity of this process, read the two sample letters of reference provided in Exhibits 4.1 and 4.2. The letter in Exhibit 4.1 was written without the foregoing procedure; the letter in Exhibit 4.2 was written as a result of that procedure.

We know very well that Martin Pierre is writing about the same person in both letters—the name's the same. But the name is clearly the only similarity between the employees described in the two letters. In the first letter, Joyce comes off like some nitwit—a corporate misfit who probably took six months to find the coffee machine. The Joyce in the second letter impresses us as a highly skilled, competent, well-rounded employee who performed her job professionally but was a victim of a corporate reorganization.

The difference, of course, is that Joyce Barton wrote the second letter,

EXHIBIT 4.1
Sample Reference Letter Without Proper Procedure

Joyce Barton
555 Park Lane
Omaha, Nebraska   77777

Dear Joyce:

ABC Company is a new member in Midwest Corporation and as such brought many changes and a new dynamic to both organizations. We believed we could place an individual like yourself with substantial technical skills but in need of managerial development at ABC Company. We found, however, that we had numerous issues which did in fact require the experience of a seasoned manager. The result was the necessity to initiate your outplacement and seek an individual with greater managerial experience.

We believe this change was necessary for the success of ABC Company and you. We support your effort in proper placement with a firm which has greater depth and can provide the opportunity for managerial development.

Sincerely,

Martin Pierre
President

and Martin Pierre accepted her draft and reproduced it on ABC Company letterhead. Is this easy? Certainly not. We've been consulting with managers and job searchers for twenty years, and some cases are tough to crack.

MEND YOUR FENCES, NO MATTER HOW BROKEN DOWN THEY ARE

Most employer–employee relationships can be patched up. Most bosses will cooperate. Most companies are as anxious for terminated employees to find

EXHIBIT 4.2
Sample Reference Letter After Proper Procedure

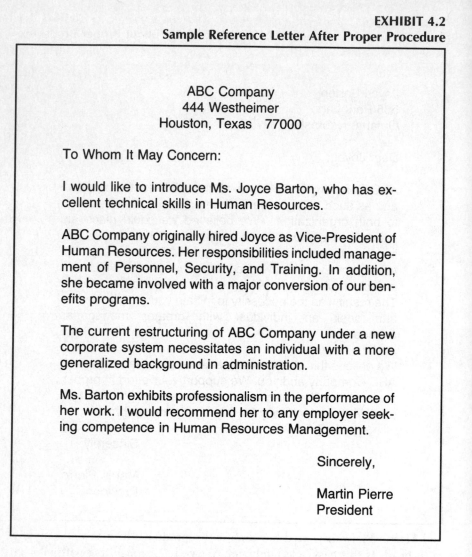

ABC Company
444 Westheimer
Houston, Texas 77000

To Whom It May Concern:

I would like to introduce Ms. Joyce Barton, who has excellent technical skills in Human Resources.

ABC Company originally hired Joyce as Vice-President of Human Resources. Her responsibilities included management of Personnel, Security, and Training. In addition, she became involved with a major conversion of our benefits programs.

The current restructuring of ABC Company under a new corporate system necessitates an individual with a more generalized background in administration.

Ms. Barton exhibits professionalism in the performance of her work. I would recommend her to any employer seeking competence in Human Resources Management.

Sincerely,

Martin Pierre
President

a new position as the individuals are. When you run into an exception to that, you must bear part of the responsibility. And you'd better accept that responsibility now if you're in that situation, because—like it or not—your next potential employer will certainly assign you guilt. If you do have a bad relationship with your ex-boss—if you parted on difficult terms—this is an area where you must use psychological leverage to your advantage. There's nothing to be gained from maintaining a negative relationship with anyone.

Our suggestion is that whenever you have a rift with someone in a job setting, bridge the gap immediately. The best way to bridge that gap is to ask for a letter of reference. Psychologically, this causes you to eat a slice of humble pie— which is good for anyone. Also, it causes your boss to rethink your work experience and, usually, to accept his or her share of the blame for the negative results of your previous relationship. Usually, the conclusion to the process is, "The least I can do now is write him a letter of reference."

We concede that there are impossible cases in which the resentment and anger simply can't be neutralized. But you can be sure that such a situation will hurt you in your job search. You'll be admitting that you don't have sufficient interpersonal skills to establish, maintain, or repair a key working relationship, and you'll be judged on that. You'll be in danger of joining that 40 percent of the job hunting population whose search keeps tripping over reference problems.

Never write off your relationship with your ex-boss, however, until you've given your best shot at getting a reference. And note that your best shot doesn't mean one phone call or a perfunctory inquiry through his secretary. It means professional persistence and courteous insistence that you expect nothing less. This is another example of what we call *psychological leverage*. If the boss refuses absolutely—and out of nothing more than 100-proof stubbornness—your psychological leverage includes the implied threat of legal action. We are unequivocally opposed to lawsuits over dismissals. They simply don't serve your best immediate or long-term interest. Here, however, it wouldn't hurt your bargaining position for the boss to realize that maliciously blocking you from securing a new position could land both him and the company in hot water.

Most of the time, however, the difficulty revolves more around pride and wounded feelings than it does around substantive or irresolvable differences between two people. A recent case in our Houston outplacement facility illustrates this most clearly:

Pete Smith, a terminated, angry former vice-president of administration, entered our program. He did not have a reference from his former boss. We told Pete that he was making a mistake by not attempting to get one. He replied that he couldn't ask for one and, moreover, that he would never ask "that [expletive deleted]" for anything. Our reasoning fell on deaf ears, and Pete lost three straight potential jobs. When he learned that a poor reference was the cause, he came to us and asked for help in getting a reference from that most recent boss. Resisting the temptation to say "We told you so," we constructed a letter of reference, laid the groundwork with a diplomatic phone call, and forwarded the material to his former boss. Without the slightest delay or protest, the reference letter was routed back to us on the company letterhead. Pete got the next job for which he interviewed.

Almost everyone underestimates the importance of a letter of reference. It can kill a job offer to not have one or to have a negative one. There are situations in which corporate policy prohibits your former boss from writing in support of your job search. Often, former employers will do nothing except confirm employment, with starting and stopping dates of service. But before you give up and accept that policy, try to work around it—in a professional manner. For example, you might be able to convince your ex-boss to sign a personal letter vouching for your performance record; the letter can be on plain bond paper or on his or her own letterhead, rather than the corporation's. This would not have the impact of a corporate letterhead reference, but it's better than no reference at all. And take heart, even when your former boss cannot or will not violate a corporate regulation, at least you emerge even on the scale. Your lack of a reference is a result of corporate policy. Your new employer will get dates only, with no comments on personality or motivation and no confirmation of your accomplishments. Although this certainly won't help you convince the potential employer that you're the person for the job, neither will it detract from your campaign.

GETTING YOUR REFERENCES TOGETHER

Most of our discussion has centered on a reference from your ex-boss, because that's typically the one that is toughest to get and hardest to control in terms of content. Getting it can be fraught with potential for conflict or at least uncertainty. That's not the only reference you'll need, however. We suggest a minimum of three—your boss, your boss's boss, and a peer. If you go beyond three, we suggest getting a letter from a subordinate next. That's extremely valuable to some employers. Conversely, you might want to go as high up in the company as possible for another reference. The higher the title—the more influence—the better. But remember, this is not just a list of names; your top executive reference must know who you are and what you did. If he or she is called, it's imperative that the responses given to a prospective employer will be consistent with what you said in the interview as well as with what your other references said about you.

Consistency becomes the key word here. It's not so much that the prospective employer will perform a cartwheel every time a positive statement is made about you. Nor will one negative comment hurt you that much. Everyone recognizes that personality conflicts exist in all workplaces.

What's critical to the process is that, on balance, the employer expects to hear a common thread emerging when your personality, duties, accomplishments, and skills are discussed. That consistency drives this entire process. And of course it is an integral part of our linkage concept, which touches every element of your job search.

HOW MANY?

Six references is the maximum you should list—and they all must be professional contacts. They all must be people who are familiar with your work experience. What your minister thinks, or your tennis partner, or your neighbor will have absolutely no impact on a prospective employer. Why should it? When do you suppose was the last time your minister gave someone a poor reference? Personal references are a waste of time and do not belong in your job campaigning tool kit.

Usually, references from your most recent employer are of greatest value. However, there are many situations when going back to earlier employers is important—for instance, when you have been with your latest employer only a short time or are still employed; when you are leaving a company that's on the rocks or an industry that's in decline; or when your previous experience is of particular value to the new position you are seeking.

In addition, when you prepare your draft letter of reference, don't get too flowery. Keep the statements job-related. Don't try to convince a reader that you are without fault or that Michener could have chronicled your adventures in the office. Keep it simple, straightforward, professional. Obviously, your former boss is not suicidal simply because you no longer work there, so don't try to make it sound as if the company can't stay in business without you.

Specifically, think of a three-phase approach to reference gathering:

- First, get the letter.

- Second, put your resume, a copy of the letter, and a brief worksheet outlining your responses to typical, tough interview questions into the hands of all of your references.

- Third, immediately upon completion of an interview that has gone well, notify your references that you believe the company is considering making you an offer and that reference-checking calls likely are forthcoming. Then highlight what was discussed in the interview and tell your references briefly about the company and the person who interviewed you, what job you're pursuing, and what qualifications from your background you highlighted during the discussions.

THE INTERVIEW WORKSHEET

The brief interview worksheet can be as informal as a piece of ruled yellow pad paper. You simply want to cover some of the key questions to which you'll respond in the interview and determine that your former associate can and will support your statements. Remember, don't try to *tell* your former boss to do this and do that. The entire process involves negotiation, communication, and flexibility. State that you will be saying that you accomplished this, this, and this. Does he have any problem with that? If so, discuss it and make your points. Walk step by step through your accomplishments at the company, reminding your former boss why you are claiming the accomplishments listed on your resume.

This process links with our earlier discussion of truth in preparing your resume. Many of our clients initially think that we encourage people to play fast and loose with the truth, to say whatever looks good in a resume. But that is absolutely not the case. You state what you accomplished in terms that make you appear as attractive as possible to the prospective employer, but you never go outside the limits of truthfulness. If you do, the negotiation step with your former boss will roadblock you.

On your worksheet, jot down typical interview questions and what your responses will be. (You'll learn later, in our interviewing chapter, that your answers to these questions will be identical from one interview to the next, so it's perfectly logical to commit them to paper.) For example, prep your reference with your responses to these questions:

- How do you know me?
- How long have you known me?
- What specific results or accomplishments have I provided for the company?
- What are my strengths and weaknesses?
- Under what circumstances did I leave?
- Would you rehire me?
- How did I get along with people?
- Did I meet deadlines?
- Do you know of anything that would disqualify me from performing the job in question?

- Is there any other information you can share?
- Is there any other person in the company who can discuss my work performance?

Remember, your references must have your resume, the worksheet, and a copy of the reference letters they have agreed to sign in their possession. Moreover, they must be on the person's desk when the reference checker calls. That's the purpose of your last-minute, postinterview phone conversation with each reference. It gets you fresh in his or her mind, and you can encourage the reference to pull out your file and be ready to confirm the responses to which both of you have already agreed.

Exhibits 4.3 and 4.4 provide examples of the cover letter and the draft of the letter of reference.

One more key point—along with your letters, carry a list of references in your job search tool kit everywhere you go. Your four, five, or six names should be listed as shown in Exhibit 4.5.

PREPARATION IS THE KEY

Put all the information in your tool kit, and you're ready to face any job search scenario with a high-impact, impeccably professional stack of assets in your corner—your resume, letters of reference, and a list of references. Be certain that you have multiple copies of each, and present them to each interviewer you meet at a company. Preparation is what job search is all about. Most often, landing a job will require multiple interviews over an extended period of time. On occasion, however, a window of opportunity will open, perhaps only for hours. That's the eventuality for which you always want to be prepared. By arriving for your interview with a tool kit full of information, you're ready for multiple interviews, you're ready for a reference check, and you're ready to entertain a job offer today. Whether or not you accept it depends on other varied factors that we'll address in subsequent chapters. In every case, however, whether it takes two hours or six weeks to draw an offer from the employer, you want to be ready. Have your references coached and prepped, with the appropriate papers on their desks—ready to support your statements and your career future.

See how our professional approach to job search unfolds—each step linked to the one before and the one to come next? You take a proactive posture to touch every base, to cover any eventuality. And you anticipate events—you don't react to them. The numbers for an employer's search work like this: Start with 250 resumes in response to an opening; screen out

EXHIBIT 4.3
Cover Letter Requesting a Reference

Date

Mr. Ed Wilkinson
President
Mako Company
35 Greenway Plaza
Houston, TX   77046

Dear Mr. Wilkinson:

I want to take this opportunity to thank you for your assistance to me during and just after my severance from Mako Company. To date I have developed a very aggressive job search, and am confident that placement is only a matter of proper timing. I have also looked into possible consulting assignments and have found considerable interest there.

My job and consulting search has presented one need for which I would like to ask your help—a letter of reference.

Based upon our prior discussion, you were pleased with my work. Your stating this fact in writing will enable me to present your reference when a request arises. I have taken the liberty of drafting a letter which you may wish to change as needed. Please provide the letter of reference on the company's letterhead.

I appreciate your assistance on this matter. If I can answer any questions, feel free to call me at xxx-xxxx.

Sincerely,

Stan Kolb

EXHIBIT 4.4
Draft of a Letter of Reference

MAKO COMPANY
35 Greenway Plaza
Houston, Texas 77046

To Whom It May Concern:

Mr. Stan Kolb was employed by Mako Company from its inception in 1969 until his recent departure, at which time he held the position of Treasurer. He was one of two individuals who helped initiate the business activities of the company, and was instrumental in its growth and success as a reputable contractor.

Stan is a very pleasant person with a friendly, cooperative attitude, which helps him to develop good personal relationships with co-workers and clients. He is knowledgeable about the industry in all business segments, from his many years of association with Mako, and through our association with a major producing company. Stan's personal integrity, professional skills, and broad-based experience enable him to contribute positively to any organizational environment.

Our corporate reorganization has eliminated Stan's division, but were we looking for someone with his skills and background, I would certainly employ him again. I recommend him as a valuable asset to any organization. Feel free to contact me for any additional information.

Sincerely,

John A. Wilkinson
President

200 on the first reading. Forward the remaining resumes to the hiring authority; screen out all but eight. Interview those eight and invite five back for follow-up sessions. Cut it to two candidates, and finally pick the winner. Except for the first cut, this screening process is seldom cut and dried. In each step of the process, there are but minute distinctions between winners and losers. That's what our philosophy is all about. We want you to be a half-step ahead of the competition.

That doesn't come easily, however. It's an outgrowth of your time and effort, hard work, consistency, preparation, and discipline. Always, the winners in any endeavor will tell you that there's a direct correlation between hard work and good fortune. And nowhere is that "hard work/good luck" scenario more evident than in job search. So put linkage into action in gathering your references, and enjoy the fruits of your extra effort as your job search builds momentum.

EXHIBIT 4.5
Sample Reference

John A. Wilkinson
President
Mako Company
5 Greenway Plaza
Houston, Texas   77046
(713)xxx-xxxx

CHAPTER FIVE

Build Your Network: Eighty Percent of *Successful* Job Hunters Can't Be Wrong

As you no doubt have already noticed, we are not at all shy about telling you what *won't* work in job search. With the same degree of confidence, when we find a technique that *does* work—such as a two-page, chronological resume or networking—we'll tell you straightaway. You now know that a two-page, chronological resume should serve as the drive wheel for your job search. But the fuel for your search engine is networking.

We're well aware that networking has fallen into disfavor among "savvy" job hunters. Many self-anointed "experts" now claim that networking is passé, that the American job market has been just about networked to death. Well, we dismiss that nonsense out of hand. Successful job hunters are like salmon swimming upstream. The one percent courageous enough to go against the current instinctively struggle to reach the river's source. Although the majority of job searchers looking for an easy placement float downstream, the *one percenters* who take control of their campaigns know that they must go against the current to get to where the jobs are. The truth is that if you wish to join our *One Percenters Club* of successful job hunters, you must unequivocally accept the concept of networking. Further, you must study it until you're a master. When you can make the telephone sing as though Chopin had scored a networking concerto for it, you will begin to break loose from the masses out there who are failing at job search. In our view, those who bad-mouth networking are selling you a rotten bill of goods—suggesting that networking is nothing more than another transitory fad in our disposable society. This reveals their purely commercial intent: Peddle it, use it, then discard it like an empty plastic soft drink container.

Then search for a new fad—another hot-button that will sell a few more books or videotapes, or schedule a few more talk shows.

Job hunters, if you swallow that—if you accept the flawed logic that networking is old and cold—you're practically guaranteeing failure in your campaign. Networking is not and never has been simply a manifestation of pop culture. Rather, it is one of three key strategies to a winning game plan in job search. For strategy A, we created the resume (yours should be complete by now). For strategy C, you will put on an interviewing performance that ensures that the employer will want to put your name in lights, to say nothing of offering you a job (you'll learn all that in Chapter 8). As important as these two strategies are, however, without networking you're trying to skip a step, a very difficult proposition indeed.

When you utilize networking, strategy B is in place. This assures proper use of linkage in your job search, and it practically guarantees that you'll be a step ahead of the rest of the world in locating and accessing job openings. Even beyond specified openings, truly excellent networkers create their own positions by identifying an employer's need, then selling their skills and background as the solution. So take our word for it; we've learned from many long, difficult counseling sessions with clients trying to make the tortuous journey from A to C without networking. Use our A, B, C strategy in your search, and let linkage build your momentum.

This is not meant to minimize the difficulties of networking. The reason this concept has slipped from its favored status among job search "experts" who are always looking for a hot fad is simply because too many people use it unprofessionally. Each time some jerk calls a company executive without a conversational agenda, without direction, and without goals, he wastes everyone's time. As a consequence, the road is that much rougher for everyone who follows. Your task will be that much more challenging.

Don't confuse the issues here, however. Just because networking is misused, abused, and trivialized by amateurs doesn't mean that you must choose an alternative. Quite simply, there are none. U.S. Department of Labor statistics prove that 80 percent of people who find jobs in this country do so by networking. In our view, that figure is probably conservative. So don't listen to the charlatans who are trying to sell books and job search fads simultaneously. Don't buy a ticket on their bandwagon. Effective networking gets jobs. The more you do it and the better you do it, the sooner you'll be selecting the best position from among several offers.

HANDLING THE NO'S IN NETWORKING

So much negativity permeates job search that people despair easily during the journey. No's are a major part of the process. We mentioned earlier the juvenile system of working through the no's and rejoicing because each no means that you're getting closer to the ultimate yes. Although this is an attempt to instill positive thinking, it overlooks the more proactive approach. Our promise to you is that when you network effectively, you do more than move toward the final yes. In fact, you modify, or even circumvent, the no's. Rather than receiving a rejection, a good networker can transform an unproductive conversation into a lead at another company, with another person—another potential job opportunity, another potential yes.

With effective networking, you take command of your job search. Certainly, there will be no's. Rest assured that you will run into jerks who won't even give you the time of day. But remember, you can make the numbers work for you. When you're making twenty-five, forty, or fifty phone calls a day, it is not so depressing to get a no, even from a 101-proof jerk. The trick is to distill out nonproductive calls after about ten seconds and move along to your next call. You'll learn the fundamentals of using the phone—what to say, what not to say, how to set goals for each day and each phone call—in Chapter 7. Our point here is that you must commit now to the philosophy of building and using a network in job search. If you're swayed by any advice to the contrary, you're only postponing success and complicating your job search.

We've counseled with thousands of clients in our Houston outplacement facilities, and we can attest to the fact that good networkers never sit idle—wallowing in self-pity, drowning in rejections. They stay up, active, and positive. They don't have time to be depressed, because they're so active on the phone. Moreover, results sustain that positive momentum. When you do networking the right way—when you fully commit to it—the constant leads and new information you obtain will guarantee that you won't be defeated by rejection. Although there are many negatives to overcome in job search, they should never dominate your life. The people who sit by the phone, depressed, are typically those who rely on search firms and newspaper ads to do the work for them. We agree that the situation is tough to go through, but at the risk of sounding unsympathetic, those people are getting out of job search just about what they put into it—nothing. That's the nature of job search when you abandon the tried-and-true principles set forth on these pages—when you won't put in the time, effort, and dedication necessary to take charge of your own campaign.

NETWORKING GIVES YOU A MARKET ADVANTAGE

The statistics from the U.S. Labor Department cited earlier—that 80 percent of jobs come from networking—become even more dramatic when you consider the following ironic pattern. Although only 10 to 20 percent of jobs are found through ads and search firms, our informal surveys indicate that about 80 percent of job searchers concentrate their searches there. These are, of course, the simplest ways to look for a job—that's what draws the majority to them. By contrast, only 20 percent of job searchers concentrate full-bore on networking.

Imagine it! If you buy into our theory, you're shopping in an area where 80 percent of the merchandise is located but only 20 percent of the shoppers. If that supply/demand market advantage doesn't convert you to networking, you're just not as serious about your job search as you may think. Our feeling is that many people who fail to buy into the concept of networking misunderstand what it is and what it isn't. The statement "Network your way into the hidden job market" can be intimidating to a novice, even if you're a novice with twenty-five years' experience in petroleum engineering, in general management, or in any other field. So let's dissect that statement:

- *Networking:* If you can talk, you can do it. Cold-calling on the phone is very difficult initially, but it's a learnable, do-able skill. If you think, "I'm an engineer, not a salesman; we don't do that" or "I'm a senior VP and chief counsel; we don't do that at this level" think again. If you want a job, you'll do it. Does networking mean talking to important people who can offer you a position? Yes, it does, but that's only one very limited fraction of the whole equation. In total, networking means talking to everyone—personal and professional acquaintances and friends as well as brand-new contacts— telling them your situation, and asking if they can assist or refer you.

- *The hidden job market:* This one throws a lot of people, and it's probably somewhat misleading. Our view is that too many people think that the hidden job market means a closed market, with all the jobs reserved for insiders or the sons-in-law of the chairmen. Without dwelling on family relationships, trust us—many board chairmen would much rather hire you than their sons-in-law. So, in fact, that job isn't hidden, it's just not public knowledge. It will come open and be filled before most people know about the vacancy. Frequently, that includes the corporate human resources department—to say nothing about search firms or readers of newspaper ads. Your challenge is to make a networking contact at the right place and the right time to learn about that "hidden" job.

LUCK HAPPENS WHEN OPPORTUNITY MEETS PREPARATION

Is all this luck? You'd better believe it is. But we guarantee that networkers who place fifty phone calls a day are the ones who always get lucky.

We all have a tendency to think of successful people as being lucky—Bob Hope, Johnny Carson, Jack Nicklaus, Larry Bird, Lee Iacocca, Donald Trump. If you're a *one percenter* who makes fifty phone calls a day, you'll have a chance to tap into some of the same kind of luck. That's what we want you to strive toward. Similarly, best defined, the hidden job market is really analogous to an iceberg. More than 90 percent of it is out of sight. But just get below the surface and you'll find out how big it is. That's precisely how the job market operates—not so much hidden as out of sight to the superficial job seeker.

The elements of success in networking center on confidence in what you're doing, coupled with the requirement that you make each networking contact a true exchange of information. People who use a networking contact to get what they want but give nothing in return are the people who are contaminating the networking landscape for the rest of us. For example, we can't stand the phrase, "I'd like to pick your brain." That's an insult to us; we infer from that statement that someone wants for free what it took us years of hard work to build.

As part of your job search, you'll be researching companies and industries, so be prepared to share that information if it's useful to your contact. Also, offer to help him with a problem if you can. And don't forget, for your hottest contacts, the Dawson & Dawson *Number One Rule of Networking: Everyone Likes to Eat.* The corollary to that is *Rule One-A: Everyone Really Likes to Eat a Free Lunch.*

Our point is that you must be prepared to give back while you receive. And commit to certain fundamentals—such as asking for one minute of the contact's time (generally, that gives you license to take three minutes). Just be certain that you don't waste anyone's time—yours or the contact's. Get in and out quickly. (We'll cover all the dos and don'ts in Chapter 7, under telemarketing.)

If you're like most people, you've probably listed five to ten people that you think can help you find a job. Our network includes 4,000 to 5,000 names. We're not insisting that yours be that extensive, but five or ten just won't get it done. If you don't have at least 100 names listed, you're not thinking creatively. Consider these sources:

- Family members
- Colleagues, present and past, and executives for whom you've worked
- Classmates, teachers, campus placement officials, and alumni
- Professional acquaintances: lawyers, stockbrokers, accountants, bankers, real estate brokers, insurance agents, elected officials, industry leaders, consultants, doctors, dentists, salespeople, and so forth
- Community members in clubs or associations to which you belong,

neighbors, church members, local merchants, fund raisers, sponsors of performing arts, and wealthy people
- Officials of professional organizations, whether or not you are a member, as well as speakers at any of their meetings
- Suppliers, previous customers, even creditors
- Editors and writers for trade journals
- The local chamber of commerce
- Anyone and everyone on your Christmas card list

Finally, don't forget your checkbook as another source. Anyone to whom you've written a check within the past year can be considered a possible network contact.

Remember, build your contact list on the strength of your acquaintanceship or friendship with each person. *Do not*, at this time, attempt to evaluate whether or not these people will be able to help you. That is a time-wasting, subjective process that is inherently self-defeating.

One of the most obvious contacts is one that is frequently overlooked— a former boss. As a result of speaking with just such a contact, one of our clients recently obtained exactly the position he was looking for.

> Henry Little wanted to move from a huge, billion-dollar company to a small, growing organization where he could utilize his entrepreneurial skills. Among the primary contacts he made was Joe Stratton, his former boss. Joe suggested a company that, as a subsidiary of a major U.S. firm, could offer him a ground-floor opportunity in a dynamic entrepreneurial environment—and one with significant financial backing. After four rounds of interviews, Henry got the job he wanted. Had he not contacted his former boss, he never would have discovered this opportunity.

Don't judge your contacts: list them and use them. Either on 3" x 5" index cards or in a loose-leaf binder, record each name, phone number, title, address, the initial contact and when and how you will follow up, plus that follow-up contact and what happened in the follow-up. Let's stop here for a key point. Job hunters and those who proffer advice on the subject wrestle interminably with the question of timing follow-ups to contacts: "How long should I wait?" Stop all that nonsense and think. Communicate. The quickest, simplest, and most direct way to resolve the question is to ask your contact. There is no set formula, no right or wrong answer. Simply ask your contact when he would be agreeable to a recontact, and note that in your record book. (Exhibit 5.1 provides a form for tracking personal/professional contacts.) Chapter 7 discusses record keeping further.

EXHIBIT 5.1
Personal Marketing Plan: Personal/Professional Contacts

NAME_____   DATE_____

PHONE NUMBER	NAME/AFFILIATION	RESULT OF CALL		
		CALL BACK	WILL RETURN	SEE RECORD

THE NEXT STEP

Now for the critical part of networking—going beyond the initial contacts. Seldom will the 100 people on your list of primary contacts actually provide you with a job lead. What they *can* do is provide you with another level of contacts. So you must develop techniques for expanding your network. Even the second level of contacts usually doesn't ring the bell. But when you broaden and deepen your network to the third tier—your tertiary network— you will begin to access viable job leads. To that end, part of every networking contact should include questions such as "Do you know who your counterpart is in XYZ company?" Again, we'll cover all the techniques of telemarketing in Chapter 7. But rest assured that you must push each contact to the limit if you're to succeed at networking. Your goal should be to get at least two or three additional names from each contact. Assuming that you start with 100, do you begin to see the impact you're about to make on the job market?

Remember, you must, *without fail*, send a thank-you letter to each productive contact. Obviously, you don't want to waste twenty-five cents on the jerks. But if a person takes the time to try to help, acknowledge that with a thank-you note and resume. Of course, if you arranged a follow-up contact with the same person, confirm that in the letter as well. The thank-you letter should be very brief, but it's essential. It confirms to the network contact that he's dealing with a pro when he's talking to you.

OTHER NETWORKING LEADS

Theoretically, the networking process should never end, but inevitably you'll hit a few days when your contact potentials seem to have dwindled. What then? Do you go into withdrawal and begin to hallucinate that you'll never find a job? Not if you use your head and develop a list of target companies besides those your personal/professional referral network helped turn up. Potentially, this is where cold-calling can really turn frigid. But don't panic—your research on the companies and industries you target will provide you with the knowledge and confidence to warm up your calls and produce new leads.

In our outplacement facility in Houston, we have an extensive library of directories and reference tools available to our corporate clients for developing their target company lists. If you do not have access to a specialized job search and career planning library to help you identify companies as targets for your new position, your public library should have many of the needed directories and other publications. There are five major reference sources for researching target companies and industries:

- Directories
- Annual reports/10K reports
- Newspapers and other current periodicals
- Professional associations
- People in general

Exhibit 5.2 provides a listing of suggested resources that are invaluable to your research. If you use them, you will never deplete your list of cold-calling prospects. When you first begin to thumb through all the directories, you'll likely be overwhelmed with the sinking feeling that you're about to look for the proverbial needle in the haystack. That is definitely not the case unless you plan to start at page 1 and work your way through page 1001—not a strategy we recommend unless you intend for your job search to go to the year 2001! Obviously, you must narrow down the target area on the basis of your preferences as well as market realities. The following are some of the criteria to consider in targeting companies:

- Type of industry
- Products/services
- Growth/decline industry
- Geography/ locality
- Job availability
- Company size
- Corporate culture/management style
- Employment policies
- Compensation/ benefit policies

Research as much information as you possibly can about a company and its requirements:

- Read materials about the company.
- Arrange a tour of the company if possible.
- Inquire about the nature of the work.
- Learn about possible job functions.
- Study job requirements.
- Ask about recruitment policies.
- Find out why management hires the people they do.
- Ask about the potential for advancement.

EXHIBIT 5.2
Sources of Company Information

Local Directories

The following are examples of Houston and Texas directories. Check with your local library and chamber of commerce for similar directories of businesses in your locality.

Directory of Texas Manufacturers (Volumes I & II)
Gulf Coast Oil Directory
Harris County Business Guide
Houston Corporate Directory
Houston–Gulf Coast Manufacturers Directory
Houston International Business Directory
Houston Organization Directory
Houston Public Companies
Texas Business: The Texas 400
Texas Top 250

National Directories

Directory of Corporate Affiliations
Directory of Executive Recruiters
Dun & Bradstreet Million Dollar Directory
MacRae's Blue Book
Standard & Poor's Register
Standard Directory of Advertisers
Thomas Register of American Manufacturers
U.S. Industrial Product Directory

Additional Sources of Information

Almanac of American Employers
American Almanac of Jobs and Salaries
Business Periodicals Index
Business Week: Scoreboard
Company reports—annual, 10-K, proxy
Dictionary of Occupational Titles
F & S Index of Corporations and Industries
Forbes: Annual Report of American Business
Forbes 500's
Fortune 500
Inc. 500
Moody's Investors Services
Special Issues Index
Standard & Poor's Corporation Records
Standard & Poor's Industry Surveys
U.S. Bureau of Labor Statistics: Area Wage Surveys
Valueline
Wall Street Journal Index
100 Best Companies to Work for in America

- Learn what you can about compensation, benefits, perks.
- Keep notes on each company you explore.

Exhibits 5.3 and 5.4 provide forms on which to list your target companies by high, medium, or low priority and to record your research notes.

THE PROCESS

In summary, think of networking as a five-step process:

- *Step 1: Prepare your contact list.* Include not just important decision-makers but everyone who may be able to help you. Also include your list of target companies.

- *Step 2: Send a resume and cover letter to each of your primary contacts.* Just because a contact happens to be your brother, you're making an egregious mistake if you assume that he knows all there is to know about you and your career. (Exhibit 5.5 provides a form to keep track of letters mailed.)

- *Step 3: Use your contacts properly.* Be aware that your network will usually think more in terms of jobs open or not open than in terms of your individual skills and background. Help keep each contact focused on you— on what you've done before and can do in the future as well as on how potential employers might use your skills and experience. Remember to offer your assistance to your contacts in any way possible.

- *Step 4: Always ask permission to use the name of your contact.* Then do just that, both in phone conversations and in correspondence. Nothing drives the networking process more quickly and more effectively than a personal reference. That's how you break through into secondary and tertiary contacts. Always open the conversation or letter with a phrase such as "A mutual acquaintance, John Robertson, suggested that I contact you." The body of the letter (or phone conversation) should very briefly summarize who you are and why you're making contact. Then close with a proactive statement about calling or visiting soon to discuss mutually beneficial ideas.

- *Step 5: Follow-up.* Again, let your contact set the schedule. Just be certain that you adhere to it and recontact each person within the agreed-upon time. Report back to your contact when a lead pans out. It's not only professional to do this, but it keeps that person aware of and interested in what you're doing and where you're going. Even if a secondary contact

EXHIBIT 5.3
Personal Marketing Plan: Target Companies

NAME_____   DATE_____

Circle to indicate priority: A (high)   B (medium)   C (low)

| PHONE NUMBER | TARGET COMPANY | DECISION MAKER (Name & Title) | RESULT OF CALL | | |
			CALL BACK	WILL RETURN	SEE RECORD

EXHIBIT 5.4
Personal Marketing Plan: Target Company Research

PROSPECTIVE JOB TITLE_____

DECISION MAKER _____

COMPANY_____ TELEPHONE_____

ADDRESS _____

RESEARCH SOURCE (person, directory, etc.) _____

SIZE (employees, sales, income) _____

INDUSTRY _____

PRODUCTS _____

GROWTH _____

ORGANIZATION/SUBSIDIARY OF _____

EMPLOYMENT POLICIES _____

_____

COMPENSATION/BENEFIT POLICIES _____

_____

CURRENT INDUSTRY INFORMATION:

CURRENT COMPANY INFORMATION:

EXHIBIT 5.5
Personal Marketing Plan: Letters Mailed

NAME_____

DATE SENT	NAME/ADDRESS	PHONE NUMBER	FOLLOW-UP DATE

doesn't develop into a job lead, when you keep your primary contacts advised, you're inevitably drawing them closer to your corner for future contacts and assistance. This is how psychological leverage works in networking. In your initial contact, you've offered to help them in any way possible. You've been thorough, courteous, and professional in following up each time, and now you're reporting back with a progress update and another thank-you.

Always keep your goals foremost in your mind for each contact. First, you want leads about openings. Failing that, you want the names of other people in the firm or elsewhere with whom you might talk. Keep pushing, deepening and broadening your network. Here's an example:

Todd Moore, a very senior executive with an extensive network, has a base of contacts that requires tremendous organization and persistence to work. Todd was getting a bit discouraged after a few months and was beginning to wonder whether he would ever find the right position. To take a new tack, we suggested approaching a couple of the firms with which he was carrying on discussions about consulting proposals. This would get his foot in the door until a permanent position could be found or created in the organization. The approach worked. Todd's aggressive networking paid off.

The realities of a transitory economy, with so many people displaced, can work to your advantage. Although your unemployed status might once have labeled you as an undesirable or a chronic problem case, unemployed people now are generally viewed as first-rate employees who are victims of the economy. Members of your network usually have been recently unemployed, know they're about to be, or are scared to death that they might be in the immediate future. As a consequence, most people are more willing than ever to help you.

This is another example of how important positive thinking is. Don't dwell on the negatives of a difficult economy. Think of how you can transform the negatives into positives. Make the situation work for you, rather than against you. Very often, this requires nothing more than an attitude change. Never underestimate the critical importance of a positive attitude. Like your resume and interview, your networking contacts will live or die on the strength of your attitude. If you expect a networking contact to be unsuccessful, we can just about guarantee that it will turn out that way. So pump up your mental state, and put your networking skills into action.

One of the hardest things to do in a job search is to continue even though you have a really hot offer in the works. Remember that no job offer is official until you're sitting in your new office on your first day!

Janice Schultz was made an offer and accepted it. She immediately abandoned her efforts elsewhere, only to discover later that the person who had made the offer did not have clearance to do so. The offer was rescinded, and Janice had a lot of catch-up networking to do.

If you internalize the principles outlined here, coupled with the tele-marketing skills you'll learn in Chapter 7, you will be headed in the right direction—swimming upstream. Remember not to pay any attention to the doom-and-gloom preachers, who are floating downstream with all the search firms and newspaper ads as flotsam and jetsam. Your route will be more difficult in the short term. It will require large measures of courage, confidence, perseverance, and dedication. But your upstream direction will lead to what smart campaigners are looking for—jobs.

CHAPTER SIX

Search Firms: How to Distinguish the Pros from the Peddlers

When we say that *you*, and only *you*, can get yourself a new job, does that give you a clue to how we feel about search firms? Certainly, that statement does not minimize the importance of the assistance others can give you in some of the key segments of job search, especially networking. Obviously, the essence of networking is help from other people. You draw upon every person with whom you've had contact to help you locate job openings a step ahead of anyone else. But your networking contacts, vital as they are, can only help you. They can alert you to openings, give you leads, or, at best, provide introductions—but they won't get you a job. And regarding search firms, we repeat that statement with emphasis: *They won't get you a job.*

Do not count on headhunters, search firms, or employment agencies to act in the best interest of your career, your future. Certainly, a high-quality, professional search organization can assist you effectively, but be sure that you don't assign too much faith in, or responsibility to, that search guy. He can assist with leads, help you understand the corporate culture, and prep you about the person with whom you'll be meeting. But never lose sight of the fact that you get a job through a winning resume, coupled with a powerful interviewing presentation.

Equally important, you must then negotiate the best deal you can get. Again, you alone can accomplish that. Negotiation is when the money's on the table, when you apply all the skills you'll learn in Chapter 9 to secure the best deal possible without jeopardizing the job offer. Your skill at this scenario will ultimately be reflected on the bottom line, every day you work for that company. This is why your trust is misplaced if you think that search consultants can guide you through the negotiation process. In every case, no matter what they call themselves, the search firm represents the company and its interests, not yours. Inevitably, the bottom line they're protecting is the employer's and their own, not yours.

We are assuming that if you elect to be involved with any search firm, it will be a top-quality, professional organization—a real pro at the business, one that works on a retainer arrangement with corporations. We suggest that you don't associate with the lower-echelon agencies that work on a contingency basis. If you must, do so very carefully. As in every phase of your personal and professional life, you will be known by the company you keep, and there's a lot of bad company in the search and executive consulting world. Not for a moment are we suggesting that no contingency search agencies are staffed with competent, ethical people. But beware of unemployed jerks who hustle telephone contacts because they couldn't find any other job. Many of them are starving on a straight commission setup.

Do you imagine that a person like that can possibly help you? Not only will most be unable to help you, but they'll tarnish your name just because you've allowed it to be associated with theirs. Admittedly, we get emotional about this point, primarily because we've seen so many people disappointed—losing job opportunities or, worst of all, getting suckered out of huge sums of money when they can least afford to lose it—all because they signed the wrong piece of paper at the wrong time in the wrong place so that some charlatan posing as an executive search consultant can line his pockets a little deeper without doing anything to help the job seeker.

DON'T STACK THE ODDS AGAINST YOURSELF

Emotion aside, however, consider the cold, hard statistics from the U.S. Department of Labor. How do people find jobs in the United States? Five to ten percent get them through classified advertisements. Another 5 to 10 percent find them through search agencies. But 80 to 90 percent locate them through networking. We've already illustrated, in the chapter on networking, how the numbers work against you when you concentrate on ads and search firms. At best, 10 to 20 percent of the jobs are there, yet that's where 80 to 90 percent of job hunters look. Other statistics on employment agencies and search firms provide an even stronger indictment against their effectiveness for you. One recent survey showed that only 2 to 3 percent of all the clients at search firms actually found positions. The greatest number of people are chasing the smallest percentage of jobs when they operate this way. Those are incredible odds to bet on, yet most job hunters do—day after day, year after year. That's how a lot of incompetents stay in the search business, along with a small cadre of outright thieves.

FINDING THE LEADERS

Briefly, here's how the search business works. At the top of the industry are the retainer firms. You find these listed in a compilation called "The Nifty Fifty," a ranking of leading executive recruiting firms published annually by *Executive Recruiter News*. There you can isolate the biggest, the best, the most reputable search organizations in American business. Associating your name with these reputable firms will not tarnish your reputation; in most cases, it will create a positive impression on an employer. An additional source for identifying executive search firms is the *Directory of Executive Recruiters*, an annual publication of *Consultants News*. Typically, a retainer firm operates with candidates who earn higher than an established minimum salary. If you don't earn more than their minimum, they won't accept your resume. Their retainer arrangement with companies is based on a one-third/one-third/one-third fee structure. They get a third of the fee when they submit a number of resumes of qualified applicants, another third when interviews are conducted, and another third when placement is accomplished.

This fee structure guarantees that they are not just peddling flesh to a potential employer. The retainer firm sends only top-flight, qualified pros on a confidential basis. There is implicit trust between the search firm and the potential employer. Obviously, you benefit from that professional association. To illustrate, a really upper-echelon retainer search firm might spend hours on the phone with a company, performing a needs analysis to discover what the company really requires in an applicant for the available position. Such firms operate with subtlety, discretion, and professionalism. They are paid for their time and professional services, not for sending an army of warm bodies from which a company can enlist employees.

In contrast, contingency search firms operate quite differently. They are at the other end of the scale. Often, this is where the incompetents gravitate. If you're an engineer, you'll likely be talking to an unemployed engineer. Or if you're a systems analyst, you'll be talking to an unemployed programmer. The search agency hires these people primarily because of their contacts in engineering or DP departments. What drives their business is acquiring new job listings from employers, not servicing you, the job hunter. The company is the customer; you are nothing but a potential peg to fit an empty hole in the search firm's revenue board. How well you fit is of little concern beyond the prospect of a fee.

Typically, when a contingency search firm gets job listings, it will be one of several such agencies with identical marching orders, hustling to get there first with the most—to get the right (or wrong) person hired so that they can snap up a fast commission and survive another thirty days. It's a dash to the finish line, and the first huckster that shows up with a warm body gets the prize. We fully understand how callous, tough, and cynical that makes us sound. And it may be depressing if your income isn't high enough to qualify you for a retainer search firm. So, then, what do you do? Do you use a contingency firm anyway? No—you do it yourself.

If you can't deal with a pro, don't waste your time with a peddler. You can do a better job working in your own interest than any of the contingency peddlers will ever do for you. If you follow our guidelines on networking, time management, positive thinking, and self-discipline, you'll do it better in every case. How does a search firm develop job listings? On the phone—cold-calling. How do you telemarket and network your way into job openings? The very same way. The difference, of course, is that when you get a hot lead, you'll jump on it one step ahead of the rest of the world. But when a contingency search agency generates a lead, they'll send you and anyone else they can scrape out of the resume file whose qualifications are even close to those listed on the job order. So it is that many people complain bitterly that job hunting is a numbers game at which you can't win. It may be—but only if you play it the lazy way, expecting someone else to do your work.

Basically, contingency firms move bodies; they shop commissions, servicing companies as their clients. They are not primarily interested in your job objectives and career goals. Consider some other claims that agencies will make to sell their services:

- *Salary information:* They'll tell you that they can help you grasp the dynamics of the marketplace—what your skills are worth under current conditions. Moreover, they'll offer to help you negotiate compensation. Don't buy that for a minute. Again, they are servicing the company, while simultaneously looking for a quick placement. You may bring skills and experience worth $50,000 to the marketplace. But if an agency can manipulate you into accepting a $40,000 offer, they'll do it every time, without regard to your income potential or needs. First, they'll talk you into accepting the $40,000 by bad-mouthing your experience and background. Quite naturally, your $50,000 skills will blow all the $40,000 competition out of the water, and you'll get the offer. The result is that you're saddled with lower compensation than it was necessary for you to take, with a corresponding setback for your future income potential. The agency gets what it wants most, of course—a fast payday.

- *Job leads:* They claim to network into job leads by the hundreds. We've already stated that, in every case, you can do a better job looking out for your own interests, but there's a more ominous overtone as well. Incredibly, once an agency gets your resume (and be alert that when you give any information on the phone, they might be writing down everything you say to compile a brief resume outline), some of these charlatans will even send an unauthorized resume to companies without your knowledge or permission. If they have your complete resume, often they will shotgun it all over the place. If you have networked your way into a job interview, it would not be unusual for your resume to have hit that company from another direction if you're also working through a contingency search firm. Not only is this unprofessional and damaging to your interests, it can lead to an ugly fee dispute. The company may believe that the hire was accomplished directly by you, but the agency may send an invoice on the strength of the resume it had sent.

Believe us, this is not an unusual occurrence. This scenario constantly plagues corporate human resources departments. If you think a contingency search firm is looking out for your best interests, just get caught in the middle of a fee dispute between such an agency and your new employer. The battle can get nasty—and you are the ultimate loser, no matter how the problem is resolved. The company hired you to solve a problem it was facing. But when you walk in with a fee dispute trailing in your wake, you become a new problem, not a solution. This can ultimately eliminate you from contention for the position.

• *Coordinating your search for more efficiency:* This is another agency tactic that can lead to a fee dispute problem. Without fail, a search counselor will say something like "Keep me posted. We're working together on your search, and we don't want to duplicate our efforts. So if you have a contact working, let me know about it." (Job hunters, if you swallow that kind of verbal effluent, we have a nice piece of land at the bottom of a lake we'd like to sell you.) Although this may sound logical and in your best interests, it most assuredly is not. When you're told, "Keep me posted—let me know where you're interviewing," the search firm is, once again, doing nothing and hoping to profit by it. The guy is fishing for an easy commission, looking to capitalize on your hard work. It's incredible, but it happens every day in the contingency search business. You notify the agency that a contact looks good, and what happens next? The search guy shoots in your resume and calls the company, claiming that he represents you in your search. That gives him the right to invoice the company if you get the job.

Obviously, that can lead to the unfortunate fee dispute scenario we just described. But there are other more immediate problems. Despite the fact that you've done the work, the search guy's claim to represent you means, in effect, that you've just acquired a 30 percent price tag on your head. How much does that assist your job search? Not much, we bet. What if, for example, you're one of three very close finalists for a position that pays $36,000 annually. By your calling that search agency to keep them posted, their fee gets added to that; you now carry a first-year price tag of $48,000, while your competition, not represented by a search firm, will come in for $36,000. What do you think of your chances now? Moreover, the worst of it is that the effort was all yours. The contingency firm did nothing for you, only for itself. You threw a possible commission right into their laps, and they likely threw you right out as a prospective employee of that company. That's the type of unethical search practice that sends our blood pressure boiling. We see it every day. It's such a waste—so damaging to your immediate search and, potentially, to your career. To summarize our discussion of search firms, we strongly recommend that unless you're in a position to utilize the services of a top-echelon retainer firm, just don't deal with search agencies.

ON THE OTHER HAND . . .

Having said that, we'll back off our fighting mark a half-step. As critical as we've been about contingency firms, let us stress, again, that our opposition to them is rooted primarily in our conviction that they just don't do very much for you. They are unable to help you more than you can help yourself. Obviously, there are some benefits in using an agency. Even if the statistics indicate that only 5 percent of people get jobs through agencies, that 5 percent is enough to qualify agencies as a valid source of job information. Many agency people are honest and dedicated, and they can help you get job leads and assist you in preparing for interviews and in critiquing your interviewing style. If you're dealing with a reputable firm and an experienced counselor, you can enjoy some benefits, as long as you're aware of and guard against the downside potential.

SOME GUIDELINES

The most important guideline in using search agencies is to adapt the way you allocate your time to the statistics we mentioned earlier. If you use search organizations, devote no more than 5 or 6 percent of your time to them. That's effective time management in your job search. This means that if you work a fifty-hour week on job search—which we classify as the minimum—you will spend no more than two to five hours a week on agency contacts. When you are with a company and looking for a job, it is especially tempting to rely strictly on search firms to conduct your search. Although the time to spend on your search is obviously limited, our cautions about allowing the search firm to control your search still apply. Use evening hours for researching target companies and early, late, and lunch hours for networking. Conducting a job campaign while you're still working requires expert time management, but it can be done.

If you elect to use agencies, be certain that you control the relationship. Be assertive. Watch out for your own interests, because its likely that no one else will. Here's an illustration:

> For family reasons, Joe Hudson was anxious to relocate from his home in Houston to Atlanta. Obviously, he was going to need a job there.
>
> Joe's first instinct was to go to a search firm. Then he thought, "If only one search firm is trying to find a spot for me, wouldn't I have less of a chance than if sixty search firms were?" So he prepared a letter of introduction and was about to send them to sixty different firms.
>
> Luckily, a friend pointed out to him the folly of that move. "Your resume will be coming at all the potential employers from every direction," he said. "They aren't going to know which search firm is entitled to the fee, and as a consequence, not one of them will consider you."

Exhibit 6.1 provides a form to list your search firm contacts. Follow these additional guidelines: Remember that the consultant, not the agency, will be responsible for your satisfaction in dealing with that firm, as well as for your success in accessing job leads through the firm. With that in mind, go to the agency (once again, be careful what you tell them on the phone) and determine who the best counselors are in your functional area. Interview the counselor, and make certain that he is professional, competent, and knowledgeable about your function. Then find out how long he's been with the company and in the industry. Learn what companies the agency represents, so that you can strategically select an agency that will best help you cover the market and best complement your search. In other words, you're taking charge of the situation. You're making sure that the agency doesn't duplicate your efforts, and you're also blocking them out of any easy fee collection. In addition, request that they never send your resume anywhere without first getting your permission. Finally, never sign any agreement with a search firm unless you absolutely and fully understand what the agreement obligates you to do. Substantial amounts of money are involved in recruitment of employees through search firms, and the contracts are

EXHIBIT 6.1
Personal Marketing Plan: Search Firms

NAME_____   DATE_____

PHONE NUMBER	SEARCH FIRM	CONTACT (NAME & TITLE)	RESULT OF CALL		
			CALL BACK	WILL RETURN	SEE RECORD

usually designed to protect the agency's right to collect a fee, even if this means that you will ultimately be responsible under a specified set of circumstances. To be safe, do not use an agency that requires you to sign an agreement.

THE PITS

Don't for a moment confuse the different segments of the industry, however. At the top are the retainer firms; on the bottom are the contingency agencies. And somewhere so low that they can't be measured or categorized are the up-front fee operators. These are the slumlords of the industry. They may call themselves "executive job search consulting services" or "individual outplacement consultants." It's easier to identify them by their method of collecting money. In short, if someone wants your money up front, he's a crook.

We don't have any problem with people getting paid for services or goods. That's not how we run our business—our clients are, without exception, corporate-funded—but legitimate companies may bill an individual job hunter for finding that person a job or even for writing a resume. We might question the practice, but there's no question about its morality or ethics. It's simply a judgment call. But the up-front fee collectors who take your money and give you nothing in return are a plague on the American job marketplace. Job hunters who are emotionally vulnerable will pay upward of $5,000, $10,000, or $12,000 and get nothing but a resume and a list of target companies that hasn't been updated since your grandfather looked for a job. *Nothing*. The best advice we can give you is, if someone wants your money for goods or services, that's fine—that's free enterprise. But if some low-life sponge tries to get your money in return for nothing but a lot of fast talk, fancy acronyms, and stacks of computer printouts, get out of there as quickly as you can. Then write to anyone and everyone you can think of—the Better Business Bureau, your representatives in Congress, your mayor, your district attorney, your state legislator. And write to us. Before our business careers end, we'd consider it the greatest professional accomplishment if we could eradicate this kind of scum from our industry.

In short, keep your money in your pocket, and don't think that anyone else can do your work for you—even a reputable search organization. Even if you conduct your job search in accordance with every one of our tough rules, you still must understand that rejection is part of the process. We believe that's one psychological motivation that drives people to rely on search firms. They think that someone else will bite the bullet, make that tough cold call, soften the ground to make the interview less stressful, and exercise that delicate, subtle pressure to negotiate the best deal possible. Meanwhile, they sit on the sidelines, hoping to enjoy the fruit of someone else's labor. And we believe it's not necessarily because of slothfulness, but rather because of fear of rejection. Whatever the motivation, such expectations are nothing but wishful thinking.

Yes, a search firm may be able to place you—not primarily to your advantage, however, but to a company's advantage. Moreover, a search firm can never do it as well as you can if you continue reading, learning, and putting our advice into action for your job search today and your career tomorrow.

CHAPTER SEVEN

Telemarketing Yourself: The Technology of Networking

Whether they are used to earning $6,000 a year sweeping floors or six-figure megabucks charting the course of an international corporation, jobless people invariably ask the same question: "Who's hiring?"

The question can be stated in several ways, but whatever sophisticated terminology the corporate quarterbacks may use to ask it, like all job hunters they gravitate toward any source of job leads. Many imagine that those leads are grouped on some master list of companies that are hiring in their particular discipline. It's amazing to us, but even senior-level human resource executives, who should know better, think that new positions will materialize on a list, like manna from heaven. Well, if you're on a first-name basis with Moses, that might happen. But if you're like the rest of us, forget it. And get to work.

Not only is the "master list" concept unrealistic, but—more important—it runs counter to our basic premise of job search. If anyone gives you a list of companies that are hiring, you immediately place yourself on the wrong side of the job search equation. About nine out of ten job hunters concentrate their search efforts in the minority slice of available jobs, diluting your possibilities for success with such lists.

From word one in this book, we've stressed that there's no revolutionary innovation, no easy path to finding a new position. The traditional methods work if you labor hard enough at implementing them. Nowhere is that more true than when you're contacting companies, generating job leads.

Is there a secret, fail-safe path to success? You bet. But it's only a secret because it's been pushed back into a dusty corner in the world of job search advice, outdated by more glamorous, high-tech instruction. It's dated, but not obsolete. Our secret, it shouldn't surprise you to learn, is *work*, then more work—coupled with dedication, preparation, discipline, planning, learning, and positive thinking. These will drive your job search, and they will ensure success. And there's not a single shortcut in this recipe. In our view, working hard means an absolute minimum of ten hours a day—we put twelve to sixteen hours a day into our business. Be prepared to put similar time and effort into your job search if you expect to succeed.

HOW DO YOU FIND THE JOBS?

You pick up the phone and call each company, each department manager, and ask if they're hiring. So who's hiring? A select few, if you follow the herd mentality. Everyone, if you learn networking and cold-calling skills. The telephone and the business letter are your communication tools in this stage of job search. We'll discuss networking and talking to employers in the context of telephone work. Incredibly, we still come across advice that it's fine for job searchers to visit employers if they're uncomfortable or inexperienced on the phone. This suggestion is so absurd that it belongs in the *Guinness Book of Records* as the world's worst advice. Stay out of your car until you begin to arrange interviews—or at least until you've cultivated a contact to the point that a lunch or breakfast meeting might be productive. But if you spend your day driving around filling out applications, you're not looking for a job—you're wasting time, avoiding your spouse and kids, or just plain cruising. We call it the *windshield mentality*. Pure and simple, if you do it, you'll still be looking for work the day the sun rises in the west.

So we're agreed, right? You'll work the telephone to find job leads. If you're a novice on the phone, before you start, go ahead and draw a sketch of a monster face and tape it to the phone. We know that's how bad it is for most people who are new to the process. That little mechanical instrument becomes the enemy. But that enemy's weapon is fear, and fear grows from a lack of confidence. Accept that. It's normal to start out a little shaky, with a degree of uncertainty, on your initial calls. That's the primary reason we suggested (in Chapter 5) that you don't call your best contacts, your closest professional friends, first. Call the strangers first; learn while you're working the coldest contacts on your list. After the first twenty or thirty phone calls, your technique will begin to develop, and you'll be ready to approach and solidify some of your hotter contacts.

Like any endeavor, however, your technique won't improve if you keep repeating mistakes. You can't slop your way through twenty phone calls, learn nothing, change nothing, and expect the next call to part the sea. As you telemarket, analyze what you say and what the reply is—what works and what doesn't work. Above all, listen. Telemarketing is a communication technique. Whenever we use an unfamiliar technique, we tend to become preoccupied with what we're saying. It's fine to script a conversation but don't fail to listen and react to the other person's comments.

Think of your evaluation process in two tiers. First, analyze your style—how you communicate your message and how smoothly you break from your preplanned script into a free-flowing conversation with your contact. Then evaluate what you say. As an illustration, suppose that you consider as the highlight of your professional career the redesign of a tool that eliminated a $23 zerk fitting. But if each time you mention your accomplishment to cold-calling contacts it generates nothing but silence on the other end of the line, that's a good indication that elimination of zerk fittings doesn't pull a lot of weight in this year's market. Change your presentation. Be flexible, attentive, and persistent. Don't stumble through your calls. Improve.

The guideposts to a fruitful, ever-improving telemarketing campaign are discipline, dedication, and goal setting. Your goal is an established number of cold calls each day. We suggest fifty, but set a goal that you can attain with discipline and dedication. If you want to start at twenty or twenty-five, fine. But commit now toward reaching that number and *improving* with each call. Never lose sight of your short-range goal with each call—an interview. Your fallback goal is to get the names of three, four, or five other people you can call.

Your command of goals and time makes this process of contacting companies work. (Exhibits 7.1 and 7.2 provide forms to help you organize your time—a daily action plan and a weekly activity summary.) Surely we don't need to justify the importance of setting goals; you undoubtedly have utilized the technique in your professional career. Just be certain that you don't abandon goal setting now that you're navigating in unfamiliar territory. You need goals now more than ever. Our favorite truism about goal setting is an often-quoted statement: "Those who do not set goals are forever doomed to work for those who do." Adapting that for job search, we can say: "Those who do not set goals are doomed to finding new positions much later than those who do."

WORK THE PHONE AND IT WILL WORK FOR YOU

This all leads to a radical departure from the ritualistic advice most job searchers revere. Everyone ventures out, forewarned and forearmed, to resist depression and to shake off rejection. But succumbing to rejection just

EXHIBIT 7.1
Personal Marketing Plan: Daily Action Plan

DATE_____

MY GOALS FOR TODAY ARE:_____

_____

_____

MY ACTIVITIES TO ACCOMPLISH THESE GOALS ARE:

7:00 _____

7:30 _____

8:00 _____

8:30 _____

9:00 _____

9:30 _____

10:00 _____

10:30 _____

11:00 _____

11:30 _____

12:00 _____

12:30 _____

1:00 _____

1:30 _____

2:00 _____

2:30 _____

3:00 _____

3:30 _____

4:00 _____

4:30 _____

REMEMBER—LOOKING FOR A JOB IS A FULL-TIME JOB!
(Record daily accomplishments on Weekly Activity Summary.)

EXHIBIT 7.2
Personal Marketing Plan: Weekly Activity Summary

NAME:_____   WEEK BEGINNING:_____

ACTIVITY	RESULTS					
	M	T	W	TH	F	TOTAL
NETWORKING Personal/professional contacts (1) Target companies (2) Search firms (3)						
LETTERS First contact/cover (4) Ad response (5) Follow-up/thank-you (6)						
INTERVIEW PREPARATION (7) (research and practice sessions)						
INTERVIEWS Informational interviews (8) Job interviews from networking (9)						
JOB OFFERS (10)						

doesn't happen to our clients in Houston if they follow our principles. Time after time, across the board of professional disciplines, they find new jobs faster than they had dreamed—and not just a job, but a better position, for more money, with a better company. Believe us, if it's possible in Houston where the oil glut has caused a steep economic slide, it's possible on the moon. If you can make it here, you can make it anywhere.

Many people are telling job hunters that cold-calling is so tough that it's all right to avoid it as a job search technique. That advice might make you feel better, but it won't help your job search. In fact, its dangerous to your career.

Your job search is not governed by the economy, any more than a salmon swimming upstream is driven by the river's current. It is a fact of American business that companies hire people every day. Companies in bankruptcy proceedings do it; companies with absolute, worldwide hiring freezes do it. By networking, telemarketing, and cold-calling, you can access those job leads.

When you do, you won't have to worry about lists of jobs or lists of companies that are hiring. In fact, you won't even have time to wish for their existence. Your positive momentum will build; you'll be busy and confident. Our point is that when you work the phones properly and get a rejection in spite of your improving technique, it's only one of fifty calls. Part of your technique is to get off the line quickly—don't beat on a dead contact. You don't have time to waste. You'll hang up believing that the company lost its chance at you, and you'll move along to the next contact.

Of course, there's a fine line between confidence and arrogance. Don't be so confident that you're rude and just blow people off the phone. But believe that you have skills and background to help that company. If it's not a good match, try the next company. Always be a pro.

There's one final point to be made as we try to short-circuit every possible argument anyone can mount about why they shouldn't telemarket. Frequently, we talk with senior executives or people in traditional professions—medicine, law, accounting—who respond, "We don't do that. It's considered beneath a lawyer's standing to get on the phone and ask for help" or "That doesn't work at my level. Companies only hire through search firms at the senior levels." All we can say is, if you think cold-calling another lawyer for help is more demeaning than going for a year without a job, then there's not much we can do to help you. Even if a position is contracted to a search firm, how do you expect to find out about it? When looking for a job, *no one* is too good or too important to utilize proven techniques to get that job. So we dismiss any protest about telemarketing. It's the most important technique you can use to find job leads. And it works for everyone, not just sales or marketing people who are pros on the phone. People who say that they cannot or will not telemarket are blocking themselves from their own potential. It works for everyone. And the skills are learnable.

TIME TO START

With that in mind, let's get started on just what you say and how you say it. We mean, literally, *get started*. This is the phase of job search when procrastination is most prevalent and most destructive. To be sure, generating momentum on the phone can be difficult. We are all prone to make three or four calls, then fiddle around with paperwork or research or some other "non-prime-time" pursuit. Soon, you'll have mused away the morning. Come noon, you can say with conviction, "This telemarketing is tough. I'm exhausted." It's easy to get caught in that trap, so set your mind now to avoid it. Set your goals and meet them. If you don't meet your goals, work on your efficiency, or shorten your horizon slightly. But your goals and time management are the benchmarks for success. Don't fail yourself.

Let's look more closely at our daily telemarketing goal of fifty calls. We're actually understating our own pace—we could place fifty calls in five hours. Initially, many calls are one-minute placement calls and the contact "will return the call." You may have to call these contacts again and again to get through. We feel that we're expert in nurturing the good calls within a couple of minutes and decapitating the bad ones in seconds. Our point is that you should set a goal you can reach, then build upon it. Both the numbers and the quality of your cold-calling should increase. As we touched upon earlier, telephoning and interviewing are your "prime-time" events in job search. They must be done during business hours. Researching, reading, responding to ads, and writing letters should be done in the evening or on weekends. This is linkage in action again. Remember our equation for where the jobs are. Networking generates about 80 percent, ads and search firms only 20 percent. That is precisely how we suggest you allocate your time. Most of job search is phone work—networking and cold-calling.

A SCENARIO FOR COLD-CALLING

To prepare for your cold-calling, we suggest that you create a written script. We have used scripts for years in developing our company's business, and the same principles apply to your job search. There are certain fundamentals of selling that every cold call should contain. Remember that job search is a selling situation. In compiling your cold-calling script, include the following elements:

- The full name of the person you're calling: We suggest that you use the first and last names in your initial contact with a secretary. If you use Mr. or Ms., it can give the impression that you're operating out of your league. And if you use the first name only, that's too familiar and inappropriate for any initial business contact.
- The name of the person who referred you (or the publication from which you got the company's name)
- Why you are calling: First, you want a job; second, you want more names.
- Why your qualifications match the needs of the company
- What your specific occupational skills are
- Why a personal meeting can be helpful to both you and the company: The incentive for the contact meeting may be an interest in your background, your industry or product knowledge, the people you know, or ideas you can share.
- A time limit: Frequently, you'll be cautioned that you should not waste the employer's time; that you should hurry and get off the phone; that two minutes is plenty, and the employer's been gracious to give you that much. All these points are valid, but the movitation's all wrong. Certainly, get off the phone quickly, and don't waste time. But it's *your* time that must not be wasted as well as the employer's time. When you accept that precept, you will have taken a major step toward understanding and implementing a telemarketing program.
- The three R's: Read, Reread, then Role-play your script with another person. That's the only way to make it work when you go on wire with the hiring authority.

Keeping accurate records of your telemarketing is as important as having a script. You probably had secretaries or clerical staffs to handle all your grunt work in the past. Well, welcome to life in job search (or in an entrepreneurial organization, for that matter). There are no overlapping layers of staff. The grunt work is now your responsibility. Be sure that you maintain a simple but effective record of company, person, secretary, what was said, and what is to happen next. (Exhibit 7.3 provides a form for keeping a record of a telephone conversation.)

Look over the following sample script. Adapt the responses with which you're comfortable, but remember that they are only script suggestions.

EXHIBIT 7.3
Personal Marketing Plan: Record of Telephone Conversation

TELEPHONE NO._____ DATE_____ TIME_____

NAME_____ TITLE_____

COMPANY_____

ADDRESS_____

_____

SECRETARY_____ OTHER NAMES_____

_____

SUBJECT_____

CONVERSATION NOTES

REFERRALS

Develop your own style, and alter that style to mesh with the personality of the person on the other end of the line.

You: Good morning, Mr. Hardsell, this is [your name] calling. Fred Goodguy at TestTude Corporation suggested that I call. Could I have a few minutes of your time?

Mr. Jack Hardsell: I'm very busy; I have only a minute. [That gives you license to take three minutes.]

You: As a result of a recent corporate reorganization at [former company], I am currently exploring opportunities for new career directions. Fred suggested that your data processing unit would double its staff this year [or that he had an extremely strong base of contacts in data processing]. [Or you read about his company's expansion plans, new product merger, or the like, in the *Wall Street Journal.*] I wonder if we might meet to discuss your expansion [or if he'd share some of his contacts].

Give him a chance to respond, then proceed on the basis of his comments.

You: To give you a better idea of my background . . . [briefly tell him those parts that will have the most impact]. Is there a need in your [company, division, department, etc.] for someone with my skills?

Asking a question helps ensure a dialogue in which you can gain as much information as possible from your contact. Again, give him a chance to respond and assist you.

Close with an invitation to lunch (if it's an exceptionally important contact) or with an attempt to set up an appointment. As a minimum, get a few referral names:

You: I really appreciate your taking time to speak with me. I understand that there are no immediate needs in your division, but can you suggest others with whom I may speak?

Even in this brief sample, some of the myriad options become evident. Our point is, don't script so closely that you fail to carry on a logical conversation. You want to preplan everything you say, but you don't want to memorize it. Every company, every call, every person will be different. You must react spontaneously, and you do that by practicing.

Count on the fact that some of the Mr. Hardsells on the other end of the phone line will be jerks. But also anticipate that a Mr. Easysell may jump at the chance to interview you and may need a new employee that day. Most people will respond somewhere between those extremes. Remember that you have immunity from the jerks; they can't hurt you. Learn to cut down their phone time to ten or fifteen seconds and move along to the next call. More likely, however, you'll find people cooperative and anxious to help. It's not a disgrace to be unemployed now. Generally, it's an experience most of the people you'll be talking to have encountered. If they haven't personally, they probably know someone close who has, or they may even expect to be unemployed soon themselves! At least, that's what the Texas economy is like. So don't feel that you're a deadbeat or that people will treat you like a degenerate because you're conducting a job search. If they try to do so, cut them off.

GETTING TO MR. HARDSELL

Back to Mr. Hardsell—if he's important enough to have valuable contacts, in all likelihood he's important enough to have a secretary. To get to him, you must first get past her, and it's her job to see that that doesn't happen. You've probably heard advice for the best way to dodge the secretary— calling before or after business hours, during lunch, and so forth. The hope is that your contact will pick up the call in person.

Those are valid tactical moves, but only as fallback positions. We always suggest that your first step should be straightforward. Although the secretary's job is to protect her boss, why not consider it your job to win her as a convert to your needs? If you're really skilled on the phone and deal with her honestly, very frequently she'll feed information that will help you catch Mr. Hardsell. Don't ever dismiss that possibility without a try. For example:

You: Good morning. Is Jack Hardsell in? This is [your name] calling.
Secretary: He's in a meeting. May I tell him the nature of the call?
You: Yes. Fred Goodguy at TestTube is a mutual acquaintance. He suggested that Jack might have some information to assist me in my job search.

We like this approach because you're limiting the information you're giving out, but you're never making a false or misleading statement. Don't try to blow smoke at the secretary—inevitably, it will smother you later. At this point, she may take your name and number for a callback (don't get discouraged if you don't punch through on the first call). If you don't hear from Mr. Hardsell that day, at least you've established the rudiments of a working relationship with his secretary. The next day, it's proper to call back and place the message again. Such callbacks are the times when your professionalism can really pay off. Each time, be courteous, supportive of her schedule and Mr.

Hardsell's, and understanding of the delay in returning your call. Simultaneously, however, be persistent. You won't be rude, but you won't be put off, either. That's how you can subtly enlist a secretary's aid.

Another possibility is that the secretary will immediately instruct you to contact the human resources department. Again, don't argue the point. Do as she asks. The call to human resources will likely be unproductive. At that point, call back Mr. Hardsell's office and ask to speak with him. When the secretary states that human resources handles this type of call, you can truthfully state that you're not asking him for a job—you want information, and you only want a few minutes of his time.

Notice that at no time do we recommend that you ask for an information interview (sometimes called a referral interview). First, this country has been "information-interviewed" to death. It's a buzzword with no buzz left. More important, it smacks of a technique that an amateur would use. You want to communicate implicitly to Mr. Hardsell that you're a pro—that you need help now, but that you're the type of person who can be beneficial to him in the future. The term *information interview* does none of that. Don't give the impression that you're stepping up in class. That's a false imagery that is especially harmful to you in job search.

The concept and content of information interviewing is fine; in fact, it's just what we're suggesting that you do. It's the terminology that drags you down with excess baggage. Stay away from it. But do get the information—and the new referrals.

Throughout this process, remember our rules of engagement in telemarketing. When you're talking to Mr. Hardsell's secretary, she may resist all efforts at charm and professionalism, proving her a formidable blocker. Or Mr. Hardsell might be predisposed to be unavailable. Or the human resources department might tell you that your name has been programmed into the computer to self-destruct if your resume comes within a mile of their building.

If that happens, fine. Your fail-safe position protects you. Each of those calls will take only seconds, and you will move along on your contact list. Again, you can't get depressed—you don't have time. Also, don't lose sight of the fact that in a large company, even if Mr. Hardsell and his formidable accomplice won't help you, they are only one of perhaps a dozen destinations for your cold call. If the company is one into which you are determined to network, cut off this contact and develop another within the same organization. And do it all within minutes of telephone time. The following situation will give you an idea how this can work:

John Powell had targeted a major company as having excellent opportunities to fit his background and skills. When his letter of introduction and cold calls to the vice president of operations produced no direct response, John decided to call one of the directors who reported to the vice president. To his surprise, the director already had his resume in hand, routed from the vice president. Using the referral from the vice president to his advantage, John had no trouble setting up a preliminary interview with the director. Had John given up on the vice president and not placed the call to the director, he might never have networked into that target company.

To cold-call hiring authorities, you first must have a company to call. Your goal is to network into a department decision maker before he lists a job opening with a search firm or in a newspaper ad. To that end, you must work through your list of personal and professional contacts. We discussed in Chapter 5 what your network is and who should be on the list. You should have built a network of more than 100 names by now. Call each one, tell them your story, and ask if they can help. Most important, get three, four, or five names from each. Your contacts with search firms should also be handled as part of your networking effort. Get names of people and companies from your executive search consultant. If he's a real pro, he'll assist your networking even though there's not an immediate fee in sight. Even when you read the newspaper ads, if you don't get a job offer from a company, try to generate additional contacts from your interaction.

NEWSPAPER ADS

When you're reading newspapers, don't stop at the ads. Other parts of the paper can be far more valuable for generating job leads. Any news report about growth, expansion, sales records, new territories, new products, or mergers and acquisitions is reason enough for a telemarketing or networking call.

Volumes of advice are available on how best to utilize ad responses. Keep in mind, however, that most of the advice comes from the Newspaper Advertising Bureau, a glorified trade association whose goal is to generate more revenue for newspapers. The fact is that classified advertising is a very low payoff proposition. Certainly, include ads in your job search, but don't build your search on them. Like search firms, they are easier to use than networking and cold-calling, but they just don't work as effectively.

If you do respond to ads, foremost among the rules is that you conform to whatever imperatives you find in the ad copy. If they want a resume, don't send some hybrid mutation you learned about from a college professor— send them your resume. If they want a salary history, put it in your cover letter (as we discussed in Chapter 3). You'll hear a lot of advice about answering *any* ad with your resume, just on the theory that if a company is hiring chemists, it may need petroleum engineers or systems analysts as well. That's fine if you have the time. But don't expect too much. Remember that, at best, classified ads are a long shot, and this lengthens the betting odds against you. Blind ads are another source of controversy. (They have only a post office box number, no company name.) Don't assume that it's a second-rate company just because it placed a blind ad. It may be a small firm without the resources to process large volumes of responses. So we're not opposed to your responding to blind ads. Our only warning is, don't answer a blind ad when you are employed. You may be asking your present employer for a job—that blind box number may be down the hall in the next department.

There's always a question about when to respond to an ad. Should you respond quickly, ahead of the rush, or late, after the crush of resumes has hit the human resources department? Our suggestion is to wait a couple of days until the crush should be over, and mail in a resume and cover letter. If it is not a blind ad, be sure to follow-up with a phone call.

Remember, like search firms, ads are only one source of job leads—and one that does not have a high degree of return. So don't waste a lot of time reading and thinking about how and when to use them. It's foolish to spend time weighing alternative courses carefully when none of the alternatives weighs much in the job search process. Spend the majority of your time with networking and cold-calling.

SMALL COMPANIES OFFER GOOD POSSIBILITIES

Keep your eyes and ears open for small, closely held, or private companies in your networking. Specifically, entrepreneurial organizations constitute fertile ground for job campaigning. We've thoroughly refuted the notion that you can find a list of jobs and companies, but now we'll retrench a fraction of an inch. To the question "Who's hiring?" we can safely answer: "Small companies." It's estimated that over 80 percent of all jobs in the next decade will be created by companies with fewer than twenty employees. The Seven Sisters may be cutting to the bone, and the Big Eight may be recycling pencils, but that's no cause to be discouraged. While the multinational corporations struggle through a transitioning world economy, remember that there's more to the job market than corporate monoliths. In fact, small entrepreneurial organizations represent the future of the American job market.

That's the up side—that small companies have the jobs. The down side is that small firms are more difficult to research for a cold contact. Most are private and aren't required to produce public records for the SEC. Once again, we don't have any magic formula to simplify your task, except to stress that the reward justifies the extra effort. You must dig, read, research, think, retrench, and keep sifting through layers of information. Start in the library. Read professional journals, all business periodicals, chamber of commerce publications, as well as municipal, county, and state compilations or guides to businesses registered for operation in your area. Always remember that at this point you're not only working to uncover job leads. You want to find out about the corporate culture, the environment, and the principals of these small organizations. Especially when you're dealing with newer, smaller companies, you must work smart and hard to develop your own information base before you even think about networking and cultivating job leads. To reiterate, once you hook one entrepreneur on the phone, even if you can't create a match, push your contact to the wall—max it out. Get five additional names. Remember, these are usually people who are successful refugees from corporate workstyles. And it's safe to generalize that they'll be more sympathetic and helpful to your networking quest.

THIS PROCESS WORKS

Networking is close to our hearts because we built our business from ground zero, living and working these same principles. Are you beginning to understand how this process eliminates the rejection syndrome that most job search consultants try to sell wholesale? Can you sense that this is a reality-based approach to creating momentum in your job campaign? We think the following chart of positive versus negative approaches to job search illustrates our point perfectly:

Approach	Attitude	Decision	Action	Emotions	Result
+	Learning experience	Try again	Keep improving	Enthusiasm	Success
−	Personal rejection	Withdraw	Quit	Fear	Failure

The chart's message is that when you get a no, it's not failure. It is an opportunity to analyze and improve your technique, an opportunity to isolate any chronic weaknesses in your presentation, and an opportunity to put your self-discipline to the test. In reality a no is more productive than a maybe in job search. "Maybe" means that you must maintain your records, follow-up on schedule, and continue to pursue what is, at best, a marginal possibility. "No" means that you can scrub the company and move along to more productive contacts.

We tell our outplacement clients that depression and failure are internally produced and, therefore, controllable. They cannot be forced upon you by the economy or the price of oil or the heartless corporation that terminated you two days before Christmas. It is your choice to be positive or negative, your decision to succeed or fail at job search. If you can buy into that philosophy, you're a candidate for our *One Percenters Club*. If you can't, that's fine, too. Keep reading as if you were skimming a Sears catalogue. That will mean fewer really smart job hunters, making it that much easier for the rest—those who intend to succeed.

As our last words on telemarketing, some "if . . . then" reminders:

If	*Then*
You are afraid to cold-call . . .	Get realistic. This is your career, your life. Pick up the phone and talk; each call gets easier.
You have a title . . .	Use it.
You have a company affiliation . . .	Use it.
You got the referral from a news story or a written report . . .	Verify the position and the name of your contact with the company switchboard first.
You can't get an interview or job lead . . .	Get three to five additional names you can contact.
You ask a question . . .	Be quiet and listen; don't be so preoccupied with your script that you fail to get the answer.
You leave a callback message . . .	Suggest the best time for a callback. Invest in an answering service or a phone recorder. Never wait by the phone.
You can't get past the secretary . . .	Try again. Then try calling before 8:00 or after 5:00.
You can't make any progress after repeated calls . . .	Ask your original contact to help you if this company is critically important in your search. Otherwise, move along to your next cold call, with your spirits up.

CHAPTER EIGHT

Interviewing: It's a Psychological Tennis Match, So Hold Your Serve

First, let's do a six-question pop quiz on interviewing for a job. Answer yes or no to each question:

1. In an interview, you exchange information. Right?
2. It's a chance for you to learn all about the company—products, services, philosophy, and corporate culture. Agreed?
3. Simultaneously, of course, the company will learn all about you—your strengths, weaknesses, hopes for the future, work style, and personal value system. Correct?
4. You'll be carefully evaluating the company and the interviewer during the process to determine whether you want to work at this place. Right?
5. You'll be prepared to discuss frankly the facts on your resume, paying special attention to a candid assessment of your reasons for leaving previous jobs. Agreed?
6. You'll tell the truth, the whole truth, and nothing but the truth. Correct?

That's the quiz. Before you score it, however, it might give you a clue to the answers if we tell you that those six statements incorporate much of the bromide that is peddled as advice on preparation for the job interview. Indeed, most job hunters (career counselors, too, for that matter) would answer yes to each question. Did you? If so, you're 0 for 6. More important, someone else has the job.

People think that they are preparing for the interview by merely laboring over a list of tough questions that they know they'll be asked. They struggle with the answers. They fret over how badly they'll be hurt by

121

discussions about weaknesses or difficult situations in their work history. They expect to provide candid information about themselves and, in turn, get the same from the employer—a true exchange of information to benefit both parties in the decision-making process. Don't think us cynical, and don't assume that we're suggesting that you be deceptive—but nothing could be further from the truth.

An interview is not an exchange of information. It is a contest in which you are a contender—a psychological tennis match. Your resume has captured the company's interest, proving that you have the technical skills and background to do the job. Now, in the interview, the hiring decision will be made. This is standard job search advice, and we certainly don't take exception to it. We do, however, want you to know how you can best extract the offer. To that end, you must understand that interviewing is an art form, a performance. Your task is to hold your serve by controlling—very subtly— the direction of the interview.

We don't trivialize the interview; we simply snap it into proper focus when we teach our clients that they must approach it as though they are contestants in a beauty pageant or a dog and pony show. In business terminology, visualize it as a sales call. But understand what the process is and what it isn't. We get occasional resistance on this point from individuals who protest, "That's a game. I don't play games." A game is exactly what it is. You can't change that fact; you can only succeed or fail according to your ability to grasp the reality of the scenario and turn it to your advantage.

The interaction isn't created to hurt or deceive anyone. This is a classic win-win situation. You want the job offer; and if you get it, both you and the company will profit. You're not there just to play a game—you're there to win the game. The payoff, of course, is that both you and the employer can win at the same game.

To accomplish that, you prepare. You do your homework. In fact, that is *The First Great Commandment of Interviewing: Plan Every Word.*

Don't say any word that won't help you get the job offer. This is not a time for reflective, introspective responses. This is a time to *sell*, to *market*. You must tell the company what it wants to hear—assuring the employer that you are confident, poised, in control of yourself and your surroundings, and with a personality that contributes to team unity and productivity. In this scenario, there really are no difficult questions, at least not for our clients. That's not an empty promise. You probably know what a devastating experience a tough interview can be, so no doubt you can appreciate what our clients typically tell us when they complete an interview. Not one or two but an overwhelming majority of our clients say with a grin, "I kept waiting for the tough questions. I was so confident of my responses that I was actually hoping for a chance to answer the objections. When I left, I thought it was nothing compared to the practice sessions the Dawsons put me through." Yes, we admit we're tough. But those conditions are dictated by the Darwinian job market. And our clients—provided that they buy into our principles—are ready for survival in any environment.

You see, each tough question is answered with a preplanned statement, and it's the same for every interview. You don't pause, reflect, stammer, then wade through an emotional response, fighting to control yourself. For each question, you've rehearsed the answer time and again, in advance. Most important, with each answer, you talk about yourself, but you do it in terms of what the employer wants to hear. Ironically, our position on interviewing runs counter to our advice about networking and cold-calling. There, we told you that scripting wasn't the whole answer. You had to prepare, but your responses had to be spontaneous and based on input from your contact.

For interviewing, however, you can plan and script your answers thoroughly and completely. Memorizing is a word fraught with danger in a situation like this, but we're suggesting that that's very nearly what you must do. Nevertheless, you must interact with the interviewer and respond to the changing dynamics of the discussion. For each tough question, develop an answer that meshes with your background, and ride that horse until you get a job offer. Unwavering consistency is critical. And when we say *every* word should be planned in advance, we mean *every* word. That ties in with *The Second Great Commandment of Interviewing: Positioning.*

With regard to individual questions within the interview, think of shooting a game of pool. Every pool shark in the world—and even every amateur—knows that the secret of success at pool is not just the shot you're attempting but the shooting position you set up for your next attempt. Ladies and gentlemen, that's also the key to unlocking the puzzle of interviewing success. With each answer, you position yourself for succeeding questions. This is how the interview becomes an exercise in control rather than a draining emotional nightmare. You allow the interviewer to rack the balls. But you make the break to control the interview. Your goal is no surprises—no questions too tough to "play."

You want to convey an image of professionalism and confident persistence. Just be careful not to be too dominant, aggressive, or rude in striving for that control. Actually, the real trick is to allow the interviewer to feel in control even though *you're* the one making the shots.

The building blocks for interviewing success are consistent with all our principles of job search—preparation, practice, research, confidence. But one imperative overrides all others in the interview—concentration. You'll probably have to develop your powers of concentration and extend the time you sustain it to a degree you've never before reached. What powers of concentration must a neurosurgeon command when he's working inside a patient's brain for eight hours? We'll never know, but it's an appropriate frame of reference. In your psychological tennis match, you must anticipate and react to every nuance of the interviewer's mental play with the same degree of intensity. Is this difficult? Without question.

IT'S NOT EASY, BUT IT CAN BE DONE

You thought cold-calling was tough! By now, you should recognize that talking into the phone is really quite simple compared to going one-on-one with the interviewer—nose-to-nose and toes-to-toes. In fact, we rank this process—especially the mandate that you concentrate, totally, completely, incessantly—as number two in degree of difficulty in the entire scope of job campaigning. In our view, only negotiating your compensation package is more subtle, complex, and difficult (and you'll learn that next, in Chapter 9).

That's the bad news. But, as always, we have good news coming along close behind. The good news is that this is the point in job search when our concept of linkage most clearly evolves from theory to reality. When you link your resume and references to your interview, you've hurdled the biggest obstacle in your path to a job offer. As we discussed in the chapter on resume writing, whenever you feel yourself getting into trouble, use your resume as an escape hatch. Moreover, you can build most of your interview answers from the contents of your resume.

For example, the single most difficult (and inevitable) question you'll deal with in an interview is "Tell me about yourself." It's in response to this open-ended inquiry that many people talk themselves out of a job offer. But if you structure your answer as we've suggested earlier—starting at the bottom of page two on the resume and moving up to the top of page one with a two- or three-minute biographical sketch of who you are, where you've been, and where you're going—you'll succeed. Quite simply, you've transformed a major roadblock into a positive image of yourself in the employer's eyes. And you're a giant step closer to a job offer.

YOUR TOOL KIT

Every time you go out on an interview, you will take your *tool kit* with you. The tool kit consists of:

- Your resume
- References
- Samples of projects
- Performance appraisals
- Background information
- Documentation of accomplishments

These are not used to cover the interviewer with paper, but if you are asked for specific items or examples of your accomplishments, you have them in your tool kit to reinforce the points you need to make.

WHAT IS THE GOAL OF AN INTERVIEW?

Let's pause here to clarify our position. Notice that we're not suggesting that you're after a *job* in the interview, only an *offer*. That's a critical distinction, and it's central to our approach to planning and implementing your campaign. We want you to get the best job you can locate, but if you take only one company to the point of an offer, if you have only one offer from which to choose, how can you possibly know which job is best for your present and future? To determine the best possible combination of duties and corporate culture, you must get multiple offers—at least three, preferably simultaneous—then weigh them and choose the best.

Before we move along toward helping you structure a win-win interviewing style that will generate multiple offers, let's deal with the six statements at the opening of this chapter. When we explain why each statement was inaccurate, we're confident that you'll share our viewpoint.

1. In an interview, you exchange information.

    No. Interviewing is a performance by you—nothing more, nothing less. It will require six to nine months for the company to determine whether or not you're suited for the corporate culture and the position. To suppose that anyone could identify a match, for better or worse, on the basis of one or even several conversations is preposterous.

2. It's an opportunity for you to learn all about the company.

    No. You'll already know everything about the company in advance of the interview, based on the information you learned from researching, networking, and cold-calling. Before you walk in, you'll understand what they do and how they do it. That's just another function of your networking. With your cold-calling skills, you learn about the company's products, services, reputation, plans for the future, and workstyle or corporate culture.

3.   The company will learn all about you.

No. Get serious. Of course that won't happen. Think for a moment about the significant other person in your life—spouse or whomever—and recall what you learned about that person during the first date of your embryonic relationship. It's a good bet that you can't even remember. Again, the employer will learn about you—your skills, abilities, ambition, personality, workstyle—gradually over the next six to nine months. If you try to tell the company all that during the interview, you're conducting job search the way Khadafy runs his country—death-wish style. If you get too deep into your personal business, we guarantee that you'll leave the interview feeling that it was a cathartic experience. We also guarantee that you won't get the offer.

4.   You'll be evaluating the company and the interviewer.

No. Not on your life—at least, not on your career. Remember, you're not there to make a decision; you're attempting to get an offer. You'll evaluate later and compare. If you don't have multiple offers before accepting one offer, you're selling yourself, and us, short.

5.   You'll discuss your work history frankly.

No. Never. Everyone's work history includes periods of difficulty, failure, or conflict, in varying degrees. But believe us, that is no one's business but your own. Tell the company what it wants to hear. You admired and respected every boss for whom you've ever worked, everyone got along great, the company was ideal, and you learned more about your profession than you could have hoped for. You're ever so thankful for all those opportunities to grow and learn. We acknowledge that this answer is full of a substance generally found in fields and collected by shovel, but we're perfectly comfortable with that (the imagery, not the actual substance). You want the job offer. So long as your resume is factual with regard to your work history and accomplishments, the employer knows what he's getting. Once again, the interview discussion is only to confirm that you're confident, capable, positive, and a potential asset to the company.

6.   You'll tell the whole truth.

No. Talk about death wishes! Tell the truth—under no circumstance should you lie to get a job. However, although telling the truth connotes honor to us, telling the *whole truth* represents stupidity. To reiterate, please don't think that we're suggesting that you play fast and loose with ethics. Never lie. Answer the questions truthfully, but do so in a manner that won't hurt you. And then stop. Don't crucify yourself with too much information. Every time, tell the truth, but stop short of telling the *whole* truth—spilling your insides all over the desk. An illustration:

Dick Ryan was interviewing for a position as division marketing manager in a major corporation. When asked about the extent of travel in a previous position, Dick proceeded to explain: "The travel was very extensive, about 90 percent of the time, which was very demanding and more than I really cared for." Although the job he was interviewing for required only 50 percent travel, Dick had raised enough doubt in the interviewer's mind about his willingness to travel that he lost his chance. Besides breaking the interviewing cardinal rule of never saying anything negative about one's former position, boss, or company, Dick offered more information than was necessary to answer the question. A better response would have been: "My last position required 90 percent travel. How much travel do you anticipate for the division manager's position?"

If you're asked, tell the truth—but respond only to what you're asked. People wander off mentally, say too much, realize they're in trouble, and then panic. They'll typically say something totally stupid because they're desperate and confused. If that happens in your interview, you're history. So the simple, fail-safe solution is, just don't say too much. Don't go out on a limb. Don't get into trouble.

To further illustrate the point in terms of business PR strategy, suppose that a company is about to introduce a new product that will gain a dramatically strong market share. Also suppose that there are three lawsuits pending against the company and a projected cash flow shortage for the next quarter. What do you suppose the company will announce in their news release? This country's ingrained values about motherhood and apple pie compel us to tell the truth. Fine—just don't volunteer information that isn't requested. Leaving some information out of your answer doesn't mean that you're a liar; you're just a smart interviewee.

GOOD ANSWERS TO HARD QUESTIONS

We've dealt with "Tell me about yourself." Now let's inject a little truth serum into another classic tough question: "Tell me about your weaknesses." You reply: "I have trouble getting along with people" or "I have trouble meeting deadlines" or "My spouse can't stand it if I work on weekends, and I don't like having to deal with that." Fine, you told the truth. What the employer will tell you now is good-bye. He may not speak it for another few minutes, but we guarantee that that response just clicked on in his mind. You're history.

Keeping those three weaknesses for our mythical job hunter, let's alter the responses 180 degrees without really changing the basis of the answers. Trouble getting along with people? Why not respond: "I do tend to get impatient with people who are deliberately unproductive." Trouble meeting deadlines? Why not respond: "I am a workaholic. I'm willing to put in however many hours it takes to get the work done." Angry spouse? Why not phrase it: "Sometimes I have to be careful—I get so wrapped up in my work that I don't give my family the time they need."

All we're suggesting is that you insist in your mind that you'll take a positive approach to every interviewing question. Work on it, practice, role-play, and conduct postinterview self-critiques (see Exhibit 8.1). For the process of self-evaluation, use the technique we call the *interviewing continuum* to facilitate an ongoing analysis. Both during and after the interview, think of the discussion as generating positive, neutral, or negative responses. On the interviewing continuum, left is positive, the middle is neutral, the right is negative. You can afford negative points on very few questions. You can get by with a few neutral responses. But the great majority must be positive. They must weigh the interviewing continuum to the left if you are to leave the impression necessary to receive an offer.

SOME TOUGH QUESTIONS

Now let's look at some typical tough questions you'll get in an interview. But before you read on, let us caution that these questions are not included for you to merely skim over. The planning and preparation of answers to them is essential to maximizing your interviewing prowess. The only way to succeed is to match your background to a positive, upbeat, convincing answer for each of these questions. Start with your resume. Know every word on it. Another key part of your preparation is company research. You should know as much about the company as you possibly can before you arrive for the interview.

Now, here are the tough questions. We'll give some sample answers, but your responsibility is to construct similar positive responses that coincide with your background:

- Would you rejoin your former company?

Most people would say yes, but this question has a hidden agenda. The interviewer wants to be sure that you'll stay on if you're hired, so your

EXHIBIT 8.1
Postinterview Self-Evaluation Form

Company _____ Interview Date _____

Name & Title of Interviewer _____

Position Interviewed for _____

Check if you felt "OK" or "very good" about certain aspects of the interview or if you felt you could have done better and "need to improve" for future interviews.

	Need to Improve	OK	Very Good
(1) Personal appearance	____	____	____
(2) Professional first impression?	____	____	____
(3) Firm handshake at start and end of interview?	____	____	____
(4) Maintained good eye contact?	____	____	____
(5) Expressed myself well by talking clearly and correctly?	____	____	____
(6) Self-confident, not ill at ease?	____	____	____
(7) Expressed interest in the job and career?	____	____	____
(8) Willingness to start at entry level or lower level and work up?	____	____	____
(9) Minimized employment barriers by presenting them in a positive light?	____	____	____
(10) Positive about my previous employer(s)?	____	____	____
(11) Demonstrated knowledge of the company and the industry in general?	____	____	____
(12) Described qualifications in a positive manner?	____	____	____
(13) Asked pertinent questions about the job?	____	____	____
(14) Presented abilities and qualifications in terms of the requirements for this job?	____	____	____
(15) Thanked the interviewer and arranged for follow-up?	____	____	____

Areas needing improvement for future interviews:

response should be something like, "I really enjoyed the opportunity to work there—it's a fine company, and they treated me very well. But it's time to move my career along to the next level. That's why I'm so interested in your firm. I'm considering opportunities at a number of excellent companies, but yours is at the top of my list."

- What makes you mad?

Look out for this one. You might say, "I really think it's my responsibility to avoid getting mad in the workplace. That drains too much productive time. But if there's one thing, it would be people who don't pull their weight, who won't strive for excellence. That may sound like I'm intolerant, but I'm not. I try to give people every benefit of the doubt, and I communicate my concerns to them before I ever get mad." Carefully note this answer. Not only does it defuse a potentially dangerous area of questioning, but it also illustrates our positioning theory. Tolerance might be a concern of the interviewer, and if it is not addressed, it might grow into a large-scale problem. But by linking it to the answer, you've controlled the interview in a professional manner while simultaneously heading off a potential problem.

- Would you relocate (or travel)?

This is an easy one. Your answer is, "Certainly, for the right opportunity." There may be only one set of circumstances for which you would relocate—Cancun for $500,000 annually—but your answer stands as accurate. If the company makes the right offer—the right opportunity—you'll relocate. It's truthful, but it keeps control of the interview in your court. Be aware, also, of the motivation for companies to ask questions about relocation and travel. The information may have nothing to do with the position for which you're interviewing, but frequently such queries originate from a list of prescribed questions to which every new employee must respond. How sad it would be if you lost a job offer because of a careless remark about not being willing to relocate, when in fact the job in question wouldn't require a move.

- Were you fired?

No matter what your circumstance, you were never fired. Rather, you were "part of a downsizing and reorganization." Always blame your condition on the economy or on organizational restructuring, not on the company or on your former boss. Similarly, you were never laid off or cut loose, nor did you "hit the bricks."

- What does cooperation mean?

"Cooperation means working with subordinates, superiors, and peers to establish an environment of excellence as a member of the team in order to meet organizational goals."

- What did you think of your boss?

"He was an excellent manager. I learned a lot from him, and we had an ideal working relationship. In fact, one of my letters of reference is from him, and I'd be glad to share it with you if you'd like." (By now, you recognize linkage—and there it is again.)

- What books have you read recently?

"*Iacocca* and *In Search of Excellence*." Always keep your responses business-oriented. Be sure that you've read the books you name in case the interviewer has also read them and asks more specific follow-up questions about them!

WORK UP ANSWERS TO THESE

With the foregoing samples close at hand, build your own responses to the following typical tough interview questions:

- Why are you interested in this industry?
- What kind of research have you done on this industry?
- What, in your opinion, is this industry's biggest problem or problems?
- What, in the short term, is the future for this industry?
- What, in the long term, is the future for this industry?
- Where, in your opinion, is the greatest growth potential?
- Where is this industry weakest?
- How do you view the competition in this industry?
- What do you consider to be the most important skill necessary to achieve success in this industry?
- What important trends do you see in this industry?
- What do you know about this company?
- Why would you like to work for this company?
- In what way can you make a contribution to our company?

- How long would it take you to make a meaningful contribution to our company? Why? (Watch out for this one. Your answer should be, "Immediately. I'll meet with all the key people and do a needs analysis.")
- How long would you stay with this company?
- Wouldn't you be happier in a smaller (larger) company or a different type of company?
- What kind of research have you done on our company?
- What kinds of measures do you use to evaluate a company?
- Why would you like to live in this community?
- What does it take to be successful in a company like this?
- In your current job, what problems have you identified?
- In your present job, what problems have you identified that were previously overlooked?
- Why are you leaving your present job?
- How would you evaluate your present firm?
- Have you helped increase sales? Profits? How?
- Have you helped reduce costs? How?
- How large a budget have you been responsible for?
- How many people do you supervise?
- What do your subordinates think of you?
- What do you like most about your current job?
- What do you like least about your current job?
- What have been your five most significant accomplishments in your job? (Refer to your resume as you respond.)
- Describe a few situations in which your work was criticized. (Here's a good example of a crossover answer. Your response to the question on weaknesses will work here as well.)
- How have you changed the nature of your job?
- Why aren't you earning more at your age?
- What are some of the most important lessons you have learned in your job?
- Describe some situations in which your efforts have been praised.
- What are the most important contributions you have made to your present employer?
- Why did you accept each of the positions listed on your resume?
- What position in our company are you applying for? Why?
- What interests you most about our product or service?
- Name five unique contributions you can make to our company.
- What is your greatest potential area for contributing to our company?
- Which is more important to you, money or position? (Your answer here is that both are important.)

- What kind of relationship should exist between managers and those reporting to them?
- What qualities and personal characteristics must a successful manager have?
- Why should I hire you?
- Describe what you feel to be an ideal working environment.
- Aren't you overqualified for this position?
- What do you look for in a job?
- What is your philosophy of management?
- What is your management style?
- What do you see as the most difficult task in being a manager?
- Why haven't you found a new position before now?
- Do you prefer staff or line work?
- What do you feel this position should pay?
- What kind of salary are you worth? (Remember your commitment to control. If you talk about worth, you've lost control. Talk about how much money you expect to earn, based on company and industry norms.)
- How much do you expect if we offer this position to you?
- Will you be out to take your boss's job? (No, you want to work with him.)
- What position do you expect in five years?
- As a manager, what do you look for when you hire people?
- Have you ever fired anyone? How did you handle it, and what were the reasons for the firing?
- Are you a good manager?
- Why do you feel you have top management potential?
- What are the "frontier" issues of your profession?
- What was the last book you read? The last movie you saw?
- How would you describe your personality?
- Are you a leader? Give examples.
- What are your goals?
- What are your strong points? (Don't answer with mundane statements about putting in a full day and getting there on time. Your strong points should include qualities such as leadership, communications, decision making.)
- Would you object to working for a woman? (If you are a man, do not say something flip, such as "Of course not. I love women!")
- What are your long-range (five-year plus) objectives?
- What are you doing to reach these objectives?
- What career options do you have at the moment?
- How would you describe success? According to your description, how successful have you been so far?

- What are some of the new goals you have recently established?
- What are your most important concerns when seeking a position?
- What is your greatest accomplishment?
- What are five unique features about you that contribute to your success?
- Describe some situations in which you have used initiative in your professional life.

If you're like most people, you've skimmed over these questions. But be certain—now or sometime before you face an interviewer—to think through and write out appropriate answers to each of them. Only then will you be prepared for an interview. Although it's a long list, don't feel overwhelmed; one answer might cover four or five different questions.

BUILD YOUR SELF-CONFIDENCE

Ironically, all the time and effort you invest in prepping for these questions will have an implicit reward even more significant than your acquired ability to respond adroitly at every turn. When you've built a series of answers that links with your resume and letters of reference, you will be fully prepared. That preparation builds confidence, and confidence builds excellence under pressure. You will send off nonverbal signals to the employer that you're a pro, ready for anything they can throw at you in the interview. We call this the *positive expectation of success.* Your nonverbal, dress, grooming, and confidence levels will close the credibility gap within fifteen to twenty seconds of the interview opening. Everyone walks in with this credibility gap. If you don't close it within a few seconds, you'll be struggling uphill for the entire session. Our clients close it. They know that they belong there; they know that they can perform in the interview. They expect to succeed.

WATCH OUT FOR . . .

In part, an abiding self-confidence is a by-product of a thorough understanding and appreciation of the following interview cautions.

Illegal Questions

How old are you? Are you married? Are you divorced? Do you plan to have more children? There's no doubt that these are illegal questions, but don't spend time thinking about what is legal and what's not. Even if a question is inappropriate, we suggest that you not dodge it. Respond briefly; then execute a linkage maneuver, pivoting on your resume, to maintain your offensive position. You might say, following a ten-second response to a poor question: "And Mr. Johnson, what's more important to us all is how my experience in a new territory, highlighted at the bottom of page one of my resume, gives me ideal experience to assume a key role in your expansion plans." A final point: Don't assume that any question is illegal. In reality, it is only illegal if information from a prohibited question is used to screen you out of a job. So don't be defiant if you get a question that's improper. You may politely say that the question is irrelevant to your ability to perform this job; then take control and turn the interview back on course. That's the best message of all—you can handle adversity, and you know the law. The employer isn't dealing with a rookie.

Two-Part Questions

Be especially alert to two-part questions. In the interview, what you say isn't the only factor of importance. The employer is also testing your retention and confidence. He wants to see if you can answer a two-part question without stopping to ask for a repeat of the second part. This is a very basic interviewing tactic, yet many people trip over it.

Hidden Agendas

Most people will face recurring objections about parts of their background. You must custom-design your response in such cases; but in so doing, you must understand that what the interviewer says isn't necessarily the issue on which he wants an answer. For example, take the 61-year-old engineer we described earlier. He kept getting objections about too much experience. That meant that he was too old. He defused the objection with his frontal assault: "I have thirty-five years of experience, and if you want an engineer with thirty-five years in the field, you're going to have to hire an older man."

Another example is a businessman who had closed down his entrepreneurial enterprise to reenter the corporate world. Repeatedly, he'd get questions about the nature of running a small business and his successes. Each time, he'd respond about the opportunities and challenges. Each time, he'd fail to get an offer. Finally, he realized that companies were reluctant to make an offer for fear that he'd leave to start another independent business at his first opportunity. So he altered his response to this: "I learned a great deal and treasure the experience. The most important lesson I can bring to your company is the lesson in time management. When you're on someone else's payroll, time management is an abstract goal. But when every minute of your day either adds to or subtracts from the bottom line, you learn time management as a business imperative, not an abstract goal." On his next interview, he got an offer.

The Secretary

Your relationship with the employer's secretary in the interview process is as important as it was during your cold-calling. Treat her with courtesy, use her name, and ask her a few questions if there's time and opportunity before the interview. In many offices, the secretary is the first person an employer will ask for feedback following an interview. Make sure that she's on your side.

Affirmative Delays

We think one of our tiniest little tricks helps our clients beyond measure in interview situations. We all know that it helps you respond better to any question if you delay for a moment before answering. But in an interview, any pause is destructive. It suggests lack of preparation on your part, and it allows negative energy to build in the room. So take your time to gather thoughts for an answer, but do it this way: As soon as the interviewer completes his question, affirm it. For example, if you are asked to list your five greatest strengths, you immediately say, "Yes, Mr. Johnson, I'd be happy to." Then you can take a couple of seconds to get your brain in gear. But to the listener, you appear to be quick, bright, prepared, ready to go in any direction immediately. This is a key element in maintaining psychological leverage in the interview. And it's really very simple to accomplish.

Grooming and Dress

Much of our job search advice is predicated on the approach of custom-designing for each company's situation. So it is with grooming. Generally, be conservative, neat, clean, and understated. If there's a choice, always go for the more muted color, the more simple pattern. But dress differently for an interview on site at a chemical plant than you would in a bank or brokerage house. We suggest that you visit a day in advance of the interview to determine corporate culture, workstyle, and dress code. Every place has a dress code—most often it's unwritten, but it's always there.

Be Punctual, but Don't Be Early

Don't show up fifteen or twenty minutes in advance of your appointment. That suggests that you're a rookie who is desperate to get this job. Tardiness is *always* inexcusable, however, so here's our original proposition for interview punctuality: Arrive at the location fifteen or twenty minutes in advance, and determine exactly where the interviewer is located and how long it's likely to take to get through the waiting area. (Is it a private secretary's office or a department full of visitors you might have to wait in line behind?) Having determined that, go to a coffee bar and spend a few minutes in last-minute preparation. Part of this preparation is a two-minute psychological drill. Tell yourself that you're the best candidate for the job because you've done your homework. You look right, you'll act right, and you feel good about yourself and about why you're there. Assert to yourself that you'll walk in with confidence. Then proceed to the interviewer's office. Time your arrival three or four minutes in advance of the appointment so that you'll be announced right on time. That's sharp and impressive. Again, the psychological leverage is evident. You've protected your interests by getting there in plenty of time to make the appointment. You've arrived on site only minutes ahead of time, yet you're calm, cool, collected, and ready.

KNOW YOUR INTERVIEWER

Let us offer a word of caution before we proceed. If you think there's enough material thus far to choke an army mule—or a job campaigner new to the task—stop now and begin digesting. Be sure that you have the basics down pat, because what follows is equivalent to a graduate school for interviewing.

Part of the process of a true commitment to excellence in interviewing is preparing and learning not only about yourself and the company but also about personality types of interviewers. If you can learn to read the person across the desk—how he lives, works, and thinks—you're really flirting with the stratosphere in the world of job search. There are four basic types:

- *The long-range planner:* Typically, this person, also known as the *intuitor*, is an economist, a forecaster, or occasionally an engineer. His job is to plan three to five years in advance, so that's how he thinks and talks. Your answers should focus on the big picture—where technology will take this industry in the next decade, and so forth. In appearance, this person will tend to be conservative but not overly concerned about minute details.

- *The analytical, task-oriented type:* This very present-oriented type of person is also called the *thinker.* Typically, he'll be very neat and well organized. Never use the word *about* with this person—he deals in specifics, not generalities. If there are numbers in your resume, be prepared to defend them. This person will tend to be very neat and controlled and immaculate in dress.

- *The people person:* This much more informal, more colorfully dressed interviewer is also called the *feeler.* He'll be interested not so much in your analytical powers or skill levels but in whether you'll be a good fit for his team. You're much more likely to be offered a cup of coffee, or even lunch, during the interview with this person.

- *The time-conscious, reactive type:* This person's environment is full of ringing phones and other interruptions. Also known as the *senser*, he really won't have time to allow you to create a full portrayal of your personality, skills, and background. Typically, he'll be coat-off, sleeves rolled-up, and harried. He's always under the gun, caught up in the activity trap, with never enough people, never enough time. He'll be looking for your ability to get things done. What he needs is a doer—someone who doesn't waste time and gets right to the point.

This is highly complex and sophisticated analysis, so don't deal with it unless you're ready. But if you are, you'll be able to structure your responses to mesh with the corporate style and the interviewer's frame of reference.

GO FOR THE OFFER

As we've mentioned before, we're not saying that you are going after a *job* during this stage of the interview. You're going all out for the *offer.* Then you will evaluate this company against the other offers you generate. If the environment is alien to you, obviously you will take another position. We're trying to train you to survive in any interviewing situation, not push you into a corporate setting with which you can't cope and that you don't like.

Finally, at the close of the interview, ask three questions: Where do you see this job in three to five years? Where do you see the company in three to five years? And where can I get more information? That's all. We don't recommend that you ask a lot of questions during the interview.

SOME LAST WORDS ON INTERVIEWING

Most Frequent Complaints About Interviewees

- Poor communication—talks too little, talks too much, rambles, is evasive, is nervous
- Poor preparation—asks no questions, has no information about company
- Vague interests—lacks career goals, is unsure of job goals
- Unrealistic expectations—is too concerned about salary, is immature, is inflexible

Most Frequent Complaints About Interviewers

- Poor communication—talks too much, is unclear, rambles, is evasive
- Poor preparation—didn't read resume, manages time poorly
- Judgmental attitude—draws conclusions or makes statements that are inaccurate or unfair
- Negative attitude—spends too much time talking about negative aspects of the job
- Dumb questions—asks questions that don't relate to the position

Your preparation and your ability to control the interview will enable you to overcome the weaknesses of a poor interviewer. Don't allow such an interviewer to cause you to lose your psychological edge. Gently lead the interviewer through the points you want to make, without letting on that you are aware of his ineptness. Like playing tennis with a rookie, if you get frustrated by the opponent's bloopers, you can easily throw the match.

Why People Are Hired

- Positive attitude
- Good presentation of skills needed by employer for the position
- Professional in all contacts, including letter, phone call, and face-to-face contact
- Good rapport with interviewer, including good discussion
- Past experience that supports qualifications for the opening
- Provides knowledgeable questions and statements about company and job opening, thus proving commitment to research
- Professional appearance, including appropriate dress, neat and clean personal grooming, friendly attitude

Why People Are Rejected

- Bitter attitude based on previous employment experience
- Limited presentation of skills, based merely on job title
- Poor appearance and demeanor
- Mistakes and misspellings in written correspondence
- Lack of confidence during interview, including stumbling over answers and not portraying a positive attitude
- Bad references
- Unqualified for the job

Your interview preparation will ensure that you avoid the points of rejection and emphasize the winning points of acceptance. The ball's in your court!

CHAPTER NINE

Negotiating the Deal You Want: Get the Money Now

As authors of this book, we have the easy job in talking about negotiating compensation. To distinguish between interviewing and negotiating, we simply end one chapter and begin another. It's imperative that you, too, make such a clear-cut distinction between interviewing and negotiating in your campaign. Your task, however, won't be nearly so simple as concluding Chapter 8 and launching Chapter 9. Not only is negotiating a tough, complex, demanding proposition—it is, we think, the most difficult of all the steps in campaigning for a job—but it is also so subtle that it takes true discernment to know when to do it, let alone what to do. Of all the facets of looking for a new position, negotiating requires the greatest measure of discipline, preparation, and confidence on your part.

Interviewing usually gets preeminent ranking among the elements of job search. Resumes, networking, telemarketing, and research do nothing more than put your body in front of the hiring authority, with a chance at the job. Certainly, we agree with that. Negotiating compensation is typically considered a part of the interview process, and without question it's the most vital part of that interview. Throughout the pages of this book, we have attempted to instill in you the belief that getting *a* job isn't difficult or particularly noteworthy. We want you to find the *best* job for you. But if you cannot or will not negotiate the best available compensation package, what might have been *the* job may unfortunately turn out to be only *a* job. In fact, you'll probably never even know the possibilities of the position if you're not prepared to take negotiation to the limit.

THE SITUATIONS ARE REVERSED

Now that we've blessed negotiating with such an aura of significance, here's the reason we've separated it from interviewing: Despite the fact that negotiations may occur at the same time and place as your job interview, the interaction between you and the employer changes radically at that point. In fact, it represents a 180-degree position shift. Throughout all the hours of interviewing—in three, four, or five discussions—you have courted the employer with your ability to contribute to the bottom line. You've been selling, selling, selling.

When negotiations begin, the company has been sold. It wants you. Now the question becomes whether it is willing to pay enough to get you. At least, the events should be in that sequence. Don't ever let any discussion of compensation begin until it's clear that the company is making an offer. In the best of worlds, you'll complete the final interview, get the offer, and shake hands on a tentative deal. Then the company will set up a subsequent interview to negotiate your entire compensation package.

In that scenario, the negotiating session will take on an entirely different tone from the employment interviews. Separating the two kinds of sessions, so that both sides can work toward a mutually satisfactory goal, is best for both job hunter and employer. Unfortunately, job search reflects life, and the best of worlds happens all too infrequently. Consequently, once an offer is made, you'll have to help orchestrate the switch from your sales presentation to negotiations. And you'll have to do that in the heat of the interview. This is where subtlety, discernment, and confidence pay off. This is also why preparation for negotiating compensation is unrivaled in its importance to your successful job search.

One point here—stop and make certain that you buy into our philosophy of negotiating compensation as well as our challenge to you to make it happen. We hope that it's evident to you that this book is about self-help; it is not designed as a "feel-good-no-matter-what-you-do" journal. Our goal is to help your career, to challenge you to work hard enough to assume command of the events of your search. Not surprisingly, our position on negotiating is consistent with that stand. Of course, you can shake hands and smile, taking whatever first offer the company makes. That's safe, easy, and perfectly suited to the standards of slothfulness that dominate the field of job search advice. But we suspect that if you've answered the challenges set forth in this book, negotiating your own compensation package won't be such an imposing roadblock after all.

Always remember that the level of compensation with which you begin your new position affects every dollar you'll earn with the company. When you shake hands on $65,000, all your future income will be calculated from that figure. Next year at this time, if the company determines that top achievers will receive a maximum increase of 10 percent, your increase will be $6,500 if you get the $65,000 you are looking for. On the other hand, if you settle for $50,000, your maximum increase just got a $1,500 cut a year in advance. Obviously, that shortfall widens every year you work at this company.

But arithmetic is easy. Negotiating is hard.

You don't just pick $65,000 out of thin air. If that were possible, why not ask for $165,000? The numbers are calculated from your research into the company and the industry—how your skills and experience are normally compensated, plus the demand for them in the current market. Back to the library. Back to the telephones. Without question, the skills required to research this question and then bring the research into action in negotiating are the most complex and require the greatest degree of precision of any you'll utilize in your search. Most important, you're relying greatly on linkage to make the negotiation process work in your favor.

The skills you acquired in the preceding chapter should have that employer leaning forward in his chair, ready to leap at the prospect of adding you to the team. However, if you've merely put on an OK interviewing presentation that convinces the company that you can do the job but nonetheless leaves you grouped with four or five other finalists, you don't have an abundance of negotiating leverage. When you've enhanced your marketability with a dazzling set of interview responses, that employer wants you. Now you're in the catbird seat, ready to negotiate with the power and authority in your corner.

THE DAWSON & DAWSON COMMANDMENT OF NEGOTIATING COMPENSATION: MONEY FOLLOWS VALUE

Your value is subjective, of course. So your interviewing performance will prove your value to the company—or at least it must convince the employer that you're as valuable as your resume and your compensation expectations promise.

Make certain, though, that you back up your newly won authority and confidence with research and preparation. The proper numbers—$65,000 or whatever—are not based on what you fancy you'd like to earn this year. And most assuredly, you won't learn the right numbers from the interviewer. So you must reactivate all your networking and telemarketing skills to establish a negotiating position. In advance, talk to people with or formerly with the company, people in the industry, trade associations in your profession, competitors and suppliers of the company. With your cold-calling skills, find out what your occupational skills will command today at that company. As much as we've belittled executive search firms, this is an area in which one you trust can help. It can be a source of accurate information about salary trends. At all costs, however, use the search firm for background information only. Do not allow the recruiter to be a surrogate negotiator. You'll lose every time. Obviously, such information has to be elicited subtly; if the search firm thinks that there is no incentive for sharing information, it won't be too open.

Besides talking with people, read. Library sources that can help in your salary research include the *Occupational Outlook Handbook,* the *American Almanac of Jobs and Salaries,* and the *Salary Guide and Job Outlook.* Don't forget periodicals; the best is the *Wall Street Journal's National Business Employment Weekly* (NBEW). In about one issue each month, NBEW publishes comprehensive salary survey information by profession.

When you get the information, don't go in with only one number in your negotiating tool kit. Take the norms for the company and its industry and create a sliding scale of compensation upon which you plan to negotiate. Almost every company in American business—and every wise job hunter—structures compensation around a three-tier sliding scale.

For example, take the $65,000 figure. In the ideal scenario, that $65,000 salary would be the end product of an initial offer of about $58,000 from the company. The company's figure results from a three-tier scale: high, low, mid-range. The high point might be $66,000, the low $56,000, with a mid-range of $60,000 to $62,000. The first offer, $58,000, is slightly below the midpoint on the scale, which is typically where companies like to bring in new employees. If you take the first offer, you'll fit nicely into the departmental budget, but you'll be about $5,000 to $7,000 poorer the first year, along with an expanding annual salary shortfall. You won't have gotten what a person with your skills and experience typically can command in the current marketplace.

Conversely, we're not suggesting that you shoot for the maximum salary on the scale right out of the starting blocks. If you drive such a hard bargain, the employer might leave the table with hard feelings that you held his feet to the fire, that you took advantage of his acute personnel need to bust a budget. In addition, keep in mind that if you hit the top of the scale to start, you have little room for increase in that position. You're boxed immediately, unless you can work your way into more job and more responsibility rather quickly.

So your goal should be to elevate that initial offer—to get into the upper range of the salary scale, but not to max out. When the interviewer mentions $58,000, you can respond with a statement such as, "I sincerely appreciate the offer, and I'm looking forward to working with an excellent company like yours. But based on my research, I was looking at a figure in the high $60's." Again, of course, you must have a sound idea of the range of the three-tier salary scale from which the interviewer is negotiating. We can't tell you every word to say, because you must develop your own style. Moreover, your responses and statements will vary, depending on the personality and style of the interviewer. So scripting a conversation is meaningless. We know what works for us—you must learn what works for you. Plan that individually—but do commit now to the time and effort necessary to research and learn the scale. Then react to the first offer with a confident and professional transition into the negotiations.

Part of the negotiating process is identifying exactly what you are to do in the new company. One of the best ways to obtain the right job for yourself is to tailor it to your specifications! For example, when you're discussing a position with a firm during a sequence of interviews, you may custom-design a job description for the position based on how you perceive the company's needs. Of course, you would want to find out whether a job description already exists, but it is not unusual—even in major corporations—for there to be no job descriptions for managerial positions.

In writing such a job description, Donna Holmes was able to create her "ideal job." She first presented it to Jim, the executive who was moving into a different division and whose job was available. Jim acknowledged the accuracy of the description and was impressed. Donna then presented the description to her prospective boss, who responded so favorably that he even added some responsibilities that enhanced the position.

It should be pointed out that Donna was wise not to assume that Jim, the executive who was leaving, would pass the description on to his boss. Had Donna not taken the initiative to do so herself, it would not have become significant in the negotiations. In this case, Donna was offered not only a job, but the precise position she had custom-designed. In addition, by clarifying the responsibilities and authority of the position, Donna was able to increase the initial salary offered on the basis of the expanded scope of the job.

Never—*never*—meekly accept the first dollar figure offered. Similarly, never accept a job offer on the spot. If the employer presses you, simply say that you must discuss the offer with your family or that you're evaluating several other offers from excellent companies like theirs (but never reveal who the other firms are). Offer to get back in touch in five days (if you need that long). If an answer is required sooner, be flexible, of course, all the way down to a twenty-four-hour evaluation period. But under no circumstances should you be coerced into saying yes on the spot. Believe us, an interviewer who won't sit still for a twenty-four-hour consideration period is nothing but trouble anyway. He's not a pro—he doesn't understand career planning or negotiations—and most likely you can look forward to the same style of crude overbearance every day you work there.

But back to the money. If you don't get it now, when your armor is spotless, when do you suppose you'll get it? The company wants you on the team, so this is your best chance—your only chance—to negotiate your best deal, perhaps to transform *a* job into *the* job. And consider, if you don't get a salary commensurate with your skills and experience, you're more than just limiting income in the short range. Conceivably, you are retarding the progress of your career tomorrow and on over the horizon. Unless you have a sure long-range benefit in sight, a cut in salary will hurt you—and badly.

Are there exceptions? Of course—acceptable trade-offs for a substantially reduced salary include:

- A chance to run a business (less money but more power)
- A highly visible job, perhaps one in the national or industry spotlight
- A chance to join the start-up team of a hot new company (short-range loss for long-term gain)
- A radical career change
- A chance to leave a second-rate company to join an industry leader
- A chance to leave a declining industry that has built up a grossly over-inflated salary structure during its boom years (for example, the oil industry today or the steel and auto industries yesterday)
- Extreme personal circumstances that dictate a geographic preference (for example, if your child has a chronic illness, and Armpit, Wyoming, has the only treatment facility in the nation, then it's Armpit, Wyoming, at any salary)

If you're preparing to accept a drastic salary reduction for any reason not listed, think hard. It's your career, your life—but you're making mistakes in interviewing and negotiating. And you're about to make a salary mistake that could hurt you for years into the future and from which your career may never recover. If you're rationalizing otherwise, you're blowing smoke on your own career. Go after the compensation that you're worth.

We're not suggesting that you're there for a holdup, but don't settle for a dollar figure that is so low that it could cripple your career's progress.

One caution: You must realize that compensation encompasses a great deal more than salary. There are other, often better, ways than dollars on a paycheck to achieve your compensation goals. Consider these options, which can increase the value of your compensation package:

- *Fringe benefits:* Standards here include health, dental, life, and disability insurance; retirement, pension, and deferred compensation plans; vacation and holidays; professional association fees; and perhaps educational and travel reimbursement. If your salary falls short, how about negotiating for a car? Credit cards? Stock options? Bonuses? Relocation expenses?

- *Performance reviews:* Schedules are usually well established for employee performance evaluations. If you can't get the money on your initial agreement, how about an earlier-than-prescribed review of your performance on the job? (Just be sure that you get it in writing!)

- *Promotions:* Examine the firm's policy on promotions, and attempt to agree on a timetable for when you can expect to move to a higher position. (This is another short-term loss for a long-term gain.)

- *Executive perks:* Another way to maintain your standard of living and your total compensation without cash is to negotiate perks, such as membership in health clubs and leisure facilities; discounts or business reimbursements on personal travel; tax, financial, and legal advice; publication incentives; and matching gifts.

Exhibits 9.1 and 9.2 provide employee benefit and relocation checklists to help you formulate a compensation package that meets your needs.

Our point is that *everything* is negotiable. This doesn't mean that you'll be successful on every item. But it means that whatever the company can do to increase the total value of your compensation is fair game to be placed on the table. For instance, benefits can dramatically affect how you come out financially. Smaller organizations usually provide fewer benefits than major corporations.

Kent Wilson recently moved from a large to a small organization. In negotiating his compensation, Kent was able to gain a 17 percent increase over his former salary because he carefully compared benefits and presented the differences to his new employer. On the basis of Kent's analysis, the new employer adjusted his initial offer to give Kent

EXHIBIT 9.1
Employee Benefit Checklist

Use this checklist to help determine benefits available.

BENEFIT	COVERAGE	PREMIUM
Major medical insurance		
Health maintenance organization (HMO)		
Dental/optical insurance		
Life insurance		
Accidental death and dismemberment insurance		
Disability insurance		
Travel accident insurance		
Retirement/pension plans		
Vacation and holidays		
Educational assistance		
Dependent scholarships		
Professional certification/association fees		
Bonus plans		
Deferred compensation (401-K)		
Tax/financial planning assistance		
Legal advice		
Company car		
Company credit cards		
Club memberships		
Publication incentives		
Matching gifts		
First-class travel in evenings		
Others		

EXHIBIT 9.2
Relocation Checklist

Use this checklist to help determine relocation benefits.

RELOCATION BENEFIT	BENEFIT LIMITATION	COMMENTS
Home purchase		
Closing costs		
Mortgage interest differential		
Temporary living expenses		
Household goods shipment		
Moving allowance		
Intransit expenses		
Duplicate housing expenses		
Storage of items		
Income tax gross-up		
Spouse employment assistance		

a total package that was substantially better than he had in his previous position.

Never assume "I can't get that" or "They have a policy against that." Remember, your challenge in the interview is to make yourself invaluable to that employer. If you've accomplished that goal, then you can approach negotiations with the mind-set, realistically, that every rule was put in place to be broken.

MAKE IT A WIN-WIN PROCESS

If you think that a tough negotiating session will alienate the employer, you're sadly mistaken—or maybe you're just copping out to evade a tough, demanding situation. In fact, the reverse is true. Our conviction is that weak, unprepared people hide behind that fear. Look at it this way. You're not out to hold up the company; you're out to join the team and contribute to a bolder bottom line for everyone. Of course, if you're rude, greedy, aggressive, and unprofessional during negotiations, you might jeopardize the offer or your future at the company. But who wants to be that way?

The whole process should be a challenge for both you and the employer, but not a bloodletting. Reach for the best, and expect the same from the employer. Attempt to orchestrate not a win-lose scenario but a win-win equation for both the company and you. Consider these additional basic negotiation tactics to achieve those ends:

• Always negotiate with the hiring authority, not with the human resources department.

• Let the employer name a salary figure first. (You're flexible.)

• Never answer the question, "What is the minimum you'll accept?" or "How much money do you need to make?" (You're not interested in minimums.)

• Orchestrate your potential job offers so that you can consider them simultaneously. This is another delicate, subtle process, but it pays off when it's done well. If you're under consideration for three different positions, it will limit your ability to evaluate each one objectively and compare them if you don't have all the details simultaneously. Insist that the first offeror wait until the next Monday for an answer. If the process is slow in the second company, you can insist that you need all the details and the offer by Friday, with your answer forthcoming Monday. And so on with the third offer. It's difficult, but it's imperative if you're attempting to select the one best job for your future. (Exhibit 9.3 provides a form for evaluating offers. It will assist you in weighing factors that are important in the evaluation of multiple offers.)

You'd have to see this process work in our Houston outplacementfacilities to appreciate how beautifully it can be orchestrated. Recall the case of the engineer who entered our program with no experience in job search. He couldn't even make a cold telephone call during his first couple of weeks. By the end of three months, he was placed in a better job from among three offers. And he skillfully arranged the sequence of events so that all three offers were on the table on a Friday afternoon. He took the weekend with his family, and selected the job he wanted. Speeding one offer up while you slow another one down is not easy, but if you apply yourself, you can adapt the proper techniques and make it happen.

Look at it this way—the entire process, whether you're negotiating compensation or orchestrating job offers to bear fruit simultaneously, really constitutes what might be called your first performance evaluation. If you're weak, unprepared, and easily overpowered—if you accept the first offer put on the table—the employer will walk away with a "victory." But believe us, it's a victory he'd just as soon do without. He will not be overly impressed with your ability. You've got the job, but not much else.

In contrast, if you strap on your seat belt and accelerate for a mutually beneficial best deal, you'll have an ally, not an enemy. Just be sure that you keep it professional, and the employer will be impressed by your performance. You've proved that you're a formidable adversary, but he's lucky enough to have you as his ally. All the complexities and subtleties that you conquered in negotiating a win-win package will now be brought to bear in the marketplace *for* his company.

If that alone doesn't convince you to get serious about negotiating, nothing will. Above all, trust in what we're telling you. This is a big step of faith, but if you do it our way, negotiating won't hurt your new relationship with the firm—it will enhance it.

For proof, look again to our firm's success rate in Houston. We're guiding displaced professionals to placement in an average of 3.2 months— and we're usually counseling clients why they should not be taking certain jobs, rather than pushing them into quick acceptance of any offer. Even with our rapid turnaround figure—which is the best in the outplacement industry—we're pushing no one into jobs. We guide them to the best jobs. Our system works. And it's best not only for you but for your new company, as well.

EXHIBIT 9.3
Evaluating Offers

For each offer, in column 1, rate each of the following criteria on a scale of 1 to 10 (1 low; 10 high) based on your *personal needs.* Column 1 will be the same for all companies. Then, in column 2, rate each criterion, again on a scale of 1 to 10, based on how well you feel *the company satisfies* those criteria. For each offer, multiply column 1 by column 2 and list that figure in column 3 (1 × 2). You can compare offers on the basis of their total scores.

CRITERIA	Offer 1			Offer 2		
	1	2	3	1	2	3
CAREER/PROFESSIONAL FACTORS						
Job responsibilities						
Adequacy of staff/support						
Title						
Promotion/personal growth potential						
Decision-making authority						
COMPANY FACTORS						
Size of company						
Company/industry history and image						
Management style (participative, directive, etc.)						
PERSONAL FACTORS						
Base salary						
Bonus/profit-sharing/stock options, etc.						
Benefits (pension, disability, insurance, vacation)						
Perks (car, memberships, etc.)						
Geographic location						
Amount of travel						
Commuting requirements						
Special expenses (commuting fares, taxes, relocation, etc.)						
TOTAL SCORES						

Once you have negotiated the deal you want and have accepted your new position, it is wise to formalize your agreement with a letter of understanding. Some companies provide one automatically as part of their new employee procedures. If your new employer does not follow this practice, you can draft one yourself. (A sample letter of understanding is provided in Exhibit 9.4.) By putting in writing all of the agreed-upon terms, you ensure that no misunderstanding can rear it's ugly head six months or a year after you have joined the company.

EXHIBIT 9.4
Sample Letter of Understanding

JOE JONES, JR., P.E.
9514 Smith Street
Spring, Texas 77004
(713) 713-7777

DATE

Mr. Frank Neimeyer
President
Can Company
9400 Drive
El Monte, CA 91731

Dear Frank:

It is a pleasure for me to accept your offer of employment as Director of Manufacturing for Can Company. This letter shall confirm and define the various agreements we have reached concerning your offer of July 11, 1986, for me to begin employment with Can Company as of August 4, 1986.

There will be a performance and salary review at the completion of my first six months. Subsequent annual reviews will be conducted during the month of August. Upon employment, I will be eligible for any company incentive programs that are available to other managers or executives within your organization. The various fringe benefits provided will begin in the normal fashion with medical benefits to begin on my first full day of employment. In recognition of the expenses involved in moving from Texas to California, Can Company will provide or reimburse for:

- Transportation, lodging and meals for my wife and me for one advance house hunting visit up to a maximum of five days.
- Movement of my household goods, and one automobile including packing, shipping and insurance.
- Transportation, lodging, meals and necessary expenses incurred for our family while driving from Texas to California.
- Lodging, meals and temporary storage of my household goods, for a maximum of 30 days, if needed prior to moving into our new home.
- Expenses related to the sale of our current residence, 9514 Smith Street, Spring, Texas, and the purchase of our new residence. Expenses shall include attorney's fees, area brokerage fee, mortgage prepayment penalty, points associated with mortgage loan and all closing costs. It is understood that these expenses shall be reimbursed up to a maximum of $16,000 and will be submitted to you within six months after date of hire.

If you have any questions or need clarification on any item, please feel free to give me a call at my residence. My family and I are very excited about the move to El Monte. Thank you for the opportunity to join Can Company. I look forward to working with you and your management team.

Sincerely,

Joe Jones, Jr., P.E.

CHAPTER TEN

Your Curtain Call: Make It a Standing Ovation

It's up to you, now, to play out the scenario. You're the scriptwriter, director, producer, and star. If you fully utilize the job search techniques described in the preceding nine chapters, there is no question that you will be a hit. Before you begin your creative act, let's review the essential elements of a successful search.

- *The principle of linkage:* Each step of your search must be linked to the previous step and the one to follow. As smooth as a play's script, your job search should be planned and directed from resume to reference letters to networking to interviewing to negotiating. Link them all and increase your job search leverage.

- *Positive thinking:* If you've ever performed before an audience, you know how debilitating stage fright can be. The effect is the same when you allow negativity to dominate your job search. You alone control your thoughts, attitudes, and actions. Use whatever techniques help you to reduce stress and maintain a positive frame of mind—motivational books or tapes, meditation, exercise, proper diet, discussing your successes with your friends and family, rewarding yourself for meeting daily goals, visualizing your new job, talking with positive people you admire, reviewing your accomplishments, and so forth. Whatever it takes, be positive.

- *Flexibility and realism:* In assessing your career options, leave no stone unturned. Changing careers, starting an independent business, exploring other industries, relocating—each option should be evaluated from the perspective of your interests, aptitudes, and personality as well as from the outlook of marketplace opportunities. If you merely skimmed the self-assessment questions in Chapter 1, take time now to think them through so that you know that your job objectives are on target.

- *Keeping your resume current:* By now you probably have your resume completed—if not, return to Chapter 3 PDQ! Recognizing that employers and employees no longer share undying loyalty and life-long career commitments, it is essential that you be prepared for your next inevitable job change. Maintain a file with your resume, performance appraisals, job description, and accomplishments. You'll find this file extremely useful for salary and performance reviews and when a new career opportunity presents itself. If you're still employed and looking, start this file now.

- *What not to leave home without—references:* You may be of the opinion that references are worthless, that no one puts stock in them, and that they are a pain to write. But if you follow our advice in Chapter 4, they become very meaningful and indispensable. Have them in your tool kit for situations in which they are required and to ensure that the individuals who are your references are properly prepared for that critical reference check.

- *Being a one percenter:* Use networking techniques to the maximum. It's okay to use search firms and answer ads—10 to 20 percent of jobs are found that way. But devote 80 percent of your time and efforts to networking. If you haven't started your personal and professional contact list, pull out those business card files, Christmas card lists, and alumni and association directories, and delay no longer.

Once you've placed yourself in your new job, maintain a networking file next to your current resume file and keep in touch with your contacts. Don't allow another five or ten years to pass—when you're in need of assistance again—before you call them. If your network is undeveloped now, vow to make it extensive for your next job search. It's up to you to be well connected.

- *Developing your personal marketing plan:* Get organized, set goals, and go for it. Pretend you're running the race of your life. You're at the starting block—*on your mark!* Fingers poised on the tape, you kick your legs and place them firmly in the blocks. Eyes focused on the finishing ribbon—*get set!* Every muscle tenses as adrenaline courses through your veins. The gun blast triggers your momentum, and you shoot off to the finish line. Can you win without training, without establishing goals, without desire? Throughout this book, we have provided forms to help you develop your personal marketing plan. It's not necessary that you use these particular forms, but it is essential that you develop some system with which you are comfortable—and use it.

- *Psychological leverage:* Whether you're on stage, in a tennis match, or running a race, your greatest advantage is being mentally prepared. Interviews are no different. Know your opponent. Anticipate every question. Beware of hidden agendas. Stay one step ahead, and use psychological leverage to keep the interview positive and general. Practice the tough questions in Chapter 8, and avoid the "red flags" at all cost. Interviewing success depends on your preparation and control.

- *Negotiating value:* Don't be afraid to ask for what you want. Whatever your concern, it won't hurt to lay it on the table. The offer is rarely "take it or leave it." If losing $5,000 on your house is what bothers you—let the company know. If your current medical insurance will lapse before the new policy comes into effect—let the company know. If your spouse would have to find a new job—perhaps the company will provide spouse relocation assistance. You are the "value"—don't sell yourself short!

- *Building a cycle of success:* Work hard, be confident, set and attain goals, be persistent, believe you will succeed. William James said it best: *"Whatever the mind can conceive and believe, it can achieve."*

That quotation appears in gold on a little gift we present to our clients when they succeed in achieving a new position. We call it our "touchstone." (For the practical-minded individual, it serves as a paperweight as well.) We have a tradition in our program to honor, with a special luncheon, each client who is placed. All executive clients are invited, and the "graduating" client is asked to speak to the group about his or her experiences during the job search—what we call "telling their story." It's an uplifting presentation for everyone, because it confirms that the system works. The newly placed client is rewarded for his or her success, and the other clients, who are still involved in the job search process, commit to succeed as well.

TESTIMONIALS TO SUCCESS

We have selected five recent successful executive placements in order to provide a cross-section of levels, functions, and experiences. All five clients told their stories at the traditional special luncheon, and their testimonials follow. If you have any doubt that what you have read in these pages works, you can believe these words—they were spoken by real-life executives who found themselves in the same position you are in and who cast their doubts aside in order to succeed. (Names of people, titles, and companies are altered to maintain confidentiality.)

Testimonial 1

My name is Tom, and I was a director of geological services for over eight years. Over my career I have been laid off twice and have been nearly laid off two other times. I was working for XYZ Oil and Gas Company up until May 4, 5, or 6. I don't really remember the date—one that I never thought I would forget. We knew cutbacks were coming. When your boss calls you in, you know it's not to ask what you think about the weather that day. When he got done with me, he ushered me into a conference room, and there was an outplacement consultant saying, "Well, Tom, you have an opportunity ahead of you." I thought, "Right—like 10,000 other unemployed geologists!" But it turned out to be really true!

In the three months since I've been laid off, I have found that my commitment to the oil industry is strong enough to get through these tough times in the business. I've spent that time, first, letting people know—individuals I knew—that I was available. That's what networking is. I spent a lot of time, also, trying to put my own oil and gas deals together. As big as Houston is, it doesn't take long for the oil community to hear things like that. One of the people I had been networking through, who was recently promoted to a vice-presidency, decided that he needed a few extra consultants on his staff on a retainer basis. The company buys all the data that you need to generate oil and gas prospects, and then as you come up with these prospects, you are paid. It's similar to a commission basis. There are enough unemployed geologists in Houston that jobs like that are almost unheard-of. When he offered it to me, I was just in a state of shock! We negotiated back and forth on it. Fortunately, I convinced them that I am worth what I thought I was worth. I will be starting on October 15.

Most important, I think that what got me into this fortunate situation was keeping a positive attitude. Of all the things I learned from this experience, that was the most important. When I was cold-calling, I called just about every company that was left in Houston, and almost everyone was real polite. Some of the people I called were more down than I was, and that was real tough. For those of you who have a marketable skill that can be used outside of the oil industry, it won't be as bad; but for a geologist, really, the only thing you are trained to do is work for an oil company. Networking I found to be real easy. Everybody that I knew was always willing to help. I went through networking and cold-calling and answering advertisements, which works to a very small degree. I was usually able to keep that positive attitude.

I just came to the conclusion that I was going to make it, and I realized that it might take a little while. There was no period that I let myself get down for more than one or two days in a row. There were days that I just said, "Okay, today I'm going to be depressed," and I would just go through the motions. That helped me get it out of my system, and I was back doing something. If you keep after it like that, something really good will happen. This really *is* an opportunity. I know that sounds a little hokey; I know because it wasn't that long ago that I was where you are and somebody else was saying that to me! But honestly, it really does work. You get the picture.

One thing that helped me was knowing that I had a niche to fill, that somewhere out there was "the position" that was just what I was looking for. After being laid off this many times, I am very hesitant about going to work for a company on a regular 9 to 5 basis. What I wanted was to be a consultant on retainer, which is exactly what I found. Granted, the retainer isn't a total compensation package with benefits, but as the industry turns around, I'll be in a position to renegotiate. That's just what I wanted to do, and everything I did in my job campaign was in pursuing that goal. Whatever your goals, always keep them in mind. At the same time, keep your flexibility. What you get initially may not be precisely what you want, but if you get close, you can work your way into exactly what you want—which includes the beach house wherever.

I'll be happy to answer questions.

Q: Do you think you can match your previous salary on this retainer arrangement?

A: My income will depend on how many prospects a year I generate. If I get the kind of support I think I will get from the company, I will be looking at a 15 to 20 percent pay cut initially, for a twelve-month period. The thing about having a retainer is that in addition to the per prospect fee, you also get an override—that is, some percentage of the production of anything you find, right off the top. If you know anyone in the oil business who is really very, very wealthy, that's how they made it—having a percentage of something. I mean, that's how J.R. does it!

Thank you all.

Testimonial 2

My name is Dick. I am going to talk about my job search in two phases— what happened to me job-wise and emotionally. I was with Engineering Systems Company for twelve years. I lost my job as vice president, human resources on June 13 of this year. The company made a decision that they were going to sell their oil and gas divisions, which was 80 percent of my responsibility. It didn't take long to figure out that my position would go away. One thing led to another, and finally I had no option in the company—June 13 was it.

Fortunately, I learned what the "hidden" job market is. The way it worked out for me is that I had five job interviews with companies. Two came from ad responses and three, including the job I got, came from networking. Next Monday I start to work for BIG Company. They have a productivity group there which I am joining as vice president, human resources. BIG is a diversified company, and oil and gas is only half of their business. It may surprise you that the person who recommended that I talk to this group was my former boss! The job was never advertised. As a matter of fact, the company has a hiring freeze! Had I not worked aggressively to ask, "Who do you know—please jog your memory—do you know anyone that I might talk to," this probably wouldn't have surfaced. So I think it's very important that you go after the "hidden" job market, both cold-calling and networking, because either way it's a percentage game. If you go for the ads, you know the jobs are open, but you also know there's hundreds of other people coming in against you. If you cold-call or network, you know there is going to be only one in a hundred jobs open, but you are one of only a few who are coming in to apply for it. And if it's a networking situation, you may come in with an endorsement which is very strong. You have a leg up on any competitor.

The second aspect I wanted to talk about was the emotional side of the situation. I don't know how it was for you, Tom, or the rest, but the only way I can describe it is—it was hell. There is one thing in particular that I found helpful, which I'd like to share with you. Have you heard about the two frogs that fell in a bucket of milk? Two frogs one evening fell into a bucket of cow's milk down on the farm. And they were saying, "My gosh, what in the world are we going to do?! There is *no way* we can get up to the edge." They swam for about an hour, and they started to get really tired, and one of the frogs said, "Man, I'm so exhausted, I can't see why I should just keep swimming like this. The heck with it." He just quit swimming and sank; that was it. The other frog thought, "Well, I know what happens when I *quit* swimming, but I don't know what happens if I keep swimming, so I'm just going to keep swimming 'til it kills me." Well, through the long night, the frog swam so hard that the milk started to churn into butter. Finally, at dawn, he was able to get some footing and he just jumped out!

That's sort of the way I felt. In other words, I didn't know when this damn thing was going to be over, but all of a sudden I had footing and I jumped out and that was all. I knew what would happen if I quit swimming—I'd probably still be in the bucket of milk!

I don't know how each of you rewards yourself on a daily basis, but I know that when I get home if I really had a tough day, I like to drink a couple of beers and think about my accomplishments. At the beginning of my search, I thought, "Well I haven't accomplished a damn thing. I don't even have a job." I couldn't enjoy drinking beer or riding my bike or any of the things I like to do. Then I started to think, "I'm just going to churn as hard as I can. If I have a day when I know that I got up early in the morning and that I worked just as hard at my job campaign and churned as hard as I could—even though it didn't produce a job offer that day—then I deserve a couple of beers." Whether it is beer, ice cream, running, or whatever, reward yourself for each day of hard work. That carried me through, and I felt the sense of accomplishment. Every day, even though I didn't have the ultimate reward—which can only be defined as a new job—I felt that I had put in my eight or ten hours that day and I deserved a small reward. Some days are worse than others, but you do deserve that reward. Hopefully, that will be of some help to you. I know that if you just keep churning, all of a sudden—bam, it's over with.

Are there any questions?

Q: Could you talk about your networking techniques?

A: I mostly "warm-called" in networking. For instance, one of my interviews was over in San Antonio with a grocery company. I was referred to the president of the grocery company by another man I knew in San Antonio. When I called, I didn't know this guy, but yet I was able to use the name of another acquaintance. To me that is a warm call. You are not just calling out of the blue. I had a name to drop, which got his attention, and that got me one interview. Initially, I wrote a letter of introduction to the person who offered me the job at BIG. He didn't know me, but yet I started off with the name of my former boss, who he did know. I used other techniques, but again, the "hidden" job market was my main objective. If I had time at the end of each week, I answered the Sunday ads from the week before. That was my strategy. And it worked!

Thanks to everyone who helped me.

Testimonial 3

My name is Jerry. This is the moment I have been looking forward to. As of Wednesday, I have accepted an offer as vice president, marketing with Genetics Company. I'll be working for their international division and responsible for opening up new markets for their seed productions in Africa and some in the Mideast. It's interesting, because back in June, when we did our practice interviews, this was essentially the position for which I practice-interviewed. It just took a while to come together.

I was trying to think of some things that might be of interest as you are just getting into your job searches. A lot of very true and worthwhile things have already been said. I know my experience in the whole job search process was a learning experience for me. I had been with ABC Company for nine years and never had really learned to do an effective job search. I feel safe to say that I would probably still be at it or would have settled for a job at McDonald's by this point. I just didn't know how to go about it. I really feel that the best part of this whole process was learning about myself—what I want to do, how to clarify my career goals, how to market myself, how to communicate effectively. Those are skills that are universal in their transferability and are going to come in very handy down the road.

I would like to share an analogy of how I think of the stages of the job search. At least in my case, it worked sort of like taking a trip on an airplane. You start out and there are the emotional aspects of departure—breaking loose from family or wherever you've been, the flurry of activity associated with getting to the airport, of boarding the plane and settling in. This is similar to the emotional turmoil you experience when you lose your job. The slow, gradual ascent is analogous to the daily routine of making your calls and writing your letters. Then things begin to level off. Along about one month into the process, you are feeling pretty comfortable with it. It gets to be almost like any other job. Then, after about two months, things began to happen for me. That's analogous to the plane beginning to descend—things start to get a little bit turbulent, and there's just a lot of activity. People begin to respond to your letters or to your leads. Finally, just before landing, it gets very turbulent—and in my case, that was one of the most difficult parts of the job search. All these people start expressing interest—in my case, four or five. I started to wonder how I was going to put this guy off while I waited for these other offers to come in. But it all worked out very nicely. A few potential offers faded out of the picture toward the end, but I ended up with two strong offers.

The one I accepted with Genetics Company is really the ideal job for me. It combines most of my career objectives. The one drawback is that it involves considerable travel. I had a struggle with that as I got to the point of making a decision—really wondering, thinking it through with my wife. Did I want to be gone 35 or 40 percent of the time, overseas for three-week stretches? We don't know that answer yet. I guess the only way to find out is to jump in and do it. I decided that it is better to find out now rather than later regret not having explored it, because this is an area that I have wanted to be involved in really since college.

For me, the key to success was networking. All the leads that materialized were as a result of contacts with former work associates or people that I had contact with in other companies through my previous job. My job objective was market development or projects in agribusiness, which is a narrow field. Obviously, there are not a whole lot of positions advertised in that area, so I had to rely heavily on networking. Actually, I found no ads in my area of interest. I wrote a lot of letters to major agribusiness companies here in the United States. The "cold" letter route did not really work for me. I got a lot of very nice rejection letters. The amusing part was how many different ways people can tell you "Thanks, but no thanks." There were a lot of very original letters from personnel departments.

The thing that really was helpful for me was getting out to visit companies. I took three trips to various parts of the country—one up to the Midwest, one to Virginia, and one up to the Northeast. I lined up interviews along the way. Some of these interviews were with people I had written to, and they had told me they didn't have anything. But I called them back, thanked them for responding to my letter, told them I was really interested in the company, and just wondered if I could stop by since I was going to be in the area. And I mentioned that I would like to learn more about their company. That was very helpful for a number of reasons. One, it kept me current in the interview process. I got some new contacts from doing that and occasionally got a solid lead out of those interviews. This emphasizes the importance of getting out and meeting with people. I think it is a very effective technique.

I am very grateful for this opportunity. I think it's been one of the most positive experiences of my whole career thus far. I don't know how many people there are out in the work world who probably wish for this opportunity, who are not satisfied with their jobs. I wasn't with my previous job. The opportunity to get off the treadmill and step back, look at what you want to do, and lay down some long-range plans is, I think, a chance of a lifetime.

Are there questions?

Q: What are some of the techniques you used for negotiating?
A: Basically it was just asking for time to make a decision. I was going through a second or third interview with some of these companies, and they would say, "Well, we are getting very close to a decision stage. We would need you to make your decision here shortly." Well I became quite a bit anxious, and I wondered how I was going to hold off the other employers. Actually, that problem never materialized. The guy who

said he was going to make a decision next week didn't end up making a decision 'til three or four weeks later. I think that may be practical wisdom—don't rely too heavily on what people say about when they will do something. In my case, the offers came through at least three or four weeks later than what they first told me. So just hang cool, and don't worry too much about it. The only other thing I would add along that line is, ask for time to make a decision. If they want you bad enough, they will be willing for you to make a sound decision. In certain situations, I was very up front with people. I told them I was considering several other positions; if I felt it was appropriate, I would tell them very specifically what I was doing. They understood. They said, "We are willing to wait; we would really like to have you, so we'll just wait and see what you find out."

Testimonial 4

My name is Carol, and I was formerly with High Top Company.

I remember when I first sat in the outplacement seminar, especially that first Friday, there were two or three people who got up from previous groups who had just been placed. They spoke to us as we are speaking to you, and some of us were a little bit skeptical. I wondered if they were paying these people to get up and tell these nice things, since this is exactly what the consultant said in our first meeting at High Top Company—insisting how great things would be. I had doubts as to whether these things really happened as clients described them, but as the weeks went by and more and more people came here and talked to the group, I realized that everybody who spoke about their job search was just like I was. They were going through some very difficult times, but they stuck with it.

I'll tell you quickly what happened with me. I was manager of an audio/video production department for High Top. Of course, with the oil industry downturn—by the way I had that line down pat about the "downturn of the economy"—but anyway, my whole department was shut down. I won't say it was a shock to me. In service departments, you always run the risk of something happening. Within three weeks of being here, I decided that I wanted to start my own production company. I had looked around Houston, and there just did not seem to be an opportunity similar to what I had. I did send out resumes left and right the first couple of weeks, almost all of which were out of state. After about three weeks, I didn't hear anything back from all of the resumes I sent out. I decided that I would try starting my own production company—at least, give it the best shot I could. So for the next three months, that's about all I did, except for sending out resumes just to keep my options open. That's another thing the consultant talked about in the seminar—"Make sure you keep your options open, and don't close any door that might help you out down the road." So I kept looking on a small scale—which, by the way, also fulfilled my unemployment compensation requirements. I called on people to work on productions, individual slide shows, or whatever. And I developed a few contracts—I was at least getting some work and building that up.

Then, about a month ago, I got a call from a large bank in Florida to which I had sent a resume the week after I got laid off from High Top. About a week later, I called them and they told me that the position had been "filled." I didn't quite believe that line, since my background was perfect for the job description. Interestingly enough, they called me back a month ago and said that they would like me to interview if I was still interested. At that time, I wasn't even sure I wanted to go interview, since I was just so set on doing my own thing. Since I had started it, I was going to stick with it. But I thought, "Keep your options open. You don't know what there is out there—plus it's a free trip!" I decided to give it a shot. I went out there and interviewed with a different person every half-hour or so for about three and a half hours, one of which was an hour-long lunch meeting. That was seven interviews. The process was really an experience for me. I felt very prepared. Before I left, I reviewed my notes that I had taken in the seminar. I had written about five or six major points when we practiced interviewing, and I studied those. I felt very comfortable when I was there.

After I came back, they called me a day or two later and said that they were really interested in me and asked me to return for another interview. They were interviewing someone else for the job in about two weeks, but they were narrowing it down to the two of us. I almost hoped they wouldn't call me. I had spent money on stationery and business cards and called all these people and had people call me back about possible productions that I could do in Houston. They invited me and my husband to come for the weekend to talk to us a little bit more and show us the area, et cetera, et cetera, et cetera. I thought, "Well, okay, I'll keep my options open." I went there this past weekend, and they were just extremely nice to us.

On Monday, after I got back, they called me and offered the position. I still didn't know if I wanted to take it. After discussing it with my husband and establishing a minimum offer which could induce us to move, I told them, "No, thank you, but I can not accept the offer." They called back the next day and upped the offer. It was *so* good I couldn't turn it down. In fact Tuesday, when they called and upped the offer, I responded immediately. I said, "Okay, I accept the offer." The representative said, "What? You're kidding—you're taking the offer now? You don't want to think about it?" I replied, "No—you've been fair with me, I'll be fair with you."

One thing in particular about the negotiations is interesting. I had contacted a company in Chicago about a possibility of a job offer which never really came about. But since I had been talking with them, I used that as some leverage with these people. I told them I was talking to some people in Chicago. Well, when they came back on Tuesday to up the offer, the representative spent about ten minutes talking about the statistics between Chicago and Jacksonville, Florida. She told me the difference in the price of housing—that the median price was $137,000 in Chicago and $89,000 in Jacksonville. She gave me the cost of living index of the two cities, the food index difference. I mean, there were about seven or eight categories that they were using to show why this was a better deal than going to Chicago. What was really a kick was that the lady expounding on Florida was from Chicago! I felt that having a little leverage really helped me. Even though I didn't actually have an offer from Chicago, I used that as a bargaining point.

Through all this, I did learn to keep my options open. I still would like to have my own business, which I am going to keep up. I've got some things I'm involved in which I can do on weekends. So I am going to keep that going just as a small business. If, down the road, things don't work out with this job, I'll always have that to go back to.

The last thing I would like to mention deals with networking ideas. I didn't know what networking was when I came here—except for ABC, NBC, and CBS. I quickly learned that you talk to your friends, your acquaintances, people that were former employers and let them all know what you are trying to do. You never know when they are going to find a friend or see something that might be of interest. That gets down to how I knew about this job. A week after I was laid off, a friend in the employee communications department at High Top called me and said she had seen an ad in a trade publication which I never read. She told me about it but had forgotten which issue it was in. Then, about a week later, the guy I was sitting next to in the seminar, who was another famous person from our group, told me about it. And *he* couldn't remember what issue it was in. Finally, after about two weeks, one of them found the magazine and sent me a copy of the ad. My point is that you never know where the possibility of a job will come from. That's why it's important to tell all your friends, your acquaintances, people you meet—don't be shy about it. If there is anything that is going to help you, it is believing that the more people who know that you are looking for a job in a certain area and who keep thinking about you, the greater the possibility that they are going to find something and tell you about it.

Any questions?

Q: Do any of your clients need advertising help?
A: No, but I have a lot of business cards which I would be glad to share with you!

Testimonial 5

My name is Bill. I started my career as a chemical engineer in a refinery in Houston. I went from refinery to refinery, from chemical plant to chemical plant. Then I left the States and spent a long time in South America building refineries and operating refineries. Eventually I worked my way to Puerto Rico, to Pittsburgh, and back to Houston. I got out of the refining business and into the coal business, which had its ups and downs. Then I got out of the coal business and went into engineering and construction, which has its up and downs, too. I worked here in Houston with two companies, then moved to Chicago where I had a nice tour of duty in the Midwest doing engineering and construction management. Then one of the nicest things I did was move to Washington. In Washington, D.C., I was president of a company that did public sector and government contracts, both engineering and construction. The company that I headed up got restructured, and then was restructured right out of existence.

At that time my wife, Glenda, and I talked about our choices. She could come join me in Washington and starve to death or I could come back to Houston. Since Glenda is president of her own company, the latter choice seemed most appropriate. We decided it was about time we stopped commuting anyway. It was a lovely decision and I'm glad we made it. I'm real happy now that I lost my job, got fired, came back to Houston and started over again. I'm also going to tell you that it was not easy. In fact, it was very hard on me to have to start over.

I remember the first day I was here, a consultant said, "Well, how do you feel about your situation?" That was the first time anyone asked how I felt about it and I determined at that point that I was going to be positive. So one word of advice—be positive throughout the ups and downs that you have in your professional career. So I started off on a positive note here.

I've always been a very pragmatic person, and I realized that I had to restructure the way I lived and the way I worked. It was very difficult. One of the things that I found very beneficial to me was that I arrived each day when the offices opened and I went home when they closed the doors. I didn't like using the telephone. The telephone was hard; believe me it was very difficult. But it's something that you must do. You have to overcome your stage fright and you have to overcome your reluctance to talk about yourself. I've done a lot of things successfully and I didn't want to tell people that I had been fired. The sooner you get over that and get it behind you, the sooner you can move on. The seminar helped me get my feet on the ground and head out and start doing my work. I didn't get any interviews at the beginning. But I just kept plugging away.

You need those interviews—they are good for your ego. There was a point when Glenda and I talked about the possibility that it was time for me to retire. But after a while you realize all the money is going out and no money is coming back in and you've got to decide if you are going to sack groceries or just what you are going to do. Eventually the interviews came, and the job offers came, and what do you know—some of them were so low that I wouldn't consider taking them. Some of them were withdrawn! I'm going to tell you that one of you is going to get an offer, and you're going to call back the next day to find out more particulars, and discover that there is no job. You're ready to negotiate, and they're going to withdraw the offer on you. And that's pretty hard to take. Memorial Day we had at least three jobs lined up—I just knew I would be working by July 1. Not one of them materialized. I worked with one company for weeks and I interviewed everybody from chairman down to project manager level. They offered a job once and withdrew it; then later they came back to me, and started talking all over again, but nothing ever came of it. And yet you need those interviews.

You need to talk to people. One of the things that I found very beneficial when I got to a real low level was to talk to people. You need their support. There are times when you just stop and talk over your situation and it helps you get through that day.

I did a lot of work at night. I did a lot of work on the weekends, and you need that. It is a full-time job. Don't let anyone tell you that it is not a full-time job.

I did some consulting work, but it didn't lead to a full-time position. I had one company that told me that they wanted to hire me but they couldn't get authorization. They wanted me to consult for awhile and then maybe they would hire me. It turned out that they took my strategic plan, which I put together for a business unit, and they are using it today. But at the end of the contract they said, "Well, I'm sorry but we can't get approval to hire you."

Another thing I would recommend is to keep in shape. You've got to be mentally in shape, but you also have to be physically in shape. Your appearance is also important. You've got to keep your wardrobe up, you've got to keep your body in good shape, and you've got to keep doing your work.

You've got to keep going—I can't emphasize that enough. I don't care how many interviews you get or how many job offers you get, you still need to be digging, going for a job, looking for those opportunities that are out there. Because you are going to have two or three interviews with one company and you are going to say, "Hey, this is it," and you will start neglecting your network, telephone contacts, your personal contacts. But if it doesn't work out, you've lost a lot of time.

The job that I have now is with an environmental remedial company. I selected it out of three offers. Along the way someone asked me if I had explored hazardous waste management. At the time I hadn't given it much thought, so I started working on it. As it turns out they found out about me from somebody else that eventually led to the interviews and that led to the job offer. So don't stop. Don't stop looking, don't stop working.

One of the other two offers I had was in Venezuela and I went to look at the job. Believe me, they needed help. They had all of their operations riding on three major projects in a country that needs a lot of work. The job is going down hill, and they are going to get thrown out of there if they don't do something about it. While I was looking at that job, a third opportunity developed. It was with another company here in town, where they wanted me to take over and run their engineering construction business.

I came back from Venezuela, and Glenda said, "You have an interview on Monday." She just told them, "Yes, Bill will be there to interview on Monday." It was Environmental Technologies, Inc., with whom I had been talking, and I didn't know if they were serious or what. As it turns out, they were very serious. I told them, "I've got to make a decision by Friday, and if you're going to play in this ball game, we've got to get with it." The vice president said it was a bad week—there were board meetings and this and that. I said, "Fine, you've got board meetings, I'll see you. If you want to talk to me, put your offer together and let's talk about it in detail. I need an offer by Thursday morning." At that point I was tired of fooling around; I had something I wanted and I was ready to take it. As it turned out they put it together and made me an offer on Thursday morning—he actually delayed it until Thursday afternoon because we ate lunch and talked about it. Because they were playing this game, they wanted to wear me out, take me out to the very end of the day. I decided to accept the job as executive vice president, business development; I will oversee things that are happening with their construction companies, their remedial companies and with their technology company. The company has big plans and is going places, and I plan to go with them. That is my story. Any questions?

Q: How do you feel now?
A: Great!

So there you have a few of the hundreds of testimonials we have heard. In a short time, you, too, can give testimony to a successful job search. Set your goal, apply the techniques, believe in yourself, and make it happen. That is how to create job search leverage. The one percent success factor is within you—use it to maximize your success. By the way, at your curtain call—when you've finished your script and attained your career goals—be prepared for a standing ovation. If you don't believe it now, perhaps then you'll know that rather than the worst thing, this is the best thing that could have happened to you! We wish you success, and we would like to hear your unique story when you've achieved your job search goals.

Ken & Sheryl Dawson

Appendix: Sample Resumes

The following are thirty sample resumes that represent various functional areas, organizational levels, and industries. For your convenience, a listing precedes the sample resumes. Although most of the resumes are for managerial, professional, or independent business positions, we have included a two-page administrative assistant resume and two samples to show our one-page format for hourly and clerical positions. All of the samples are actual resumes from our client files. Names of applicants and companies have been altered to maintain confidentiality.

1) SENIOR MANAGEMENT

NAME
Address
Home: Phone #
Office: Phone #

OBJECTIVE

Senior Management

SUMMARY

Over twenty years experience in the chemical industry involving assignments in general management, commercial, engineering, operating and research positions.

PROFESSIONAL EXPERIENCE

Current Corporate Involvement: Administratively responsible for the following XYZ subsidiary companies:

> XYZ Oil - Vice President
> XYZ P & M - Vice President, Chemicals
> XYZ Chemicals - President & Director
> XYZ Eastern Realty - President & Chairman of the Board
> XYZ Belgium - Director

XYZ PROCESSING & MARKETING - Houston, Texas   1984-Present

Vice President - Chemicals
Complete profit center responsibility for XYZ Polymers with $300,000,000 sales per year.

- Improved profitability by $14 million in one year despite declining market.

- Negotiated sale of company assets.

- Directed marketing of all chemical products from refinery with total annual sales of $200,000,000.

- Managed administrative responsibilities for four additional XYZ subsidiaries.

- Reduced operating costs by $14 million.

- Improved product quality by initiation of formal statistical quality control program.

- Optimized product mix by emphasizing higher added value products.

- Selected by the Texas Water Rights Commission as the only processing plant on the honor roll.

174

XYZ CHEMICAL - Houston, Texas   -   1982-1984

President and Chief Executive Officer
Complete responsibility for $250,000,000 per year company.

- Changed company's primary thrust from processing to marketing resulting in company becoming the major supplier to Goodyear and Firestone.

- Improved profitability by $22 million in one year.

- Negotiated sale of company assets.

- Improved operating levels from 15% of capacity to 80% of capacity.

- Reduced operating costs by 15% or $6 million per year.

- Operated profitable chemical trading company in Europe with revenues of $50 million.

- Successfully negotiated contract for the sale of $30 million per year of chemicals to Saudi Arabia.

- Commercialized two new technologies for the production of ocetenes and isobutylenes resulting in increased profitability.

Various Assignments   1962-1973, 1974-1982
Areas of responsibility included management of marketing, purchasing, technical services, engineering and operating functions.

ENVIRONMENTAL SERVICES, INC.   1973-1974

Regional Manager
Complete profit center responsibility for western region of industrial waste disposal business with total annual operating budget of $30 million.

- Accomplished complete turnaround of company including restaffing key positions and introduction of proper controls.

- Overcame past problems to establish company as reputable, dependable supplier of waste disposal servicers by improving operating reliability.

- Improved financial performance from loss position to profitability in a 16 month period of time.

EDUCATION

B.A., Rice University, Houston, Texas - 1961
B.S., Chemical Engineering, Rice University, Houston, Texas - 1962
Stanford Executive Program - 1980

AWARDS

Patent for Dehydrogeneration of Butanes
Who's Who in South and Southwest
Who's Who in Industry and Commerce

2) GENERAL MANAGEMENT

NAME
Address
Home #
Business#

OBJECTIVE

General Manager

SUMMARY

Over twenty years of broad based industrial experience which included:

- Two years as general manager.
- Seven years in operations management with heavy emphasis in international plant management.
- Nine years in sales and marketing management including international sales.

PROFESSIONAL EXPERIENCE

RTX, INC. - Dallas, Texas   1981-Present

Vice President, Director Valve Operations (1983-Present)
Responsible for marketing, sales, manufacturing, financial control and engineering for worldwide valve organization.

- Developed the strategic plan for growth of the valve organization, which included short term existing product growth and long term new products development.

- Restructured the international sales and distribution organization to effectively meet the demands of the changing competitive environment resulting in a 14% gain of market share.

- Introduced global sourcing and rationalization of production to reduce manufactured costs and improve distribution flexibility, which resulted in saving $750,000 annually.

Vice President & Director - Operations (1981-1983)
Responsible for manufacturing, purchasing, materials management, quality and engineering for U.S. and Mexican operations.

- Introduced employee participation (Quality Circles) to the Houston plant which led to 14% reductions in cost of quality and productivity improvements.

- Created product line focused manufacturing operations which enhanced the employee participation program and supported the overall reduction effort.

- Reduced inventory by 28% in a 12-month period.

176

- Reduced manufacturing through-put time from 16 weeks to 6 weeks with 60% reduction in work-in-process in one department.

- Redesigned raw material and manufacturing processes to reduce finished product cost by 40% in one department.

REDA Pump Company - Bartlesville, Oklahoma   1977-1981

Manager Branch Plant Operations
Responsible for all operations management and customer service activities in nine U.S. and foreign plants.

- Restaffed branch management positions by hiring eight U.S. and foreign nationals.

- Improved customer service levels from 50% to over 96%.

- Introduced MRP dependent parts forecasting as a tool for inventory control and reduction.

- Reduced inventory by 40% in U.S. plants.

- Improved inventory records accuracy from 75% to 98%.

- Built three new plants to provide expanded customer service to new market areas. Each plant located in Marshall, Texas, Singapore and the Persian Gulf employed between 100 and 140 people.

- Published a complete Standard Process Instruction book that resulted in uniformity of production methods and quality worldwide.

INDUSTRIAL TECTONICS, INC. - Ann Arbor, Michigan   1969-1977

General Manager
P & L responsibility for mechanical power transmission product line.

- Established a national distribution network.

- Added eight product lines and manufacturing capability to serve U.S. market.

WAUKESHA BEARINGS COMPANY - Waukesha, Wisconsin   1963-1968

Was promoted through several positions including: Plant Engineer/Quality Control Supervisor, Field Service Manager, Supervisor of Engineering and Sales, and Sales Manager.

EDUCATION

B.S. - University of Michigan, College of Engineering, 1958
B.B.A. - University of Michigan, College of Business, 1959

3) BUSINESS DEVELOPMENT

NAME
Address
Home #
Business #

OBJECTIVE

Director, Business Development

SUMMARY

Over twenty years extensive experience in marketing, commercial development and new ventures, marketing research, planning and diversification. Demonstrated ability to communicate and work successfully with all levels. Proven ability to contribute to profitable growth in diverse areas of responsibility.

PROFESSIONAL EXPERIENCE

CHEMICAL CORPORATION - Houston, Texas   1977-Present

Director Corporate Planning (1984-Present)

Developed business, investment and diversification strategies for a $7 billion energy and chemicals firm.

- Assessed business unit competitive strengths and weaknesses and formulated strategic actions to take advantage or improve position.

- Directed task force analysis that resulted in a $230 million acquisition.

- Persuaded management to adopt an alternative approach to a $110 million acquisition for geographic diversification, saving in excess of $30 million.

- Advised Executive Committee on market trends affecting business units and developed financial models to forecast profits under differing scenarios.

- Forecast product and raw materials supply, demand and pricing to provide a framework for operational planning and budgeting.

Manager of Marketing Strategy (1981-1984)

Key member of team managing a division's largest business. Developed business plans and marketing strategies for existing products and new specialties.

- Increased profits 10-15% by installing a customer evaluation system and improving mix and targeting.

- Managed the introduction and sales development of new specialty products adding over $1 million per year in gross profit.

- Conducted market and economic studies that guided a $40 million investment in new production facilities.

- Increased share in selected markets by creating targeted sales programs and guiding product development.

- Coordinated objectives of operating units to achieve business unit goals and prepared forecasts, business plans and budgets.

Manager of Marketing Research (1977-1981)

Established and managed the function with a $500,000 budget and a staff of 3. Prepared business plans and market evaluations for consumer and industrial products. Purchased and managed all consultants' services.

- Surveyed consumer needs and attitudes which led to the introduction of a new line of automotive chemical products increasing penetration into chain store accounts.

- Conducted advertising research that guided creative development and exposure budgeting of a $4 million national television campaign.

- Developed international competitive analysis and forecasting systems for division products.

SPECIAL PRODUCTS COMPANY - Chicago, Illinois   1975-1977

Manager of Market Research

Established and managed the function for an international specialty chemical business.

- Developed marketing plans for an important new product with potential earnings in excess of $1 million per year.

- Provided economic analysis and market guidance for major R&D programs.

EDUCATION

MBA, University of Louisville - 1968
MS in Chemical Engineering, University of Louisville - 1961
BS in Chemical Engineering, University of Louisville - 1960

PROFESSIONAL AFFILIATIONS

American Marketing Association
Commercial Development Association
American Gas Association
The Planning Forum

4) PROJECT MANAGEMENT

NAME
Address
Home #
Business #

OBJECTIVE

Project Manager

SUMMARY

Over twenty-two (22) years of experience in engineering, engineering supervision, marketing and project management in the energy industry.

PROFESSIONAL EXPERIENCE

MAJOR CORPORATION   1965-Present

Project Manager - Houston, Texas (1986-Present)

- Performed project management on 78 projects, including pipeline replacements, major pipeline expansions and multiple unit compressor stations, which ranged in size up to $15 million.

- Developed construction contract documents for 17 major projects and provided development of project management procedures and standards.

- Represented Project Management on the rewrite of Engineering Standards resulting in improved consistency and quality of projects.

Project Engineering Manager - Omaha, Nebraska (1983-1986)

- Developed project proposals, qualification documents and contract documents for outside clients resulting in favorable negotiations and project implementation.

- Facilitated project development and evaluated energy projects ranging up to $150 million including 2 ethanol plants, 5 cogeneration facilities, 4 refuse-to-energy plants, 1 geothermal project, and more than 10 natural gas facilities.

- Coordinated marketing effort that screened over 400 potential clients which resulted in a gas field development joint venture.

- Developed marketing activities to contact 170 major pipeline companies which identified potential clients and projects for marketing activities.

- Sold and provided design, project and construction management for a 4,000 and a 6,000 horsepower compressor station for outside clients.

- Originated Engineering Standards for use on outside client projects.

- Sold more than $.2 million of SGA analog studies.

- Received performance bonus for project management and marketing activities in 1985.

180

<u>Director of Engineering</u> - Omaha, Nebraska (1982-1983)

- Supervised pipeline engineers in design of 2 compressor stations, 3 district offices, 4 meter stations, 15 microwave sites and 832 miles of 42" pipeline resulting in minimal design problems during construction.

- Developed and implemented commissioning plan, prepared the pipeline purging procedures and provided start-up assistance for the pipeline project resulting in timely initiation of project construction.

- Received a performance bonus for pipeline project.

<u>Project Manager</u> - Omaha, Nebraska (1981-1982)

- Performed project management for meter and compressor stations, district offices, motel and restaurant, microwaves and pipeline restoration within budget.

<u>Director - Civil and Mechanical Design</u> - Houston, Texas (1979-1981)

- Supervised 13 engineers in design of pipelines, compressor stations, treating facilities, plastic film plant and petrochemical facilities.

- Developed Engineering Standards and Guidelines for Houston office.

<u>Mechanical Supervisor</u> - Omaha, Nebraska (1978-1979)

- Supervised engineering staff in the conceptual design of pipeline facilities.

- Coordinated development of the Project Management Plan, cost and schedule controls and technical standards for pipeline project as required by ANGTS.

<u>Project Engineer/Engineering Specialist</u> - Omaha, Nebraska (1970-1978)

- Designed over 50 compressor stations with more than 100,000 horsepower, 4 peak shaving plants, $6 million polyolifin pilot plant, Selexol CO_2 removal plant, and directed design/safety audits of 2 LNG plants.

<u>Engineer/Project Engineer</u> - Omaha, Nebraska (1965-1970)

- Developed and performed testing for new equipment and facilities including compressors, valves, pipe coating, measurement and operating systems.

EDUCATION

Masters in Business Administration, University of Nebraska
BS Mechanical Engineering, University of Tulsa

REGISTRATION

Professional Engineer, State of Nebraska

PROFESSIONAL AFFILIATIONS

American Society of Mechanical Engineers

NAME
Address
Home #
Business #

OBJECTIVE

Vice President, Strategic Planning

SUMMARY

More than 17 years broad manufacturing management experience with emphasis on financial, marketing and business planning.

PROFESSIONAL EXPERIENCE

WESTON INTERNATIONAL - Phoenix, Arizona   1979-Present

Director, Business Planning
Reporting to Division President, coordinated the development and implementation of division business plans. Served as business manager for the subsea product line with responsibility for formulating objectives and plans; coordinated subsea budgets and programs in engineering, sales, and manufacturing. Served on management committee which reviewed critical issues, set division goals and objectives, and approved and monitored action programs. Supervised market research department of three people who performed all division market research.

- Negotiated joint venture agreement with major Norwegian manufacturer which resulted in a $8.0 million order and established Weston as one of two major suppliers to the Norwegian market.

- Served on the team which negotiated first license agreement for the manufacturer of API products in China which resulted in establishing the company as the favored vendor for the offshore China market.

- Guided company's successful entry into and penetration of the subsea wellhead and tree market. Weston has achieved 10% market penetration and is well positioned for future growth.

- Developed and implemented a computer sales forecasting system which provided timely information for the development of manufacturing schedules.

- Monitored performance in plans and recommended corrective actions to minimize inventory build-up during business downturn. Designed market program to eliminate $1.0 million in excess inventory.

- Developed focused market program to expand customer base resulting in over 40 new accounts added over two years.

- Served as primary contact with the Valve Manufacturers Association for the development of the program to track industry sales which permitted accurate assessment of market share by quarter.

- Coordinated the development and presentation of Weston strategy for major capital investment program which the corporation approved.

STONE INTERNATIONAL - Pittsburgh, Pennsylvania   1977-1979
General Industries Operations (GIO)

Manager, Business Planning
Reporting to Operations Vice President of Planning, managed the merger/ acquisition analysis of selected companies and monitored the performance of divisions to plan and highlight key strategic issues in each division.

- Developed acquisition strategy for Italian subsidiary of Stone which resulted in the attempted acquisition of two companies.

- Developed the strategy to shutdown a product group within GIO which eliminated a potential business loss.

- Managed the product group during the shutdown to ensure that all customer commitments were completed while meeting time and financial objectives.

STONE INTERNATIONAL - Morgantown, West Virginia   1972-1977
Faucet Division

Director, Business Planning
Reporting to Division President, managed the development of business plans which emphasized short term variance analysis and corrective action programs. Promoted to positions of Division Financial Analyst and Manager, Cost and Statistics prior to assuming directorship.

- Implemented system to control all pricing discounts on a daily basis from remote warehouses which maintained pricing within 0.5% points of goal.

- Implemented system to coordinate sales forecasts with production plans on a monthly basis. On-time shipments were held at 97% with inventory turnover in excess of 3.0 turns.

- Coordinated the development of strategy to reorganize and recapitalize the division resulting in corporate approval and funding.

STONE MANUFACTURING - Pittsburgh, Pennsylvania   1969-1972

Staff Manufacturing Engineer
Assigned projects as internal consultant to assist with manufacturing problems.

STONE MANUFACTURING - DuBois, Pennsylvania   1968-1969

Industrial Engineer
Performed duties of Plant Industrial Engineer.

EDUCATION

B.A., Economics, Bucknell, University - 1968

6) SALES AND MARKETING

NAME
Address
Home #
Business #

OBJECTIVE

Marketing Manager

SUMMARY

Over twenty years professional experience as a marketing generalist with a strong technical background and excellent communications skills. Broad experience and education (MBA) in planning, forecasting, market research, and product development.

PROFESSIONAL EXPERIENCE

BAY AREA, INC. - Mobile, Alabama   1981-Present

Manager Special Projects

- Conceived, researched, and supervised the introduction of a new product line which increased the sales of one of the subsidiaries by 15%.

- Established methodology which reduced the over-60-day accounts receivables from 37% to 21%, saving the division over $150,000 per year.

- Saved the division over $700,000 by discovering billing inaccuracies and inventory discrepancies. Designed and installed controls to prevent reoccurrence.

- Prevented the loss of over $500,000 by persuading management to forego expansion into a market that subsequently collapsed.

- Developed a marketing plan for a subsidiary which resulted in a 28% year-to-year increase in sales and a reduction in manpower and travel expense.

- Planned, designed, and produced effective advertising brochures and catalogues, thereby saving 70% on use of outside sources.

BROWNING CORPORATION - Dallas, Texas   1974-1981

Contracting Sales Manager (1979-1981)

- Surpassed contacting sales goals by 35%.

- Negotiated and supervised $2,000,000 per year in sub-contracts resulting in savings of over 20%.

184

- Negotiated out-of-court settlement with a governmental entity resulting in savings of over $200,000 while protecting company image.

- Developed costing procedures which identified problem areas resulting in 15% savings.

Developmental Products Sales Manger   (1976-1979)

- Researched and developed a product and a market which now produces 25% of the total profitability of this division.

- Developed a market for a previously discarded scrap material resulting in increased sales of over $100,000 per year.

- Coordinated efforts of the research staff and field sales to improve existing products resulting in increased sales.

Sales Representative   (1974-1976)

- Won sales contests while serving as a salesman.

- Chosen as Salesman of the Year in second year of employment.

- Received the only promotion in the sales force during tenure.

XTA CHEMICAL COMPANY - Dallas, Texas   1971-1974

- Earned numerous sales awards while functioning as a manufacturer's representative to grocery wholesalers and packaging materials concerns.

KENNEDY INDUSTRIES - Ft. Smith, Arkansas   1964-1971

- Progressed from Sales Trainee to General Manager of a subsidiary for this lumber related manufacturer.

EDUCATION

MBA, Marketing and Management, University of Oklahoma,
Norman, Oklahoma - 1956

BBA, Marketing and Finance, University of Oklahoma,
Norman, Oklahoma - 1954

AS, General Engineering, St. Gregory's College,
Oklahoma City, Oklahoma - 1952

NAME
Address
Home #
Business #

OBJECTIVE

Public Relations Manager

SUMMARY

More than 25 years experience in internal and external communications including seven years with daily newspapers, six years as an editor of an international magazine and 14 years in public relations and public affairs practice and administration.

PROFESSIONAL EXPERIENCE

CAPITAL, INC.   1978-Present

Manager of Public Relations - Houston, Texas (1981-Present)

Reporting to Executive Director, Corporate Communications, managed worldwide public/media relations operations for 100,000-employee conglomerate with $15 billion in sales in 12 distinct industries in 56 countries.

- Assumed direction of 1987 "Special Event" resulting in 30% increase in participants and first-time live coverage by seven radio stations. Increased print coverage while keeping overall costs at previous-year levels.

- Conceived and implemented an information system to provide key executives overnight print and electronic media reports affecting the company's businesses.

- Planned and directed public relations program dealing with the controversial acquisition of the assets of Cone Company resulting in favorable acceptance by the U.S. Justice Department, customers, dealers, the financial community, employees and the media.

- Developed crisis communications procedures resulting in favorable, fair treatment by the media during crisis situations, including massive employee layoffs, anticipated hostile takeover attempt, gas well blowouts, toxic chemical spills, railroad tank car explosions, aircraft fatalities and leaking underground storage tanks.

- Reduced manpower requirements and cut media inquiry response time significantly by conception, development and implementation of a computerized communication and information system tailored to public relations and public affairs operations.

- Introduced and directed development of computerized budget and tracking system for corporate gifts totaling $5 million annually.

Press Relations Manager Washington, D.C. (1978-1981)

● Established Washington presence with the media.

● Acted as company spokesman.

D & E CORPORATION - Washington, D.C./Memphis, TN   1976-1978

Director, Public and Industry Relations

● Conceived and directed a nationwide grassroots public and government relations project. Resultant legislative change enabled the company to grow from a privately-held, unprofitable airline to a publicly-traded profitable organization. Received stock bonus equal to 150% of annual salary.

● Established public relations, government relations and employee communications departments which eventually totalled 19 professionals.

TECHNOLOGY PUBLICATION - New York, New York   1970-1976

Associate Editor/Evaluation Test Pilot

● Covered Civil Aeronautics Board, Department of Transportation, White House and State Department actions affecting the aerospace industry.

● Conducted evaluation test flights and prepared articles on foreign and U.S. military and commercial aircraft ranging from light single engine aircraft to the supersonic Concorde.

AEROSPACE CORPORATION - Wichita, Kansas   1967-1970

Press Relations Representative

● Developed and implemented media relations plan for publicizing company systems on the Apollo spacecraft and lunar landing module.

● Assumed responsibility as check pilot for editors who flew company products for flight evaluation stories.

● Published four-color marketing magazine targeting military/aerospace customers.

EDUCATION

Southwestern University, Georgetown, Texas - Journalism (1958-1960)

University of Houston, Houston, Texas - History/Government (1962-1963)

8) HUMAN RESOURCES

NAME
Address
Home #
Business #

OBJECTIVE

Director of Human Resources

SUMMARY

Over sixteen years of managerial and administrative experience in the human resources field with two Fortune 500 corporations including in-depth knowledge of:

- Salary and Benefits
- Pro-active Employee Relations
- EEO/Affirmative Action
- Labor Relations Law
- Manpower and Organization Development
- Managerial, Technical and Professional Staffing
- Human Resource Information Systems
- International Administration

PROFESSIONAL EXPERIENCE

NORTHWEST SUPPLY COMPANY - Seattle, Washington   1981-Present

Manager, Human Resources - Distribution Division

- Established self-sufficient human resource department to support 125+ oilfield supply stores worldwide; initiated individual personnel folders.

- Employed key professionals and specialist in each major human resource area resulting in 75% improvement in relocations processing time, 40% reduction in insurance claim processing time, reduction of EEO/unfair labor practice charges to zero, and established computer system for reporting employee information.

- Travelled to 85% of the stores, and counseled employees on salaries, benefits, insurance, retirement, and thrift plan programs.

- Coordinated creation and implementation of a store manager training program resulting in 50% fewer employee complaints and a new employee performance appraisal which minimized subjective evaluations.

- Conducted in-depth formal organization revisions for the company covering 6,000+ employees domestically and 75 expatriates which established a standard policy and method in all divisions for the first time.

- Formulated and implemented an emergency evacuation plan for our expatriates and established a computer program which increased productivity in administering the international payroll program and resulted in an annual savings of $30,000.

U.S., INC.   1968-1981

<u>Personnel Manager</u> - Industrial Group, Dallas, Texas (1977-1981)

- Coordinated professional and technical staffing efforts resulting in an average annual hiring of 500+ which met or exceeded annual objectives.

- Coordinated and assisted in creating a new compensation strategy which was implemented in vital front-end manufacturing group and resulted in reduction of annual turnover from 94% to 35%.

- Conducted counseling from a pro-active standpoint for three major profit centers with 5,000+ employees resulting in zero unionization attempts and reduction of EEO charges from an average of 40 per year to less than 10 in three years.

<u>Personnel Manager</u> - San Salvador, El Salvador (1975-1977)

- Established plant personnel department and employed bilingual nationals in key human resource functions resulting in successfully training a Salvadorean replacement within two years.

- Conversed on two occasions with the president of the country and numerous times with his key ministers resulting in excellent relations and minimizing government interference in company business.

- Accomplished the hiring goal of 1,500 within the first six months of plant start-up.

<u>Staffing and Employee Relations Manager</u> - Sherman, Texas (1970-1975)

- Managed all staffing activities for a plant of 3,500+ averaging more than 400 new hires per year to successfully support this labor intensive operation.

- Countered two union reorganization attempts by the IUEW and the IAM resulting in a continued ability to conduct business free of third party interference.

<u>Manufacturing Supervisor</u> - U.S. Equipment Group, Dallas, Texas (1968-1970)

- Supervised 60-100 assemblers building classified government equipment on a $31 million contract where successful completion resulted in two additional contracts worth over $80 million.

MILITARY

USAF Captain, Air Traffic Control Officer (1963-1968)
Spent four years in several overseas locations

EDUCATION

BBA, Personnel Management, North Texas State University,
Denton, Texas (1963)
MBA, 18 hours completed; Braniff Graduate School,
Dallas, Texas (1971)

NAME
Address
Home #
Business #

OBJECTIVE

Information Systems Management

SUMMARY

Over fourteen years experience in information systems including office systems, applications development, systems software, data base administration, supervision and project management.

PROFESSIONAL EXPERIENCE

INTERSTATE SUPPLY COMPANY - Tulsa, Oklahoma   1981-Present

Supervisor - Office Systems

- Directed staff of five professionals in planning, analysis, development, and implementation of automated office systems.

- Implemented integrated office system for use by CEO, CFO, Division Presidents, Division Controllers, and Accounting staff which facilitated financial planning, reduced information float, and improved productivity.

- Increased effectiveness and efficiency of Office Systems staff and users by implementing an Information Center where company personnel could receive advice, training, and assistance with office systems technology and information retrieval systems.

- Analyzed requirements and implemented numerous personal computers and word processors which improved productivity of users.

- Assessed impact of office systems technology on long-term cost of a new building and participated in planning the new office complex for company.

- Managed data processing training throughout the company and reduced training costs 50% while improving coordination and procedures without reducing level of training.

DIGICAN CORPORATION - Mobile, Alabama   1978-1981

Projects Manager - Text Processing (1980-1981)

- Originated Office Automation Program, managed project teams and provided consulting services to all levels of management for processing textual material and for improving clerical and professional productivity.

- Implemented office system in Legal Division which increased clerical productivity.

- Designed, developed, and implemented a Docket Control System to track status of cases, cost, attorney caseload, attorney time, and critical docket dates to provide improved control over cases by Legal Division management.

- Analyzed requirements and implemented systems to reduce costs and improve productivity in Word Processing, Records Administration, and Micrographics.

Project Leader - Text Processing (1978-1979)

- Designed, developed, and implemented a litigation support system which was used to successfully appeal a $5 billion suit.

- Worked extensively with Legal Division and outside attorneys to use litigation support system in other major suits.

TEXAS OIL COMPANY, El Paso, Texas   1970-1978

Systems Analyst (1975-1978)

- Served as Data Base Administrator for new personnel system written under IMS. Designed data base; designed and programmed one sub-system; acted as technical advisor to other teams working on the project.

- Participated in development of a litigation support system for a joint venture of major oil companies to defend against the FTC's suit to break-up the major oil companies.

- Designed a Document Control System to track and control documents taken from company's files in response to subpoenas and interrogatories.

Programmer Analyst (1972-1975)

- Generated and maintained operating systems. Performed various hardware/software evaluations and implementations to reduce costs and/or increase system availability.

- Implemented and maintained CICS, DMS, and ITS. Advised and assisted programmers in the effective use of these systems.

- Acted as head of Systems Software during long-term disability of Supervisor. During this period, developed three-year plan for the group.

Programmer (1970-1972)

- Designed, programmed, implemented, and maintained various Corporate financial systems.

EDUCATION

B.S., Production Management, University of Arizona - 1970
Completed college in two and one-half years while working full-time
and was awarded three scholarships.

10) DATA PROCESSING

NAME
Address
Home #
Business #

OBJECTIVE

Programming Manager

SUMMARY

Over twelve years of diversified and progressive data processing experience with the last seven years in oil field manufacturing and services. Excellent working knowledge of all functions of mainframe, mini and micro data processing. Analyzed, designed and implemented major data processing systems for finance, marketing and manufacturing.

PROFESSIONAL EXPERIENCE

CN COMPANY - Houston, Texas   1981-Present

Manager of M.I.S. (1985-Present)
Managed a data processing organization of ten exempt and non-exempt employees with annual sales of $107 million.

- Managed an IBM 4341 group II mainframe shop with an annual operating budget of over $1 million.
- Recommended and supported all data processing equipment and services for international plants and sales centers resulting in a 20% increase in sales.
- Consolidated two IBM mainframe data centers to save $700 thousand per year in operating expenses.

Systems and Programming Manager, Corporate M.I.S. (1984-1985)
Managed a systems and programming group of 15 exempt employees with annual sales of $250 million.

- Replaced or brought in-house all data processing services from vendors which resulted in a savings of $75,000 per year in computing costs.
- Recommended, purchased and supported the use of personal computers in all departments of the company which resulted in a 25% reduction in turnaround time and a 35% increase in overall efficiency.

System Group Manager (1981-1984)
Managed a system group of eighteen exempt employees with annual sales of $300 million.

- Supervised the installation of M.S.A. General Ledger, Accounts Payable and supported upgrades to M.S.A. Payroll resulting in a 25% reduction in overall costs and a 50% improvement in customer services.
- Supervised the installation of a tool and gauge tracking system that saved the company $75,000 per year in lost or stolen tools and gauges.

OILFIELD EQUIPMENT COMPANY - Houston, Texas   1979-1981

System and Programming Manager (1980-1981)
Managed a systems and programming group of ten exempt and non-exempt employees with annual sales of $100 million.

- Managed remote site data processing which supported one $50 million plant in Houston, a $30 million plant in Tyler, and a $20 million plant in England.

Senior System Analyst (1979-1980)

- Created a new work-in-progress system that reduced computer run time by 50%.

UNIVERSITY - University Town, USA   1977-1979

System Analyst, Major Medical Research University

- Designed and programmed a contract bid system used in purchasing supplies and material for the University. This system was written to comply with state regulations.
- Designed and programmed a sports medicine system used in analysis and prevention of high school football injuries. The data from this system is helping coaches and trainers cut down on the number of football injuries.

S & S CONSTRUCTION - Birmingham, Alabama   1973-1977

Programmer Analyst

- Designed and programmed reports used for weekly, monthly and yearly payroll processing. This system was used to pay construction workers in multiple states working on multiple jobs and resulted in full compliance of state and federal payroll laws.
- Programmed a customer master profile system for AAA of Alabama which increased revenues $50,000 per year.

EDUCATION

Have attained 70 credit hours toward data processing degree and planning to complete B.S. degree by Fall, 1988.

HARDWARE

Mainframe: IBM 4341/VM/VSI, IBM 3033/MVS, IBM 370/158/MVS, IBM S/38 Model 12, IBM System 34, IBM System 3, Honeywell 2050A/1250, Honeywell Level 6

Micros: Datapoint, IMB PC, IBM PC/XT, IBM PC/AT, Compaq, Novell Network

SOFTWARE

COBOL, RPG, RPG II, CICS, IMS, Focus, TSO, SPF, Panvalet, Syncsort, Librarian, CMS, DMS, Mark IV, OS/JCL, Roscoe, Total, MSA/GL/AP/Payroll, CARMS A/R, ANSYS CAD System, ISAM, VSAM, DYL260/280

11) FINANCE

NAME
Address
Home #
Business #

OBJECTIVE

Chief Financial Officer

SUMMARY

Financial executive with over 20 years of progressive experience as Controller, Treasurer, and CFO in manufacturing, distribution and service businesses ranging from $50 million to $650 million sales. Four years with "Big 8" CPA firm.

PROFESSIONAL EXPERIENCE

GRANT COMPANY - Houston, Texas   1980 to Present

Vice President, Finance (Chief Financial Officer) (1982 to Present)
Reporting to the CEO, responsible for vice president and manager level positions including strategic planning and management information systems. Member of board of directors.

- Developed a strong working relationship with the CEO and line management to contribute to increased sales of over $650 million internationally.

- Restructured and upgraded financial organization, improving timeliness, accuracy and consistency of information; reduced employees from 100 to 80 while business was growing.

- Evaluated and changed reported financial information required to run the business resulting in fewer, more concise reports.

- Acted as economic advisor to the management team for purchases, sales and liquidations of more than 20 businesses worth over $325 million.

- Brought credibility to MIS program by organizing the department and developing and adhering to long-range plans.

- Administered preparation of SEC Information Return for public spin-off of business to company shareholders; presented plans to financial community.

- Saved over $1 million of taxes annually by restructuring corporate legal entity; reduced foreign taxes over $4 million.

- Directed a change in computer technology saving over $700,000 annually.

- Designed and negotiated a unique financing arrangement resulting in a $62 million sale and high ROI.

194

Vice President/Treasurer (1980-1982)

- Rearranged banking system to improve cash flow; strengthened local banking; and developed foreign and U.S. short and long-term credit lines.

- Decentralized cash processing which reduced employment and increased control.

- Consolidated pension fund management into master trust program which reduced paper work and improved administrative control.

- Developed a capital control manual resulting in improved project decision making process.

DIVERSIFIED CORPORATION   1965-1980

Group Controller (Chief Financial Officer) - Petroleum Group, Houston, Texas (1977-1980)

- Directed Divisional Controllers through a dotted line organization, consistently realizing annual objectives.

- Directed major manufacturing and distribution systems development programs completing them on time and within budgeted cost.

- Developed a capacity analysis model used to support capital expenditures which eliminated overstatement of projected ROI.

Division Controller - Petroleum Division, Houston, Texas (1971-1977)

- Developed financial, administrative and system functions to accommodate growth of business from $35 million to $200 million. Expanded manufacturing from four to ten locations, four foreign.

Division Controller - Packing Division, Green Bay, Wisconsin (1968-1971)

- Participated in a plant wide work-measurment program, and implemented it in the controller's department.

- Designed and implemented accounting, reporting and control systems in new foreign plant.

Accounting Manager/Operations Controller - Green Bay Plant
Green Bay, Wisconsin (1965-1968)

EDUCATION

CPA, State of Michigan - 1965
BBA (Accounting and Economics) Northern Michigan University - 1962

PROFESSIONAL AFFILIATIONS

Financial Executive Institute
American Institute of Certified Public Accountants
National Association of Accountants

12) TREASURY

NAME
Address
Home #
Business #

OBJECTIVE

Treasurer

SUMMARY

Over twenty years of responsible positions within the functional areas of treasury and finance.

PROFESSIONAL EXPERIENCE

BRIGGSWELL, INC. - Omaha, Nebraska   1983-Present

Vice President and Treasurer

- Developed an industry expert program to enhance investor relations in which recognition of company expertise became known.   Institutions now own over 58% and trade over 93% of the company's stock.

- Prepared and delivered all presentations to the Finance Committee of the Board of Directors on financial plan, policy, and funding arrangements.

- Negotiated and closed faster than any U.S. corporation a large $2.5 billion acquisition loan.

- Saved $1.2 million in interest cost by purchasing "interest rate cap" for seasonal working capital borrowings.

- Served as director of 32 domestic and foreign subsidiaries including captive insurance and finance companies.

- Evaluated leverage buyout, "shark-repellants", asset sales and major acquisition alternatives which resulted in recommendation of $2.3 billion acquisition which ultimately was accomplished.

- Earned a superior investment return on $400 million investment portfolio as measured by SEI.

- Revised asset mix guidelines reallocating increasingly risky real estate investments.

- Initiated the utilization of immunization and indexing concepts.

THE CONTINENTAL CORPORATION - Houston, Texas   1979-1983

Assistant Vice President for Corporate Finance

- Reviewed all non-operating cash uses exceeding $25 million for strategic implications, likelihood of exceeding minimum investment return objectives and ability of current management to successfully implement project resulting in sound capital investment and acquisition decisions.

- Negotiated 35 loans, 18 with multi-bank syndicates, all having more favorable pricing to the Company.

- Borrowed over $200 million in Euro-currencies to finance pipe and ship purchases, and developed foreign currency hedging programs which protected over $40 million in currency gains.

GARDNER-TUCSON COMPANY - Dallas, Texas   1974-1979

Treasurer

- Developed and implemented the methodology for measuring and managing foreign currency exposure which during 1978 resulted in a $2.3 million after-tax reduction of the cost of covering worldwide economic exposure.

- Strengthened the process used to invest extra cash in the United States, Canada and England. During 1978 the domestic portfolio achieved a return 38 basis points above the top fund in the Donoghue Money Fund Report.

- Conceived and successfully implemented an advanced computerized cash management system which was subsequently purchased by one of the largest international banks.

- Conceptualized and directed the implementation of cash disbursement techniques which reduced working investment by $12 million.

OILPORT CORPORATION - New York, New York   1967-1974

Held a series of progressively challenging positions involving corporate finance, cash management, international financial management, new business financing, financial and investment planning.

MILITARY

Captain, EDP Systems Manager, U.S. Army Materiel Command, 1965-1967

EDUCATION

MBA in Finance, Wharton School of The University of Pennsylvania, 1963-1965
BBA in Accounting, University of Notre Dame, 1959-1963

NAME
Address
Home #
Business #

OBJECTIVE

Accounting Manager

SUMMARY

Over fifteen years of diversified accounting and financial experience with extensive involvement in financial reporting, cost accounting, inventory control, budgeting and forecasting.

PROFESSIONAL EXPERIENCE

STEEL & WIRE COMPANY - Houston, Texas   1982-Present

Accounting Manager/Controller
Managed group office and plant accounting functions for $85 million manufacturer operating five plants. Supervised ten employees in accounting, data processing, credit and collections.

- Improved inventory control and cash management by developing a Lotus 123 financial planning and forecasting model, which improved forecasting productivity by 300% and eliminated two clerical positions.

- Converted five decentralized, manual general ledger/accounts payable systems to a centralized computer system (IBM System 36 and MAPICS software), eliminating four plant accountants.

- Reduced month-end close from fifteen to eight working days and year-end audit field work by three weeks.

- Maintained $7 million receivables balance below 40-days outstanding and accurate valuation of inventories which averaged $10 million.

- Invested daily cash balances which ranged in size up to $2 million.

- Supervised preparation and review of monthly divisional and consolidated statements and prepared annual divisional and consolidated budgets and forecasts and monthly forecast revisions.

B & R COMPANY - Houston, Texas   1981-1982

Manager, General Accounting
Supervised fifteen people in general accounting, sales invoicing, fixed assets and accounts payable.

- Coordinated period close and preparation of financial package for management in nine working days.

- Coordinated preparation of quarterly balance sheet forecasts and monthly review of actual-to-forecast reports as well as preparation of fiscal year-end financial package, audit schedules and account reconciliations for auditor review.

- Served as member of project team which evaluated and chose new general ledger and accounts payable software to simplify accounting systems.
- Wrote and implemented accounting control procedures resulting in improved systems.

MED LABORATORIES - Houston, Texas   1977-1981

<u>Cost Accounting Supervisor</u>

- Coordinated purchasing, engineering, and manufacturing data for annual preparation of standard cost buildups.
- Served as member of MRP implementation team which contributed to improved material planning.
- Converted standard-cost accounting system from service bureau to online, time-sharing system resulting in a more efficient system.
- Supervised semiannual physical inventories and reconciliation to general ledger and provided monthly cost analysis on closed work orders.
- Provided cost accounting support for ECO, design review, and new product sign-off meetings.
- Prepared year-end audit and tax packages and assisted in preparing annual plans and updates.

INTERNATIONAL, INC. - Houston, Texas   1975-1977

<u>Financial Manager</u>

- Supervised payroll, accounts payable, and accounts receivable.
- Supervised transition from manual ledger and payables to service bureau resulting in more cost efficient system.
- Maintained accrual and cash books on a job cost and departmental basis.
- Managed $350,000 revolving line of credit and prepared cash forecasts.
- Prepared year-end audit package for audit.

MCM, Inc. - Houston, Texas   1973-1975

<u>Tax Accountant</u>

- Accrued and paid sales taxes and property taxes to 25 states.
- Prepared Canadian federal tax return and assisted with U.S. federal returns.

EDUCATION

CPA, 1981
MS, University of Houston, Houston, Texas, 1976
BS, Spring Hill College, Mobile, Alabama, 1970

NAME
Address
Home #
Business #

OBJECTIVE

Director Investor Relations

SUMMARY

Over twenty-five years experience in financial operations of which the last eight years have been concentrated in investor relations.

PROFESSIONAL EXPERIENCE

DYNAMICS COMPANY - Houston, Texas   1984-Present

Manager of Investor Relations

Managed the company's investor relations program with major emphasis directed towards the institutional investor and sell side analysts. Planned and prepared management presentations for the domestic and European financial communities and assisted in the preparation of the quarterly and annual reports as well as other financial communications.

- Directed all phases of the program which was ranked number three by the financial analysts federation.

- Interfaced with sell side analysts and potential institutional investors resulting in increased published research by major and regional brokerage firms and an expanded institutional shareholder base.

- Maintained contact with holders of more than 100,000 shares; monitored stockholdings on a daily basis receiving direct feedback for management on the major holders' position and any unusual accumulation or sale of the company's stock.

- Initiated investor relations program directed toward the individual investor which resulted in less than 20% of the stock being held by institutions.

H & H COMPANY - Salt Lake City, Utah   1978-1984

Manager, Corporate Financial Relations

Responsible for the development and implementation of an investor relations program directed towards the individual investor.

- Cultivated analyst contacts with major sell side wire houses and regional retail brokerage firms expanding the company's retail shareholder base.

- Originated advertising and corporate profiles on the company in Research Magazine which generated over 25,000 requests for additional information on the company and a substantial increase in the value of the stock.

- Recommended two stock splits which brought the price of the stock down to more attractive levels for the retail investor and gave the stock wider distribution.

SHARP CORPORATION - Houston, Texas   1963-1978

<u>Assistant Treasurer</u> (1977-1978)

Managed the cash movement and short term investments of the corporation and its subsidiaries.

- Participated in the installation and managed a remote disbursing system creating substantial savings through the utilization of additional float.
- Invested up to $400 million in excess funds generated by the remote disbursing system which made a substantial contribution to net income.

<u>Assistant Treasurer, Interstate Corporation</u> (1973-1977)

Responsible for all banking payroll and debt administration functions.

- Transferred all Interstate Treasury operations to Houston, merging them with corporate operations resulting in stronger centralized control.
- Initiated the repurchase of debt and preferred stock in the open market satisfying sinking fund requirements and earning rates of return in excess of 20%.

<u>Senior Budget Analyst</u> (1970-1973)

Responsible for the consolidated cash function of Interstate Corporation.

- Implemented a new corporate cash forecast establishing more effective cash management.

<u>Budget and Rate Analyst</u> (1963-1970)

Assisted in preparation of rate filings and the corporate budget; participated in a newly formed special studies group evaluating potential acquisitions.

EDUCATION

B.A. Business Administration and Banking, Colorado College,
Colorado Springs, Colorado - 1961

PROFESSIONAL AFFILIATIONS

National Investor Relations Institute
American Gas Association; Investor Relations Subcommittee

15) RISK MANAGEMENT

NAME
Address
Home #
Business #

OBJECTIVE

Director, Corporate Risk Management

SUMMARY

Over twenty years of progressively responsible positions in casualty insurance and risk management.

PROFESSIONAL EXPERIENCE

TOP, INC. - Houston, Texas   1971-Present

Manager, Casualty Insurance and Claims (1982-Present)

Formulated corporate policy on insurance and loss control. Negotiated with brokers and carriers when insurance was selected as the risk management vehicle. Reviewed and negotiated contracts to assure proper insurance and indemnity provisions to protect the corporation.

- Saved more than $2 million in annual insurance premiums by recommending self-insurance to several operations.

- Served as corporate contact for brokers and underwriters of primary casualty, excess liability, directors' and officers' liability, pension trust liability and comprehensive crime coverage resulting in acceptable premiums through disclosure of appropriate underwriting information.

- Interpreted coverage for insurance contacts in operating divisions, assuring that complex claims were reported and monitored for prompt settlement or appropriate defense.

- Drafted "Pro Forma" standardized commercial contracts for use throughout the corporation thereby reducing exposure to litigation.

- Reviewed proposed state and federal legislation for its impact on the company's operations and developed the corporate position for the governmental affairs department to assure that legislation detrimental to the company's interest was opposed and legislation favorable to the company actively supported.

- Instituted computer generated premium and loss information program interfacing with insurance carrier's claim data base; program enabled machine tracking of high value/high risk cases and produced summaries of losses by line of insurance such as product liability to determine its potential effect on the exhaustion of the policy aggregate.

- Authorized the corporate "Accident Reporting, Claims and Insurance Manual", improving and standardizing communication between the corporate office and operating divisions on insurance and claim activity.

- Developed and presented contract review classes for staff, improving ability to evaluate commercial contracts and assure adequate protection for the company.

- Directed all aspects of claims against the corporation, working closely with staff attorneys as well as outside counsel, which resulted in vigorous defense of questionable claims and reasonable settlement of valid claims to save loss expense.

Senior Administrator Insurance and Loss Control Department (1975-1982)

Responsible for administering the entire corporate casualty department.

- Initiated a premium allocation system which assured that each operating entity was charged fairly based on its loss history.

- Originated a guaranteed cost premium allocation basis enabling the divisions to close books on insurance expense annually.

Administrator Property and Casualty Department (1971-1975)

Responsible for the Corporate Casualty Insurance Programs.

- Formulated corporate policy and procedures concerning casualty insurance.

CASUALTY & SURETY COMPANY   1966-1971

Held a series of progressively challenging positions in underwriting.

EDUCATION

B.A., University of Texas, Austin, Texas - 1965

PROFESSIONAL AFFILIATIONS

Deputy Member, Risk and Insurance Management Society (RIMS), Houston Chapter
Member of Risk Management Council, Machinery and Allled Products Institute
Workers' Compensation Specialist, National Governmental Affairs Committee, RIMS
Co-Chairman, Membership & Finance Committee, Texas Self - Insurance Association
Member, Legislative Drafting Committee, Texas Self - Insurance Association
Director, Texas Self - Insurance Association

CIVIC ACTIVITIES

Board member, Volunteers in Assistance,
TOP, Inc., Houston, Texas

State of Texas Certificate of Appreciation
"for exceptional and distinguished volunteer service,"
April 1981

16) PURCHASING

NAME
Address
Home #
Business #

OBJECTIVE

Purchasing Manager

SUMMARY

Over eight years of broad based Materials Management experience in Purchasing and Planning for an international industrial manufacturing corporation.

PROFESSIONAL EXPERIENCE

DENVER SUPPLY COMPANY, DIVISION OF ATC, INC.   1979-Present

Purchasing Agent (1983-Present)

- Planned, directed, reviewed and controlled the activities of the Purchasing Department servicing the entire plant (500 employees, maximum).

- Developed new sources of supplies and conducted vendor negotiations resulting in benefits favorable to the company.

- Adopted aggressive position with vendors resulting in on-time delivery performance improvement of 15% and quality performance improvement of 25%.

Senior Production Planner (1982-1983)

- Supervised Production Planning Department.

- Planned and controlled all product lines manufactured at plant for optimal operations.

- Managed customer on-time deliveries which increased performance from 70% to 80%.

- Wrote departmental procedure manual for Materials Management resulting in more consistent application of procedures.

Planner - Special Projects (1981-1982)

- Coordinated effort between Materials Management and Systems which further advanced departmental computerization.

- Originated requests to improve systems.

- Trained Materials Management employees in computer system applications.

<u>Assistant Production Planner, Order Coordinator</u> (1979-1981)

• Planned and controlled product line by matching production to sale order requirements resulting in reduction of past due backlog.

• Performed all phases of Production Planning: released orders for production, placed purchase requisitions, initiated new work orders, etc.

• Achieved cost reductions of approximately $350,000 through negotiations with vendors.

• Conceived and developed new purchase order numbering system which identified vendors by purchase order number and improved expediting efficiency by 75%.

• Researched and developed overseas vendors which reduced plant raw material cost by 50% - 60%.

EDUCATION

M.B.A., University of Houston, Houston, Texas
Concentration: Accounting
Grade Point Average - 3.79

B.B.A., University of Houston
Concentration: Operations Management
Grade Point Average - 3.89

PROFESSIONAL AFFILIATIONS

American Production and Inventory Control Society
Served on Board of Directors 1981 and 1982 - Houston Chapter
Served as Secretary and President - University of Houston Student Chapter

National Association of Purchasing Managers

HONORS

CPIM - Certified in Production and Inventory Management - Fellow Level
CPM - Certified Purchasing Manager
Mensa
Received B.B.A. Magna Cum Laude
Beta Gamma Sigma and Phi Kappa Phi Honor Societies as an undergraduate

17) ENGINEERING

NAME
Address
Home #
Business #

OBJECTIVE

Engineering Manager

SUMMARY

Over thirty years experience in process plant engineering; the last eleven years in the management of major projects. Extensive experience in pressure vessel sizing and design and process flow sheet development.

PROFESSIONAL EXPERIENCE

THE RUSTIN COMPANY - Los Angeles, California   1956-Present

Engineering Manager (1973-1976 and 1980-Present)
Managed the engineering effort on assigned projects.

- Provided the technical direction and management skills required to achieve the goals established for projects.

- Assured that projects were efficiently engineered, designed and controlled against budget and schedule.

- Audited the work to ensure adherence to technical quality and conformance to specifications and regulations.

- Served as the spokesman for engineering in technical discussions with clients, vendors, other Rustin operations, and third parties.

- Wrote VSPC Basic and IBM PC Basic programs which promoted the use of computers in the group and resulted in more effective project management.

- Directed up to 10 Engineering Managers and Project Engineers on assigned projects.

- Worked on an integrated refinery project which included desalting, hydrodesulfurization, heavy oil cracking, HF alkylation, and dimersol units; ethylene units; distillate Ultrafiner; Ultracker; Ultraformer; Alumina Digestion; and proposals for Delayed Cokers, Heavy Oil Crackers, Fluid-bed Catalytic Crackers, Asphalt Residual Treating units and Synthetic Fuels units.

FCCU Task Force Leader (1979-1980)
Responsible for finding and solving potential problems in 10 catalytic cracking units which were about to start up.

- Developed the plan and program for systematically auditing the units for potential problems.

- Directed the work of 10 process and mechanical engineers assigned to the team.

- Recommended changes in work procedures and technology to avoid future problems.

Project Manager (1977-1979)
Responsible for leading the company-wide effort on assigned project.

- Established the goals for the project.

- Determined the staffing needs and controls required to ensure the project met contractual, cost, financial, schedule, procurement, engineering, construction contractor, and operating requirements.

- Modified plans, procedures and work activities when necessary which overcame obstructions to project progress.

- Represented the company when interfacing with the client on contractual matters.

- Worked on two side-by-side FCCU revamps, two new Orthoflow FCCU's, and a Phillips HF Alkylation Unit.

Systems Engineer (1972-1973)
Converted a process flow scheme into a mechanical reality.

Process Engineer (1967-1972)
Created the detailed process design of ethylene plants.

Vessel Analytical Engineer (1962-1966)
Responsible for converting process data for vessels to a physical entity.

Vessel Mechanical Engineer (1956-1962)
Transformed a vessel analytical design to a mechanical entity.

EDUCATION

BCHE, The City College of New York, New York, New York - 1950

PROFESSIONAL REGISTRATION

Registered Professional Engineer in Texas, Louisiana, and New York State.

PROFESSIONAL ASSOCIATIONS

American Institute of Chemical Engineers, Member

18) OPERATIONS

NAME
Address
Home #
Business #

OBJECTIVE

Operations Management

SUMMARY

Over twelve years experience in operations and engineering management with specialization in the contract drilling industry.

PROFESSIONAL EXPERIENCE

SEACOAST DRILLING COMPANY, INC.   1974-Present

Vice President of Operations - Houston, Texas (1981-Present)
Managed the operational performance, financial results and personnel of four division offices and fourteen onshore and offshore drilling units.

- Served as director of six subsidiary companies, domestic and international, with total revenues of $100 million.

- Developed a preventive maintenance program and support group which reduced daily maintenance costs by 25%.

- Redesigned and implemented a safety program which reduced lost time accidents by 60%.

- Developed and maintained client contacts that resulted in a 72% utilization rate over the last three years.

- Directed exploratory trip, feasibility study, contract negotiations, and mobilization of National 80 UE land rig to Columbia, resulting in an annual revenue of $3.5 million.

- Participated in negotiating for and securing a three-year contract for a jack-up drilling unit in Brazil, resulting in annual revenues of $12.4 million.

- Supervised four operational managers and rig crews of 500 operating from offices in Brazil, Columbia, California and Louisiana.

- Participated in the installation of a Hay System for job rating and a Performance, Planning and Evaluation program for all operational management level personnel resulting in improved performance evaluation.

- Developed an operations engineer training program designed to take recent college graduate engineers through formal on-the-rig training resulting in improved preparation for operations management positions.

- Developed and presented annual merit budgets, training requirements, and career plans for all operational management level personnel resulting in substantially improved organizational development.

General Manager - Houston, Texas (1980-1981)
Supervised three operations managers and three operating offices located in Natal, Brazil; Macae, Brazil; and Bakersfield, California. Operations included one jack-up drilling unit, one semi-submersible drilling unit offshore Brazil, and three 20,000 feet land rigs in California. Drilling contracts for these units produced annual revenues of $30 million and required operational staffs of 25 people and rig crews of 200.

- Worked directly with a consulting firm to develop an in-house well control course and school to meet the requirements of the Minerals Management Service.

- Designed the specifications for and negotiated with the manufacturer for the purchase of a Simtran DS-100 well control simulator resulting in substantially improved operations.

Drilling Superintendent - Lafayette, Louisiana (1979-1980)
Managed the daily operational results of one jack-up, one self-contained platform, and one land drilling unit.

- Supervised six toolpushers and drilling crews of 125.

- Prepared operating budgets and capital budgets for these three units; approved all expenditures and monitored daily cost on these units to ensure operations within budget.

Senior Engineer - Houston, Texas (1974-1979)
Participated in expansion of Seacoast rig fleet from seven drilling units to fourteen. Project Engineer on location in shipyard during construction of one semi-submersible drilling unit, one jack-up drilling unit, two minimal space platform drilling units, and three 20,000 ft. land drilling units. Total capital of these projects was $63.5 million.

- Developed specifications, solicited bids, evaluated proposals, and purchased equipment for these units within budget.

- Served as Project Engineer during biannual dry-docking of tender units and during shipyard repair of one semi-submersible and two jack-up drilling units.

- Participated in preparation of bids for potential drilling contracts by performing engineering cost studies for platform and jack-up drilling units to maximize profitability.

EDUCATION

B.S., Mechanical Engineering, University of Texas, Austin, Texas - 1974

PROFESSIONAL AFFILIATIONS

Director, International Association of Drilling Contractors, 1983-Present

19) MANUFACTURING

NAME
Address
Home#
Business #

OBJECTIVE

Manufacturing Manager

SUMMARY

Over twenty years of management experience including: Production, purchasing, stores, receiving, sales, accounting, quality control, planning and scheduling.

PROFESSIONAL EXPERIENCE

MONSOON INDUSTRIES, INC. - Tulsa, Oklahoma   1980-Present

General Manager, Mesh Plant (1982-Present)

- Managed a $13 million annual operating budget in the mesh plant with 100 employees.

- Increased annual production from 20,000 tons to 42,000 tons utilizing the same equipment while reducing personnel by 10% which was a result of better planning and scheduling with less downtime.

- Reduced manufacturing cost by 25% over a two-year period.

- Implemented a quality control program which reduced customer complaints to near zero and resulted in over 50% decrease in product rejects.

- Established spare parts store room for control of critical equipment replacement parts resulting in a 30% increase in equipment reliability.

- Initiated and supervised modifications to existing equipment which increased production of a broader product range.

Director of Purchasing (1980-1982)

- Organized purchasing from three different companies into a central purchasing department with procurements in excess of $35 million.

- Established and wrote a policies and procedures manual for purchasing and receiving which resulted in improved standardization.

- Developed new sources of supply and achieved significant cost reductions through negotiations with vendors on larger volume.

- Purchased all material for three manufacturing plants and 21 branches including resale of material not manufactured by Monsoon.

- Managed the receiving departments at two manufacturing plants.

210

CORE INDUSTRIES - Charlotte, North Carolina   1978-1980

Corporate Pilot

- Transported corporate executives and company personnel on company aircraft.

- Arranged travel, hotel and limousines for corporate executives.

- Performed various accounting assignments including reconciliation of bank statements and expense reports between flights.

TRIANGLE TEXAS STEEL - Beaumont, Texas   1973-1978

General Manager, Office Services (1976-1978)

- Initiated, established, and maintained a central record keeping system for accounting, purchasing, and engineering which resulted in improved management control.

- Approved purchases of office equipment, supplies and forms which ensured smooth operations within budget.

Assistant Director of Purchasing (1973-1976)

- Involved in establishing purchasing and receiving procedures in a new $150 million steel mill.

- Developed sources for domestic and foreign purchasing of $50 million in equipment and spare parts.

MARIO OIL COMPANY - Houston, Texas   1963-1973

General Manager

- Managed all aspects of heating oil business including sales, accounting, personnel, planning and scheduling resulting in profitable operations.

MILITARY

U.S. Naval (Reserve) Active Duty: 1959-1961

EDUCATION

Columbia Commercial College, Columbia, South Carolina -
Two years in business administration with concentration in accounting

Miller Aviation School, Columbia, South Carolina -
Flight Instructor - MEL, DFI, CFI-I, CFI-MEL

Aero Flight, Florence, South Carolina - Commercial Pilot - Instrument

Winyah Aviation, Georgetown, South Carolina - Private Pilot

Beech Aircraft, B-100 Turbo Prop School

20) QUALITY ASSURANCE

NAME
Address
Home #
Business #

OBJECTIVE

Quality Assurance Manager

SUMMARY

Over fifteen years Quality Management experience in fabrication environments including eleven years as a Certified Quality Engineer. Eight years experience in computerized Quality Service.

PROFESSIONAL EXPERIENCE

HYDRAX COMPANY - Milwaukee, Wisconsin   1982-Present

Quality Engineer

- Established statistical process controls for design, manufacturing and product analysis which improved productivity and quality conformance.

- Tested, statistically analyzed, and approved over $40 million of capital equipment which ensured manufacturing capabilities.

- Developed statistical software logic for internal electronic probes thereby reducing cycle times by 25%.

- Established multi-plant computerized quality reporting system which reduced management report time lag from days to hours.

- Developed X Bar and R charts for machine operators which reduced internal quality failure cost by 10%.

- Initiated use of statistical software on personal computer which increased data analysis capability and reporting by over 100%.

OXELL RIG & EQUIPMENT COMPANY - Tulsa, Oklahoma   1980-1982

Senior Quality Assurance Engineer (1982)

- Supervised three quality technicians who provided MRB documentation and discrepant material dispositions resulting in a 25% reduction in inspection rejects.

Quality Assurance Engineer (1980-1982)

- Integrated computer business operating system into multi-plant environment allowing consolidation of $1 million of duplicate inventory.

- Justified and installed CMM which resulted in a reduction in scrap cost of $100,000.

212

STONING INTERNATIONAL - Jackson, Tennessee   1979-1980
Power Tool Division

Senior Quality Assurance Engineer

- Participated in inventory reduction out-sourcing project resulting in unprofitable product line write off.

- Developed statistically designed experiments resulting in 40% savings in gear hobbing line.

NATIONAL STERILIZER COMPANY - Montgomery, Alabama   1978-1979

Quality Control Engineer

- Expanded quality departmental operating procedures to meet Federal GMP requirements and UL audits.

- Developed customer response check list which ensured product acceptance.

AFFILIATED PRODUCTS CORPORATION - Opelika, Alabama   1975-1978

Quality Control Manager

- Controlled $100,000 budget for two departments during rapid sales expansion.

- Trained floor inspectors in metric conversions.

BMY CYCLE DIVISION - Little Rock, Arkansas   1971-1975

Quality Supervisor (1971-1975)

- Initiated visual defect coding for line repairmen reducing rework cost by 25%.

Tooling Engineer (1971)

- Designed assembly fixture which reduced frame rework cost by 10%.

EDUCATION

Bachelor of Science in Industrial Management,
University of Arkansas, Fayetteville, Arkansas - 1971

University of Arkansas, Little Rock, Arkansas, graduate work in statistics.

PROFESSIONAL

Certified Quality Engineer, American Society for Quality Control, 1974
Recertification, 1977, 1980, 1983

Member American Society for Quality Control - 1972

NAME
Address
Home #
Business #

OBJECTIVE

Inventory Manager

SUMMARY

Over 14 years experience in organizing and coordinating activities associated with the development, procurement, warehousing, distribution, and maintenance of company and customer inventories. Skilled in developing the objectives of a materials organization to support the needs of other company organizations, such as manufacturing and sales.

PROFESSIONAL EXPERIENCE

AMERICAN SUPPLY COMPANY - Austin, Texas   1975-Present

Supervisor - Repair Parts Warehouse (1983-Present)

Managed a repair parts warehouse consisting of three persons and a $3.5 million inventory.

- Initiated warehouse operating procedures while adhering to company budget restrictions, reducing inventory by 44%.

- Compiled and evaluated repair parts information from six service centers reducing a proposed inventory by 50%.

- Developed operating objectives with strong emphasis on company goals and which incurred no lost time accidents.

- Provided timely repair parts analysis, allowing company president to announce new warehouse service to customers, which netted $670,000 in annual sales.

- Conducted the first computer aided physical inventory at this facility, reducing time requirement by 40%.

Materials Supervisor - Machinery Centers (1981-1983)

Coordinated with company's materials manager and sales manager all activities involving machinery center rig packages.

- Managed the materials activities of five fabrication centers across the country in coordination with the sales organization which effectively met customer demands for custom-designed rig packages.

- Maintained up-to-date equipment scheduling information instrumental in the completion of 45 rigs over a one-year period.

214

- Interacted with company's information systems specialists to obtain company-wide computer visibility of the center's $8 million repair parts inventory.

- Reduced excess inventory at machinery centers by $1 million a year through computer visibility and circulation of surplus lists.

Supervisor, Materials - Machinery Center (1975-1981)

Supervised material department of 10 people and an average inventory of $15 million. Purchased rig package components and maintained work order files.

- Coordinated shipping and receiving activities with fabrication and service departments allowing for the completion of an average of 10 to 12 drilling rigs per year.

- Developed a specific warehouse layout for the efficient retrieval of assembly materials leading to a 14% increase in job profit margins.

- Initiated monthly safety meetings for department which solicited employee participation resulting in only one lost-time accident in five years.

- Developed specific job descriptions for all positions within the department resulting in better communication of responsibilities and improved personnel placement.

F.W. SHEPHERD COMPANY - Lafayette, Louisiana   1974-1975

Assistant Manager

Supervised operations of eight departments in the store with total inventory of $500,000.

- Purchased and maintained seasonal merchandise with annual budget of $85,000.

- Erected store displays and handled in-store sales promotions resulting in improved sales.

- Chaired store shrinkage committee, resulting in a 6% drop in lost merchandise.

- Interfaced directly with customers regarding merchandise disputes resulting in favorable resolution and improved customer relations.

EDUCATION

B.S. Business Administration - 1973
Course Major: Marketing
University of Southwestern Louisiana
Lafayette, Louisiana

NAME
Address
Home#
Office #

OBJECTIVE

Geologist

SUMMARY

Over seven years of experience in development and exploration petroleum geology. Diverse background with an emphasis on economic evaluation of prospects and operational responsibilities.

PROFESSIONAL EXPERIENCE

BEST PETROLEUM COMPANY   1981-Present

<u>Staff Development Geologist</u> - Houston, Texas (1984-Present)

Participated in field task force assigned to South Pelto Field, Offshore Terrebonne Parish, Louisiana. Integrated geologic information with engineering and geophysical data; interpreted depositional and post-depositional geologic history to reconstruct development of field and identify remaining prospects.

- Recommended sale of marginal properties and reconditioning or plugging of marginal producers resulting in substantial cost savings.

- Evaluated joint interest ventures, farm-in and farm-out proposals submitted by other companies meeting all deadlines.

- Performed well data evaluations on exploratory and development wells both onshore and offshore; recommended completion or plugging and abandonment to management.

- Participated in partner meetings with domestic and foreign oil companies and wrote notes documenting results of meetings.

- Provided information on drilling wells to management and partners contributing to sound management decisions.

- Specified needed services and recommended service companies to be used on company operated wells resulting in optimum operations.

- Coordinated West Texas activity between the regional office in Odessa and the division office in Houston which ensured smooth operations.

Staff Exploration Geologist, Economist Specialist - Houston, Texas (1982-1984)

Participated on team of landmen, engineers, geologists and G&GL personnel to prepare economic analyses of proposed development and exploration wells in the eastern division to maximize profitability.

- Prepared farm-out analyses with back-in options and conversions from ORRI to WI.

- Assisted in preparation of quarterly and annual reports reflecting economic results of drilling operations.

- Created and maintained a computer system with FOCUS to track the status of farm-out wells and organize information into reports.

Staff Geologist - Odessa, Texas (1981-1982)

Performed wellsite duties on development and exploratory wells drilled in the Permian Basin Region.

- Correlated logs, constructed cross-sections and updated maps to reflect the results of drilling.

- Represented company at Railroad Commission hearing on Hobo Field in Borden County, Texas; prepared necessary exhibits and supervised drafting.

- Assisted R&D project to create a natural gas liquids storage cavern in southeastern New Mexico.

Geologist-in-Training Program - Tulsa, Oklahoma (1981)

Trained in subsurface and surface mapping methods, geophysics, well log interpretation and quality control, stratigraphic methods, computer applications, economics and reserve estimation, contracts, and hydrodynamics.

- Contributed to both overseas and domestic projects during assignment in the corporate office.

EDUCATION

Bachelor of Science Degree in Geology
University of Texas-Permian Basin - 1980

Associate in Science Degree
Odessa College, Odessa, Texas - 1978

Associate in Arts Degree - Business Administration
Odessa College, Odessa, Texas - 1978

23) HOSPITAL ADMINISTRATION

NAME
Address
Home #
Business #

OBJECTIVE

Hospital Administrator

SUMMARY

Cost conscious administrator with over twelve (12) years of broad based health care experience. Possess a unique blend of interpersonal skills, financial/ management accomplishments and clinical experience.

PROFESSIONAL EXPERIENCE

MEDICAL HOSPITAL - Houston, Texas   1979-Present

Administrative Director of Radiology (1984-Present)

Directed a capital intensive, highly technical, $14 million revenue center with 125 employees and significant medical staff involvement for a tertiary care university hospital licensed for 908 beds.

- Increased contribution margin by over $1,500,000 (22%) in two years by marketing outpatient services and limiting expenses to a 0.7% increase.

- Developed and implemented an accounting structure to detail procedure costs by creating separate revenue and expense reporting for six major radiology product lines.

- Implemented an in-house radiology engineering program which created an $84,000 (11%) positive variance in equipment repair and maintenance expenses for Fiscal 1986.

- Coordinated the planning, acquisition and installation of capital equipment and facility renovation projects which totaled over $10 million including C.T., M.R.I. and Angiography.

- Chaired a hospital task force that developed policies and procedures which improved capital equipment priorities and acquisition decisions.

- Established a comprehensive quality assurance program which involved on-going monitoring by all first-line supervisors and resulted in favorable inspections by the State Health Department, Health Care Financing Administration and the Joint Commission for Accreditation of Hospitals.

- Instituted a comprehensive cross-training program which enhanced service to a patient population of increasing acuity without increasing staffing complement and reduced overtime hours by 21% in two years.

- Participated in a Radiology Workload Measurement Study which established national productivity standards.

<u>Operations Administrator</u> (1983-1984)

Coordinated hospital operations by functioning as the administrative representative to employees, medical staff, news media, law enforcement agencies and other health care institutions.

- Successfully negotiated sensitive transfer arrangements for patients through a Class I Trauma Center with the nation's largest air ambulance system.

- Prepared the hospital for a favorable JCAH inspection by serving on a mock survey team.

- Contributed to top level administrative staff meetings and various hospital committees.

<u>Oncology Research Coordinator</u> (1979-1983)

Managed the administrative and nursing functions of a clinical cancer research program in whole body hyperthermia involving the services of oncology, anesthesiology, vascular surgery and the operating room.

- Planned and coordinated the establishment of an outpatient chemotherapy clinic which improved patient care and reduced treatment costs.

EDUCATION

Masters in Health Care Administration - 1982
Texas Woman's University, Houston, Texas

Bachelor of Science in Nursing (with distinction) - 1979
Cornell University, New York, New York

Bachelor of Arts in Psychology - 1975
Fairfield University, Fairfield, Connecticut

PROFESSIONAL AFFILIATIONS

American College of Health Care Executives
American Hospital Association
Texas Hospital Association
American Health Care Radiology Administrators

LICENSURE

Registered Nurse, State of Texas

24) ENVIRONMENTAL SERVICES

NAME
Address
Home #
Business #

OBJECTIVE

Environmental Services Management

SUMMARY

Over twenty years extensive environmental and general management experience.

PROFESSIONAL EXPERIENCE

ENERGY, INC. - Houston, Texas   1984-Present

Director, Natural Resources

Performed general management responsibilities for Coal Company and Water Company including marketing, engineering, properties and land.

- Directed an extensive coal marketing program resulting in the sale of a 80 million ton coal reserve in a very depressed coal market.

- Formulated a coal lease amendment strategy which resulted in reducing landowner royalty by one-third in over 80% of the leases in a 120 million ton coal deposit.

- Implemented the dismantling of a coal company from 35 employees without a single adverse incident to the company.

- Directed the successful development of one of the largest multi-purpose water rights under intense public and regulatory scrutiny.

COAL COMPANY - Houston, Texas   1978-1984

Chief Engineer

Responsible for the recruitment, hiring and supervision of a staff of engineers and geologists involved in resource evaluation, mine planning and design.

- Managed the preparation and submittal of eight fuel supply proposals to potential industrial and utility customers resulting in favorable contracts.

- Analyzed and acquired computer software for geological modeling, mine planning, and economic analysis of coal properties which resulted in significantly reducing manpower and response time for proposal preparation.

- Planned and managed the development of ten coal deposits from an inferred to a proven reserve status.

ENERGY, INC. - Houston, Texas   1973-1978

<u>Manager, Environmental Affairs</u>

Formulated and implemented policy and conducted corporate wide seminars and meetings on environmental matters.

- Coordinated the development and implementation of Spill Prevention Control and Containment procedures for oil and hazardous material in all company divisions significantly reducing corporate exposure.

- Analyzed and negotiated changes in proposed regulations issued by EPA and State Environmental agencies resulting in manageable compliance.

- Formulated and implemented an internal Environmental Audit Program which has since become standard in the industry.

POWER COMPANY - Houston, Texas   1970-1973

<u>Environmental Engineer</u>

Responsible for business development, conceptual engineering, and technical report writing in the chemical and petroleum industries.

- Consulted with the American Petroleum Institute Environmental Committee on Oil Spill Cleanup Technology contributing to state-of-the-art recommendations.

- Conducted extensive assessment of sulfur oxide scrubbing technology resulting in implementation of the latest techniques.

- Provided extensive expert witness testimony before the Public Utility Commission resulting in favorable representation of the company.

EDUCATION

MS Civil Engineering, New Mexico State University, 1967

BS Civil Engineering, New Mexico State University, 1966

PROFESSIONAL AFFILIATIONS

Professional Engineer, Texas, Louisiana, Pennsylvania

Faculty Advisory Committee, New Mexico State University

Member, Houston Engineering and Scientific Society

NAME
Address
Home #
Business #

OBJECTIVE

Process Consultant

SUMMARY

Over twenty years experience in process development, evaluation, troubleshooting, plant start-ups, and selling ideas to top management. Proven track record of innovation and problem solving.

PROFESSIONAL EXPERIENCE

T & T COMPANY - Omaha, Nebraska   1969-Present

<u>Vice President, Administrative Services</u> (1983-Present)
Directed division with annual budget of $26 million and 500 employees. Total O&M costs lowered 5% in two years. Responsible for: information services, employee relations, strategic planning, technology evaluation, general services.

- Initiated and directed transition from Burroughs to IBM. Introduced new technology which reduced costs and provided management information for deregulating market.

- Completed first comprehensive computer security analysis; developed and tested contingency plan.

- Created an information management team of key company managers which ensured business priorities were met by computer services.

- Controlled cost increases of health plans to less than 5% (projection was 18% per year) by implementing flexible plans and HMO's.

- Organized competitor intelligence and evaluation system which anticipated threats and screened potential acquisition candidates leading to merger.

- Initiated program to build new natural gas markets through new technology; for example, contracted with six Japanese companies to jointly develop and test gas engine heat pumps in U.S. market.

- Managed decentralization of general services from Corporate to division and reduced total facilities cost of $6.5 million by 3%.

<u>Manager, Corporate Planning & Market Research</u> (1980-1983)
Reported to Executive Committee. Responsible for identification, evaluation and reporting of threats and opportunities of new technology.

- Analyzed energy prices, markets and supplies; innovated program to forecast impact of market changes on corporate earnings resulting in improved corporate planning.

<u>Manager, Engineering Planning</u> (1977-1980)
Directed project scoping, evaluations and financial analysis for all major projects.

- Managed start-up of first-of-a-kind polypropylene plant after facility initially failed to operate; capacity and quality brought up to design in five months and plant reached 130% of guarantee in one year.

<u>Director of Chemical Engineering</u> (1974-1977)
Directed process selection and engineering for polypropylene, polyethylene (high density, low density, and linear low density), coal gasification, LNG, natural gas liquids extraction and fractionation, sulfur, and gas treating plants. In charge of coal gasification technology transfer at Lurgi's Frankfurt Office, Sasol, and Westfield, Scotland.

- Convinced top management that licensed polypropylene process would not provide adequate catalyst removal and led development on a crash basis of a new process. Sold the need to use the new process even though plant construction had started resulting in successful plant completion.

<u>Senior Project Engineer</u> (1969-1974)
Headed office in Germany for 600 million lb/year polyethylene technology transfer and new process development. Stayed with project through successful start-up.

CHEMICAL CORPORATION - Hopewell, Virginia; Geismar, Louisiana   1964-1969

Lead process engineer for worldwide fertilizer processes and contractor selection contributing to construction of two grass-roots complexes. Start-up manager for 1000 TPD ammonia plant and offsites. Process engineer for low pressure methanol plant for which a patent was granted in 1968. Lead engineer for Indonesian plant site selection and for process design for MEA, DEA Hot Carbonate, and Selexol acid gas units.

EDUCATION

M.S., Chemical Engineering, University of Arizona - 1963
B.A., Chemistry, Dartmouth College - 1961

PROFESSIONAL

American Institute of Chemical Engineers
American Chemical Society
Gas Research Institute - ITAC Committee
American Gas Association - Advanced Technology Committee

26) AGRIBUSINESS CONSULTING

NAME
Address
Home #
Business #

OBJECTIVE

Agribusiness Consultant

SUMMARY

Over fourteen years professional experience in agricultural consulting and management covering a host of agricultural disciplines on both domestic and foreign operations. A strong background in technical investigations and feasibility studies, with an excellent knowledge of applied agriculture.

PROFESSIONAL EXPERIENCE

GROWTH, INC.   1979-Present

<u>International Agricultural Manager</u> - Houston, Texas (1983-Present)

Investigated international agricultural diversification opportunities requested by company divisions and foreign countries.

- Performed feasibility studies/reports on such topics as land improvement techniques, transportation and marketing, agriculture, leaf protein extraction, speciality crops, as well as grain and row crops to promote company's diversified business activities in various international operations.

- Coordinated on-site collection and reviewed available data through contacts with various ministries; analyzed the political and economical environment to adapt or modify western agricultural operations to meet the requirements and abilities of host countries; and prepared financial projections including rate of return for feasibility studies/business plans.

- Reported to TDP and USAID on progress of five prefeasibility studies and handled billings which resulted in collection of $270,000 fees for successful completion.

- Reviewed and assisted in implementing 200-acre herb and spice project which employed 50 to 75 people on Vieques Island, Puerto Rico.

- Reviewed and assisted in implementing a Tunisan date exportation project which resulted in the utilization of previously unmarketable invert dates.

<u>Project Manager</u> - Sudan, North Africa (1979-1983)

Developed and managed on-site all phases of a Sudan farming operation. Responsibilities included selecting equipment; reclaiming soil; coordinating drilling activities; assembling and installing a lateral move irrigation system; selecting crops; preparing land; recommending fertilization; scheduling irrigation and implementing a financial control system.

- Acted as liaison between government officials, joint venture partner and company which helped to insure a successful operation in a difficult working environment.

- Established safety and preventive maintenance programs for farm equipment which extended the usable life of the equipment an average of five years.

- Trained local farmers in Western technology resulting in their adapting new land leveling and irrigation principles which then allowed them the option to mechanize operations.

- Hosted foreign governmental delegations to advise and promote company objectives.

RESEARCH INSTITUTE - Sultanate of Oman   1977-1979

<u>Farm Manager</u>

Managed government dairy farm, increasing irrigated area from 50 to 550 acres using center pivot and side roll systems and increasing dairy herd from 30 to 200 head.

- Introduced mechanized farming and harvesting techniques to handle the expansion.

- Recommended and received approval to change management from government to private control which turned the farm into a higher producing and more efficient operation.

AGRICULTURAL TECHNOLOGY COMPANY - McCook Nebraska   1974-1977

<u>Consultant/Area Manager</u> - Colorado

Served as consultant to Eastern Colorado farmers building contracted area from 0 to 20,000 acres in three years. Consulting recommendations involved establishment of fertilizer programs; insect scouting for critical level of control; crop variety selection; irrigation scheduling; and equipment calibration.

EDUCATION

B.S., Agronomy
Colorado State University - Ft. Collins, Colorado - 1974

27) PETROLEUM CONSULTING

NAME
Address
Home #
Business #

OBJECTIVE

Petroleum Consultant

SUMMARY

Over thirty years experience in the petroleum industry; the last seventeen in positions of increasing managerial responsibility in operations and engineering.

PROFESSIONAL EXPERIENCE

PETROLEUM COMPANY   1953-Present

Eastern Division Drilling & Production Manager - Houston, Texas
(1981-Present)

Managed technical staff of 62 people with varied disciplines and controlled outlying staffs of 125 technical personnel. Responsible for production of 80,000 barrels of oil and 450 million cubic feet of gas per day; in addition, responsible for 21 gasoline plants processing 500 million cubic feet per day.

- Instituted control of partner operated properties billing our company approximately $25,000,000 per month by developing a speciality group supported by computer and analysis systems not previously in effect. Recovered in excess of $250,000 per year due to revisions.

- Reduced material inventory from $47,000,000 to $32,000,000 by upgrading the quality of the staff and by increasing emphasis on inventory control.

- Supervised evaluation of properties for both purchase and sale valued at over $100,000,000. Initiated and expedited program for disposing of "marginal" properties in order to improve productivity of the staff.

- Started strict monthly capital budget controls for $75-100 million budget with computer printout revised to useable informational format.

- Critically reviewed oil and gas reserves yearly, enabling division to increase amount of reserves 10 percent annually over that previously estimated.

- Improved both written and verbal communications with accounting section, which caught errors and misunderstandings previously missed.

Midcontinent Region Engineering Director - Oklahoma City, Oklahoma
(1976-1981)

Supervised organization of 40 engineers, 20 professionals and 45 skilled workers. Responsible for the design, maintenance, and control of 1200 oil and gas wells, 9 gasoline plants, 72 compressor stations, and 40-60 drilling wells per year, with a capital budget of approximately $25,000,000 per year.

- Upgraded and centralized staff in an extremely competitive job market; handled a 50 percent increase in workload, with just a 20 percent increase in staff.

- Initiated and trained a speciality gas measurement group to reduce unaccountable gas loss of 10,000,000 cubic feet per day by 50 percent.
- Introduced financial control by reorganizing operational and financial data in more informational format and instituting monthly reviews.
- Reduced energy consumption by 5 percent.
- Participated in coordinated effort with corporate staff in design, construction, and start-up of three gasoline plants and over 40 compressor installations.
- Managed drilling programs for 40-60 wells per year to ensure profitable operations.

Oklahoma City District Superintendent - Oklahoma City, Oklahoma (1974-1976)

Supervised a group of 250 operational personnel. Responsible for the production of 10,000 barrels of oil and 60 million cubic feet of gas per day; for 8 gasoline plants and systems processing 125 million cubic feet of gas per day; and for operation of 1 - 3 drilling rigs.

- Instituted cost control measures, which reduced the rate of operating cost increases from approximately 15-20 percent per year to 8-10 percent per year.
- Anticipated increased emphasis on environmental restraints and either upgraded or eliminated facilities that would be affected.
- Started monthly field superintendents' meetings at their field locations which allowed them to share procedures and other information.

Oklahoma City District Engineer - Oklahoma City, Oklahoma (1969-1974)

Supervised a staff of 15 engineers responsible for the design and technical review of both oil and gas production operations and gasoline plant and gas gathering systems operations.

Staff Reservoir Engineer - Bartlesville, Oklahoma (1965-1969)

Analyzed properties for purchase, sale, and contributions to units. Functioned as chairman or member of committees formed to evaluate these projects.

- Served as recruiting and college contact with several universities in Oklahoma, Texas, and California resulting in successful recruiting relationships.

Progressively Responsible Engineering Positions - (1953-1965)

Designed and supervised installation of oil and gas equipment for oil and gas drilling, flowing, pumping, gathering, pipelining, and water flood installations.

EDUCATION

B.S., Petroleum Engineering, University of Tulsa
Tulsa, Oklahoma - 1953

NAME
Address
Home #
Office #

OBJECTIVE

Administrative Assistant

SUMMARY

Over eighteen years of broad-based experience in the secretarial and clerical fields utilizing a variety of office skills including administration of a word processing system. Certified as a Professional Secretary.

PROFESSIONAL EXPERIENCE

KELLER CONSTRUCTORS - Houston, Texas   1983-Present

<u>Senior Secretary to Vice President of Technical Services</u> (1984-Present)

- Provided administrative and secretarial support to technical services staff.
- Composed and managed correspondence and travel arrangements.
- Coordinated transition from IV Phase word processing system to Prime Producer word processing system. Reduced downtime of word processing systems approximately 75% by identifying and resolving problems.
- Restructured and amended training manual to facilitate more effective in-house word processing training resulting in productive use of equipment within one week of training.
- Instructed two secretaries in the Houston office and four secretaries in the Birmingham office in the use of the Prime Producer word processing systems resulting in production on the system within one week of training.
- Trained and supervised temporary personnel in the company's systematic, standardized secretarial functions.
- Reduced costs of departmental office supply purchases by 40% as a result of acquiring source at lower prices.
- Provided word processing to produce subcontract documents, start-up procedures, sales presentations, publications, and estimating efforts to a staff of 25-30.

<u>Secretary, Proposals Department</u> (1983-1984)

- Provided word processing and general secretarial support to proposal and estimating staff of 8-15.

Floater (1983)

- Provided secretarial support in various capacities as needed throughout the company.

TEMPORARY AGENCIES - Houston, Texas   1979-1983

Worked as a temporary for several local agencies in various capacities instituting computerized accounts receivable/benefits systems; seven months as personal line rate/underwriter for agent.

JOHN GREGORY & COMPANY - Houston, Texas   1976-1979

Secretary

- Rated and processed personal lines insurance policies and claims.
- Served as liaison between company and client and assisted in customer accounting/bank reconciliations.

INSURANCE COMPANIES - San Antonio, Texas   1974-1976

Rater/Coder

- Served as policy typist and engineering audit clerk to ensure timely follow-up of agent and policyholder requests.

UNIVERSITY - Houston, Texas   1973-1974

Accounting Clerk II

- Processed invoices to ensure accurate and up-to-date accounts receivable.
- Processed accounts payable invoices to meet payment schedule and obtain discounts; prepared, organized and processed purchase orders for all such invoices.
- Maintained inventory on cardex system, researched vendor statements and composed reconciliation correspondence.

RETAILER, INC. - Houston, Texas   1969-1973

Accounts Payable Clerk/Purchasing Secretary

- Held progressively responsible positions in the accounting department.

EDUCATION

San Jacinto College, Pasadena, Texas - 1985 to Present (40 hours)
San Antonio Jr. College, San Antonio, Texas - 1974-1976 (18 hours)
Insurance Institute of America - 1975-1976 (11A 21 and 11A 22)

PROFESSIONAL

Certified Professional Secretary - May 1985
CPS Society - member

29) SECRETARIAL SUPPORT

NAME
Address
Home #
Business #

OBJECTIVE

Secretary

SUMMARY

Over seventeen years experience in various administrative and secretarial positions including twelve years experience in telecommunications, including telex and PBX operations.

PROFESSIONAL EXPERIENCE

HYSON COMPANY - Denver, Colorado   1980-Present

Quotations Coordinator (1984-Present)

- Coordinated the transfer of all material and equipment between various company locations resulting in timely and cost-effective use of company assets.
- Prepared weekly sales revenue report on all tubular products which was used by company management to develop sales strategy.
- Prepared response to customer claims which resulted in improved relations and reduced claims costs.

Secretary to Purchasing Manager (1984)

- Prepared all purchase orders for the buyer to ensure timely and accurate placement of orders.
- Prepared all telexes for the Tubular Division to assist in smooth communications to outside offices.

Senior Clerk (1983-1984)
Assisted Supervisor of Office Services in coordinating the move of the Tubular Division to a new location resulting in a smooth transition for all employees.

Senior Telex Operator (1980-1983)
Responsible for the operation of all telex equipment for the company.

COTTOCO - Dallas, Texas   1971-1980
Telecommunications Operator

EDUCATION

Kilgore High School, Kilgore, Texas - 1967

PROFESSIONAL SKILLS

IBM PC - Displaywrite II; IBM PC/XT - ASAP Symphony
Lane 5000 Telex Machine; RCA Mach 4 Telex Machine
Xerox Telecopier Machine; Dex 4100 Telecopier Machine

NAME
Address
Home #
Business #

OBJECTIVE

Maintenance Repairman

SUMMARY

Over twenty-five years experience in mechanical and electrical machine repair and plant maintenance utilizing a variety of mechanical skills including: troubleshooting, electrical, hydraulic, air and mechanical repairs.

PROFESSIONAL EXPERIENCE

LATTRELL CO., INC. - Houston, Texas   1968-Present

Maintenance Repairman

- Interpreted electrical, hydraulic, and mechanical machine schematics, drawings and prints.
- Set-up and operated TL's, VTL's, automatic and numerical controlled NC lathes, single and multi-spindle drills and milling and boring machines.
- Diagnosed causes of mechanical and hydraulic malfunctions utilizing ohmmeters, ammeters, and voltmeters.
- Conducted tests to verify correction of machine malfunctions.
- Involved with start-up and operated plant machinery including heat, ventilation, and air condition units, air compressors, caustical cleaning units, metal chip crushers, paint line conveyors and dip tank operations, water well and fire pump emergency equipment.
- Welded various metals using oxygen/acetylene and arc welding equipment.

SEARCY FORD TRACTOR - Columbus, Texas   1966-1968

Mechanic

Repaired farm tractors and machinery from major overhaul on engines, transmissions, and hydraulic systems to welding and tune-ups.

COLUMBUS HIGH SCHOOL - Columbus, Texas   1960-1966

Mechanic

Rebuilt or replaced engines, transmissions and brakes; tuned-up school busses and other machinery. Welded (arc or oxygen/acetylene) parts and equipment.

EDUCATION

Columbus High School, 1957
U.S. Army Ordinance School, 1957-1959
Maintenance Electricians License, 1980

Index

Ability(ies), 16, 27, 29, 122, 126, 129, 134, 135, 151
  problem solving, 32
  to achieve goals, 28
  to communicate, 7
  to control the interview, 139
  to do a job, 41, 55, 57, 135
  to provide service, 51
Acceptance of job offer, 61
Accomplishment(s), 1, 28, 46, 52, 55, 56, 60, 72, 73, 74, 103, 108, 124, 126, 132, 134, 155, 156, 161
  in dollars and percentages, 53, 54
  summarize, 65
  values, 47 (*see also* Achievement)
Accomplishment statement(s), 50, 51, 54, 55, 56, 155, 156, 161
  bullets, 52
  examples of, 52, 53
  qualitative, 46, 52
  quantitative, 46, 52
Achievement, 54 (*see also* Accomplishment)
Action(s), 32, 46, 54, 57, 104, 119
Action verb(s), 54
  list of, 50, 51, 52
Ad(s) (*see* Classified advertisement)
Ad response(s), 60, 117, 160
  sources, 9
Advancement, 16, 58, 87
Advertisement (*see* Classified advertise-ment)
Advice, 32, 35, 36, 37, 67, 81, 84, 103, 104, 105, 107, 115, 117, 121, 122, 123, 136, 142, 156, 167
  career, 27
  cold calling, 110
  legal, 147
  worst, 106 (*see also* Job search, advice)
Agency(ies), 97, 101
  as source of job information, 100
  claims by, 98, 99, 100
  executive counseling, 96 (*see also* Executive consulting)
  guidelines in using, 100, 101, 102, 103
  signing agreement, 102, 103
  (*see also* Contingency firm; Employment agency; Executive consulting service; Executive recruiting firm; Executive search firm; Retainer firm; Search agency; Search firm)
American Almanac of Jobs & Salaries, 14
Annual report/10K report, 87

Answer(s), 40, 41, 121, 123, 127, 134, 137, 146
  planning and preparation of, 128
  to tough questions, 128, 130, 131
Answering service, 41, 120
Appearance, 129
  poor, 140
  professional, 139
Applicant(s), 41, 44, 55, 57, 97
Application(s), 106
Aptitude(s), 29, 32
Assessment(s), 8, 9, 28, 32, 121
  future career, 14
  past career, 12
  personal, 10
  questionnaires, 10–24
  self, 10
Attitude(s), 29, 32, 61, 93, 119, 140, 155
  controllable, 3
  negative, 7
  positive, 139
  problem, 3
Authority, 2, 30, 143, 145
  hiring, 2, 35, 36, 39, 58, 78, 112, 117, 141, 150

Background, 3, 6, 29, 31, 37, 57, 74, 80, 89, 98, 110, 112, 114, 116, 122, 123, 128, 135, 138, 165
  check, 67
  falsify, 55
  military, 56
  professional, 67
Background information, 124, 144
Behavior, controllable, 3
Benefit(s), 16, 20, 28, 32, 36, 47, 54, 57, 89, 100, 148, 149, 152, 154, 159
  fringe, 147
Better Business Bureau, 26, 103
Bottomline, 47, 95, 96, 136, 142, 150
Budget, 8, 144
  job search, 7
Bullets (*see* Accomplishment statement)
Business venture (*see* Independent business)

Campaign(er) (*see* Job campaign)
Campaigning, 141
Candidate(s), 38, 55, 56, 58, 137
Career(s), 1, 5, 13, 27, 32, 38, 40, 53, 57, 89, 95, 100, 104, 107, 110, 119, 120, 126, 129, 130, 142, 163, 167
  changing, 155

233